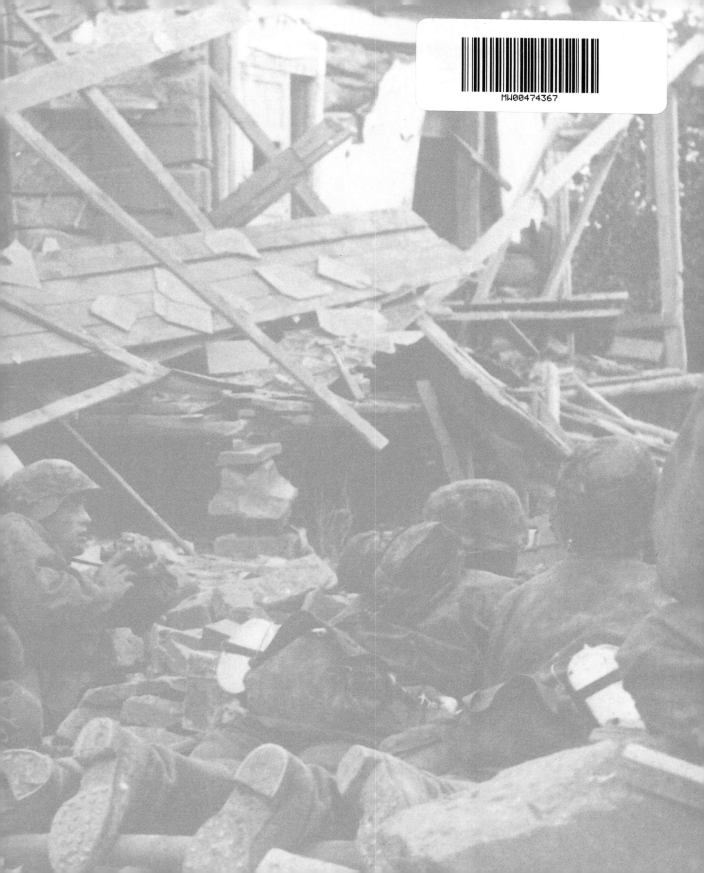

THE
SS
1923–1945

WORLD WAR II DATA BOOK

THE SS

1923–1945

THE ESSENTIAL FACTS AND FIGURES FOR HIMMLER'S STORMTROOPERS

CHRIS McNAB

amber
BOOKS

First published in 2009 by
Amber Books Ltd
Bradley's Close
74–77 White Lion Street
London N1 9PF
www.amberbooks.co.uk

ISBN: 978-1-906626-49-5

Project Editor: Michael Spilling
Design: Brian Rust
Picture Research: Terry Forshaw

Printed in Thailand

PICTURE CREDITS

Art-Tech/Aerospace: 182
Art-Tech/MARS: 60, 78/79
Cody Images: 2, 6/7, 9, 10 (bottom), 11 (top), 23, 31, 32/33, 38/39,
   48/49, 51, 55, 58, 74, 80/81, 100, 108, 112/113, 119/121, 128,
   170/171, 180/181
Corbis/Austrian Archives: 45
Getty Images/Popperfoto: 148/149
Getty Images/Time & Life Pictures: 11 (bottom)
Photoshot: 11 (2nd bottom)
Public domain 10 (top 4), 11 (2nd top), 111

All maps Patrick Mulrey © Amber Books

CONTENTS

CHAPTER 1

The Origins and Rise of the Schutzstaffel

The SS grew out of violent conditions. In the immediate aftermath of World War I, Germany was a politically and socially fractured nation. Violence approaching the scale of a full-blown civil war ran through Germany's towns and cities, as right-wing Freikorps and left-wing revolutionaries battled for control. Governments were unstable mixtures of competing interests. The German people were living in economic despair.

Out of this turbulent era emerged the Nationalsozialistische Deutsche Arbeiterpartei (National Socialist German Workers Party; NSDAP), with Adolf Hitler at its head. Hitler, sensing his vulnerability in a partisan world, needed his own elite bodyguard, and thereby sowed the seeds of the SS.

■ Hitler, Himmler, Heydrich, Hess and other members of the National Socialist hierarchy attend an early rally at Nuremberg. Note that here the SS men are carrying out their ceremonial duty as Adolf Hitler's personal bodyguard.

Freikorps Foundations

The origins of the SS lie in the turbulent conditions of post-World War I Germany. What would become the SS emerged from a range of paramilitary forces all vying for control in Germany's towns, cities and political institutions.

The end of World War I did not bring peace in Germany. Hundreds of thousands of soldiers returned home from the war, many unemployed and often nursing right-wing grievances against the Social Democrat politicians who had forced the Armistice and driven the Kaiser from office. Conversely, German society had equally strong left-wing revolutionary elements, inspired by the Russian Revolution of 1917 and looking to create their own socialist state in Germany through the power of the workers.

Freikorps

The competing ideologies produced an extreme left-wing/right-wing polarization in Germany, which expressed itself in open warfare in contested regions of the country. While the left-wing revolutionaries formed themselves into ad hoc combat formations, the right-wing produced the *Freikorps* (Free Corps). The *Freikorps* were units of ex-army and navy soldiers that collected themselves into coherent units, some eventually reaching brigade strength and armed with artillery, armoured cars, the full range of small arms and even tanks. Under the terms of the Versailles Treaty, Germany had been limited to an army of just 100,000 men, yet the *Freikorps* constituted an 'off-the-books' army, each formation loyal to a particular commander rather than the state. (They were devotedly named after the commanders, e.g. *Freikorps Ritter von Epp* and *Brigade Ehrhardt*.) Although internally disciplined, and ostensibly guided by anti-Bolshevik ideology, the *Freikorps* were brutal and bullish organizations, as much armed rabble as purposeful soldiers. Their anti-Bolshevik battles spread from Germany out into Poland and the Baltic states, and were permitted by the Allies mainly because they feared Communism more than they feared the *Freikorps*. Moreover, the historian G.S. Graber sees in the *Freikorps* the violent predecessor of the SS:

The Freikorps anticipated almost everything which was to happen under the general direction of the SS in Europe during World War II. The only difference was one of organization. The SS streamlined and coordinated a series of attitudes to which sporadic expression was given by the Freikorps in Germany, Poland, and the Baltic states between 1918 and 1921. All the hatred, brutality and ruthlessness were there to see 20 years before the mass murders of World War II took place. Himmler and his civil service applied technology and the full weight of State to prejudices and attitudes which had existed previously.

(Graber, 1978)

Graber sketches the SS as an organization continuing *Freikorps* traditions, just refining and organizing the same dark energies. Yet the *Freikorps* were not destined for long-term power. A *Freikorps* putsch in 1920 was overturned by a workers' strike, and anti-Communist adventures in Latvia ended in defeat and withdrawal. The *Freikorps'* days of influence drew down – they were dissolved in 1921 – but remnants of the organization would remain as a thorn in the side of the Weimar Republic for years to come.

Himmler and the Nazis

While the *Freikorps* had been flexing their muscles, a new and ideologically sympathetic political force was emerging in Germany. Formed in Bavaria in 1919, the

SS ORGANIZATION, 1926–28	
SS-Gauführer	*Number of Staffeln (Squadrons)*
SS-Gauführer Berlin-Brandenburg	2
SS-Gauführer Franken	4
SS-Gauführer Niederbayern	3
SS-Gauführer Oberbayern	4
SS-Gauführer Rheinland-Süd	5
SS-Gauführer Sachsen	4

HEINRICH HIMMLER – ESSENTIAL FACTS

■ **Heinrich Himmler became the second most powerful man in Nazi Germany, after Hitler himself. Not only did Himmler control an entire army in the form of the *Waffen-SS*, his authority also extended across all police and security services in the Third Reich, and over the running of the concentration/extermination camps.**

Birth:	7 October 1900
Death:	23 May 1945 (suicide)
SS ID number:	168
Place of birth:	Munich
Father:	Joseph Gebhard Himmler
Mother:	Anna Maria Himmler (née Heyder)
Siblings:	Gebhard Ludwig Himmler (b. 1898); Ernst Hermann Himmler (b. 1905)
Personal relationships:	– Margarete Siegroth, married 3 July 1928. One daughter (Gudrun) in 1929; later adopted a son. Separated (without divorce) in 1940 – Hedwig Potthast, became Himmler's mistress from 1941. Two children: son (Helge) in 1942 and daughter (Nanette Dorothea) in 1944
Military service:	11th Infantry Regiment (Bavarian) (1917–18)
Education:	Munich Technical College (1919–22)
Key pre-war positions, 1918–39:	– NSDAP member (c.1923) – Deputy Reichsführer-SS (1927) – Reichsführer-SS (1929) – Head of Gestapo (1934) – Chief of German Police (1936)
Key wartime positions:	– Reichskommissar für die Festigung des Deutschen Volkstums (Reich Commissioner for the Strengthening of the German Nation) (1939) – German Interior Minister (1943) – Commander-in-Chief of *Ersatzheer* (Replacement Army) (1944) – Commander-in-Chief of *Heeresgruppe Oberrhein* (Army Group Upper Rhine) (1944) – Commander-in-Chief of *Heeresgruppe Weichsel* (Army Group Vistula) (1945)

Deutsche Arbeiterpartei (German Workers Party; DAP) was a nationalist, anti-Bolshevik and anti-Semitic organization that grew steadily in membership and influence. Its rising star was former army corporal Adolf Hitler, a charismatic and energized individual who changed the party's name to the more familiar NSDAP. Hitler became party chairman in January 1922, and rapidly expanded its popularity beyond its Munich powerbase.

While the the NSDAP grew, one Heinrich Himmler was also making his way in the world. Nothing about Himmler's character said much about his dark future. Born in 1900 in Munich, he grew up into a slight, bespectacled man with a pedantic and thoughtful nature. Having missed active service in World War I, he then studied agriculture before feeling the pull of the *Freikorps*.

KEY MEMBERS OF *STOßTRUPP ADOLF HITLER,* 1923

Julius Schreck (1898–1936)
Freikorps member and one of the *Sturmabteilung* (SA) founders. Became personal bodyguard and chauffeur to Hitler and was a founder member of the *Stabswache*. Leader of the *Stoßtrupp Adolf Hitler* (1925), and *Reichsführer-SS* from 1925 to 1926. Died of meningitis in 1936, ranked *SS-Oberführer*.

Christian Weber (1883–1945)
Former groom. Became leading figure in the Nazi Party during its years in Bavaria. Implicated in shooting of a Munich Social Democrat politician in 1921. Later President of the Regional Parliament of Upper Bavaria (1939).

Ulrich Graf (1878–1950)
A former miller and butcher who became a founding member of the Nazi Party. Personal bodyguard to Hitler from 1920 to 1923. Wounded in the 1923 Beer Hall Putsch. Member of Munich City Council (1925) and elected to *Reichstag* in 1936. Became an SS officer, rising to the rank of *SS-Brigadeführer* in April 1943.

Emil Maurice (1897–1945)
Clockmaker by profession. Early member of the DAP and NSDAP. Joined the *Ordnertruppe* (Monitor Troops) in 1920, serving as a protection officer at Nazi meetings. Prominent figure in the SA. Took some of Hitler's early dictations of *Mein Kampf*. Performed killings in 1934 blood purge of SA. Member No 2 in the SS. Rose to *SS-Brigadeführer*.

Sepp Dietrich (1892–1966)
Joined NSDAP in the early 1920s. Made commander of SS bodyguard in 1928. Elected to *Reichstag* in 1930. SS command positions: 1st SS-Panzer Division *Leibstandarte SS Adolf Hitler*; 1st SS-Panzer Corps; Sixth SS-Panzer Army. Rose to *SS-Oberstgruppenführer und Generaloberst der Waffen-SS*.

Rudolf Hess (1894–1987)
Freikorps member (1919) and (NS)DAP member. Participated in Beer Hall Putsch (1923). Took down much of Hitler's dictation for *Mein Kampf*. Hitler's private secretary (1925), elected to *Reichstag* (1932), Deputy *Führer* (1933). Parachuted into Britain in 1941 on apparent peace mission.

Joseph Berchtold (1897–1962)
Former salesman. Joined DAP in 1920. Became early member of SS in 1925. In 1926 took over from Julius Schreck as *Reichsführer-SS*, although only held the position for one year. Replaced in this position by Erhard Heiden.

Erhard Heiden (1901–33)
Early member of Nazi Party. Joined the SS in 1925, and quickly demonstrated leadership potential. Advocated separation of SS from SA. Appointed *Reichsführer-SS* in 1927. Disgraced for Jewish associations. Arrested by the *Sicherheitsdienst* (SD) in 1933, and executed.

Hermann Fobke (1899–1943)
Joined NSDAP and SA in 1923. Participated in the Beer Hall Putsch (1923), and was imprisoned alongside Hitler. Rose to rank of *SA-Sturmbannführer*. *Gauleiter* of Hannover-Süd (1925–27) and *Gauinspektor* for *Gau* Pommern (1934–?). Barred from political activity in 1939.

Karl Fiehler
Joined DAP in 1920. Participated in Beer Hall Putsch (1923). *Ortsgruppenleiter* (Local Group Leader) in Munich from 1927 to 1930; *Reichsleiter* (Reich Leader) of the NSDAP. Rose up the ranks of the SS to reach *SS-Obergruppenführer* by 1942. Served on staff of *Stab Reichsführer-SS* (RFSS) until November 1944.

The SA and Origins of the SS

The SS would formally emerge under the authority of the Sturmabteilung *(Storm Detachment; SA), the paramilitary wing of the National Socialists. Yet in a few years the SS would snap itself off from SA authority, owing its allegiance to Hitler alone.*

Swastika on our helmets
Black-white-red armband
Storm Detachment Hitler
Is our name.

This early song of the SA indicates both its loyalty to Adolf Hitler and, through its imagery, its close associations with the future Nazi Party. And yet it is ironic that eventually Hitler would destroy the SA leadership by using one of its very own offshoots – the SS.

The SS, as we shall see, grew from very small acorns when compared with the massed ranks of the SA. Its

advantage over the latter, however, was an integral connection to Hitler, the man who was destined to hold supreme power in Germany.

Bodyguard units
The SA, like the SS, was at its roots a bodyguard unit. At the beginning of the 1920s, DAP/NSDAP political meetings were physically lively affairs that not infrequently ended in violence. To this end, the Party formed its own bodyguard to protect its speakers. Its first incarnation was the *Rollkommando*, composed principally of *Freikorps* members

(particularly those from the powerful *Brigade Ehrhardt*), which in turn became the *Zeitfreiwilligen* (Time Volunteers), principally manned by *Reichswehr* troops from the 19th Trench Mortar Company. Soon the unit once again rebranded itself, this time as the *Ordnertruppe* (Monitor Troops). However, such titles could attract unwelcome attention, hence they wryly renamed themselves the 'Sports and Gymnastics' section to prevent their being monitored by the Allied Control Commission.

In late 1921, the DAP bodyguard unit finally received a more enduring title – *Sturmabteilung* (SA). It was to move quickly beyond mere bodyguard duties. Modelled directly on the organizational structure of the German Army, the SA became an army unto itself, a paramilitary wing of the DAP dedicated to protecting its own and fighting Communist groups.

The SA, its members dressed in distinctive brown uniforms (hence their 'Brownshirt' nickname), would go on to become an intimidatory organization of 400,000 members by 1932 and 2.9 million members by August 1934. It provided the Nazi Party with conspicuous muscle to back its political rise to power, but this did not mean it flowed easily into Hitler's ambitions. Although an NSDAP-affiliated organization, the SA was independent and revolutionary in

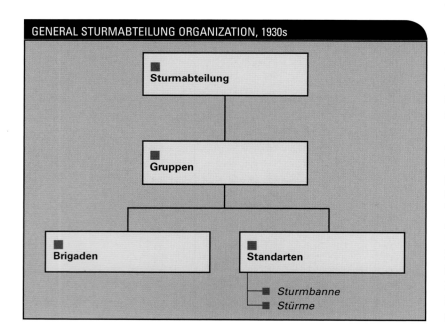

GENERAL STURMABTEILUNG ORGANIZATION, 1930s

- Sturmabteilung
- Gruppen
- Brigaden
- Standarten
  - Sturmbanne
  - Stürme

SS ORGANIZATION, 1930

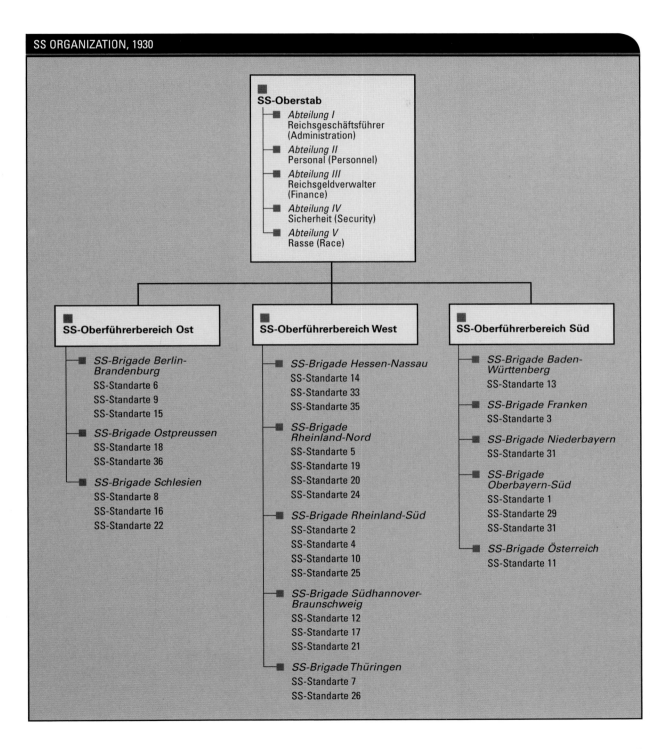

SS-Oberstab
- *Abteilung I*
  Reichsgeschäftsführer
  (Administration)
- *Abteilung II*
  Personal (Personnel)
- *Abteilung III*
  Reichsgeldverwalter
  (Finance)
- *Abteilung IV*
  Sicherheit (Security)
- *Abteilung V*
  Rasse (Race)

SS-Oberführerbereich Ost

- *SS-Brigade Berlin-Brandenburg*
  SS-Standarte 6
  SS-Standarte 9
  SS-Standarte 15
- *SS-Brigade Ostpreussen*
  SS-Standarte 18
  SS-Standarte 36
- *SS-Brigade Schlesien*
  SS-Standarte 8
  SS-Standarte 16
  SS-Standarte 22

SS-Oberführerbereich West

- *SS-Brigade Hessen-Nassau*
  SS-Standarte 14
  SS-Standarte 33
  SS-Standarte 35
- *SS-Brigade Rheinland-Nord*
  SS-Standarte 5
  SS-Standarte 19
  SS-Standarte 20
  SS-Standarte 24
- *SS-Brigade Rheinland-Süd*
  SS-Standarte 2
  SS-Standarte 4
  SS-Standarte 10
  SS-Standarte 25
- *SS-Brigade Südhannover-Braunschweig*
  SS-Standarte 12
  SS-Standarte 17
  SS-Standarte 21
- *SS-Brigade Thüringen*
  SS-Standarte 7
  SS-Standarte 26

SS-Oberführerbereich Süd

- *SS-Brigade Baden-Württenberg*
  SS-Standarte 13
- *SS-Brigade Franken*
  SS-Standarte 3
- *SS-Brigade Niederbayern*
  SS-Standarte 31
- *SS-Brigade Oberbayern-Süd*
  SS-Standarte 1
  SS-Standarte 29
  SS-Standarte 31
- *SS-Brigade Österreich*
  SS-Standarte 11

spirit, composed largely of gangs of thugs who bowed more to their officers than to Hitler per se. Although the position of *Oberster SA-Führer* (Supreme SA Leader) was filled by various Party loyalists, including Hermann Göring in 1923 and Hitler himself in 1930–31, the formative influence was Ernst Röhm, a violent homosexual determined to ride to power on Hitler's political coat-tails. Röhm was a close friend of Hitler from the earliest days of the Party struggle, and had effectively become the quartermaster of the DAP paramilitaries.

The relationship between Röhm and Hitler changed dramatically in the wake of the failed Beer Hall Putsch of 1923, a forcible DAP/SA attempt to seize power that achieved little but landing the Nazi hierarchy (including Hitler and Röhm) in prison. The SA was banned, but kept alive simply by temporarily renaming it the *Frontbann*. When Hitler emerged from prison in December 1924, he noticed that Röhm seemed to building up his own fiefdom via the SA, potentially undermining Hitler's authority in the future. The undercurrents of the SA were anti-capitalist, anti-Army and anti-establishment, and Hitler was none of these things. In short, the SA was as much a threat to Hitler as it was a support, and he realized that he needed his own personal bodyguard as a counterweight.

The birth of the SS
The true foundations of the SS predated the Beer Hall Putsch. In March 1923, Hitler ordered the formation of the *Stabswache* (Headquarters Guard), distinguished from the SA

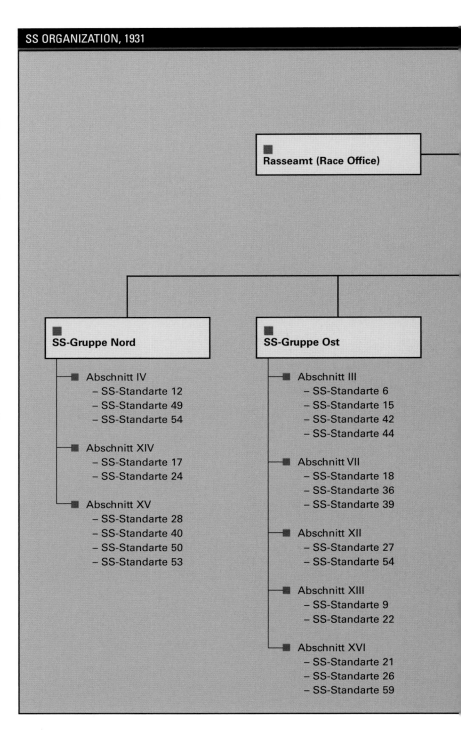

SS ORGANIZATION, 1931

Rasseamt (Race Office)

SS-Gruppe Nord

- Abschnitt IV
  - SS-Standarte 12
  - SS-Standarte 49
  - SS-Standarte 54

- Abschnitt XIV
  - SS-Standarte 17
  - SS-Standarte 24

- Abschnitt XV
  - SS-Standarte 28
  - SS-Standarte 40
  - SS-Standarte 50
  - SS-Standarte 53

SS-Gruppe Ost

- Abschnitt III
  - SS-Standarte 6
  - SS-Standarte 15
  - SS-Standarte 42
  - SS-Standarte 44

- Abschnitt VII
  - SS-Standarte 18
  - SS-Standarte 36
  - SS-Standarte 39

- Abschnitt XII
  - SS-Standarte 27
  - SS-Standarte 54

- Abschnitt XIII
  - SS-Standarte 9
  - SS-Standarte 22

- Abschnitt XVI
  - SS-Standarte 21
  - SS-Standarte 26
  - SS-Standarte 59

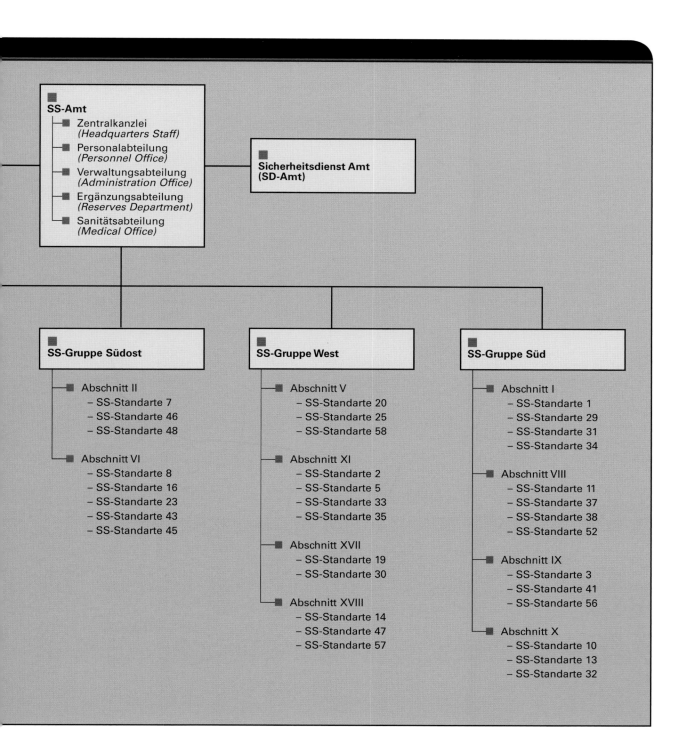

SS-Amt
- Zentralkanzlei
  (Headquarters Staff)
- Personalabteilung
  (Personnel Office)
- Verwaltungsabteilung
  (Administration Office)
- Ergänzungsabteilung
  (Reserves Department)
- Sanitätsabteilung
  (Medical Office)

**Sicherheitsdienst Amt
(SD-Amt)**

SS-Gruppe Südost

- Abschnitt II
  - SS-Standarte 7
  - SS-Standarte 46
  - SS-Standarte 48

- Abschnitt VI
  - SS-Standarte 8
  - SS-Standarte 16
  - SS-Standarte 23
  - SS-Standarte 43
  - SS-Standarte 45

SS-Gruppe West

- Abschnitt V
  - SS-Standarte 20
  - SS-Standarte 25
  - SS-Standarte 58

- Abschnitt XI
  - SS-Standarte 2
  - SS-Standarte 5
  - SS-Standarte 33
  - SS-Standarte 35

- Abschnitt XVII
  - SS-Standarte 19
  - SS-Standarte 30

- Abschnitt XVIII
  - SS-Standarte 14
  - SS-Standarte 47
  - SS-Standarte 57

SS-Gruppe Süd

- Abschnitt I
  - SS-Standarte 1
  - SS-Standarte 29
  - SS-Standarte 31
  - SS-Standarte 34

- Abschnitt VIII
  - SS-Standarte 11
  - SS-Standarte 37
  - SS-Standarte 38
  - SS-Standarte 52

- Abschnitt IX
  - SS-Standarte 3
  - SS-Standarte 41
  - SS-Standarte 56

- Abschnitt X
  - SS-Standarte 10
  - SS-Standarte 13
  - SS-Standarte 32

soldiers by black caps displaying the death's head emblem (this feature looked back to the wartime *Sturmbataillone* assault units), plus the shared swastika armbands. Internal politics meant that the *Stabswache* did not last long, and later in the year Hitler formed the *Stoßtrupp Adolf Hitler* (Shock Troop Adolf Hitler). This group was a mixture of Party hardmen and Hitler loyalists, and included some characters that would become salient figures of the Nazi era, including Rudolf Hess, Ulrich Graf and Josef 'Sepp' Dietrich. The *Stoßtrupp Adolf Hitler* was not a large organization – it is unlikely to have numbered more than 20 people – and its existence was cut short with the failure of the Beer Hall Putsch later in the year.

What these early bodyguard units had demonstrated was Hitler's desire to have elite units dedicated to his service, not to the service of a broader organization. Hitler himself spelled out the reasons behind the creation of the SS during a discussion in January 1942, in which he also explained the practical origins of the SS:

Being convinced that there are always circumstances in which elite troops are called for, in 1922–23 I created the 'Adolf Hitler Shock Troops'. They were made up of men who were ready for revolution and knew that one day or another things would come to hard knocks. When I came out of Landsberg [the prison in which Hitler had been held], everything was broken up and scattered in sometimes rival bands. I told myself then that I needed a bodyguard, even a very restricted one, but made up of men who would be enlisted without restriction, even to march against their own brothers. Only twenty men to a city (on condition that one could count on them absolutely) rather than a suspect mass.

(Quoted in Trevor-Roper, 2000)

Taking former members of the *Stoßtrupp Adolf Hitler*, Hitler created a new bodyguard called the *Schutzstaffel* (Protection Squadron; SS); the name is likely to have been coined by Hermann Göring. The historian Gordon Williamson here outlines both the early structure and the ideological bias of the fledgling SS formation:

The Schutz Staffel, or SS, was to be a select band of no more than 10 men plus an officer in each district, the exception being the capital Berlin, which was permitted an SS unit of twice the normal size. These SS men were to be specially selected, and only those of sober habit, aged 25 to 35, of good standing with no criminal record, of good health and robust physique would be considered. More importantly, however, each SS recruit would owe his unswerving loyalty not to the Nazi Party but to Adolf Hitler personally.

(Williamson, 1994)

Commanded by Julius Schreck, the SS was a diminutive force, but an important one. In appearance there was little to distinguish it from the SA, apart from a black tie. Yet it signalled that Hitler perceived himself as more than just an important cog in the Party machine, and also reflected the tensions between Hitler and the unwieldy SA. (Note that Hitler relieved Ernst Röhm of the SA leadership in 1925.)

These were early days for the SS, however, and its future was hardly assured (Hitler himself was in a politically precarious position at this time). Between 1925 and 1929 the SS grew to a membership of around 1000, but there was unhappiness in

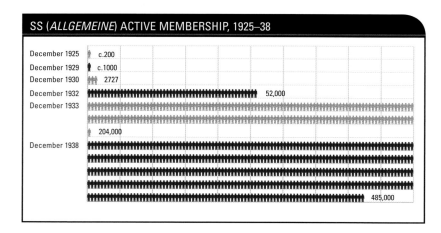

SS (*ALLGEMEINE*) ACTIVE MEMBERSHIP, 1925–38

December 1925	c.200
December 1929	c.1000
December 1930	2727
December 1932	52,000
December 1933	204,000
December 1938	485,000

the ranks. Hitler, to placate SA leader Franz Pfeffer von Salomon, had placed the SS under control of the *Oberster SA-Führer*, resulting in the SA imposing manpower restrictions on the SS. (The SA leadership restrained the SS units to 10 per cent of the size of local SA equivalents, and only permitted SS units to be established if the local SA group was at full strength.) Playing second fiddle to the SA demoralized both the SS rank and file and its leadership.

In 1929, however, SS fortunes changed with the appointment of Heinrich Himmler to the post of *Reichsführer-SS*.

Himmler takes over

As we have already noted, there was little in Heinrich Himmler's early years that explains why one day he would become the second most powerful figure in Germany, a man not only in charge of an independent army (the *Waffen-SS*) but also ruler of police and security forces at home and in the occupied territories. He would also be the man with overall jurisdiction for the Holocaust.

Born into a middle-class Catholic family in Munich in 1900, Himmler had a childhood and early education that were models of normal life. World War I galvanized his imagination, and like many youths he pushed his father into granting him permission to join the military. He entered the 11th Infantry Regiment (Bavarian) *Von der Tann* in 1917, becoming an officer cadet just in time for the war to end and leave him frustrated at a lack of combat experience.

Post-war, Himmler studied agricultural science at Munich

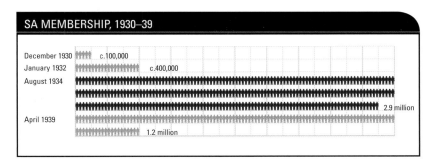

SA MEMBERSHIP, 1930–39

December 1930		c.100,000
January 1932		c.400,000
August 1934		
		2.9 million
April 1939		
		1.2 million

University. The subject matter would be an enduring love of Himmler's, who equated the countryside with good character and honest living, as well as being fascinated by the elements of breeding and genetic manipulation that came with animal husbandry and crop growing. (Himmler is known to have said, in 1942, 'Cowards are born in towns, heroes in the country.') Himmler was a rather frail, studious figure, but he now showed elements of character significant to his historical notoriety.

Himmler had an extremely ordered, bookish mind, and enjoyed rationalizing and solving problems in a rather detached way. (During his time in the Army, he had spent time as an orderly room clerk.) He was a good self-publicist, who attempted to educate the people he met with his theories on race, politics and society. Furthermore, Himmler showed a distinct interest in Nordic legend and mythology, with which the SS would later be imbued in its symbolic and ritualistic aspects.

Fuelled by a desire for adventure and belonging, Himmler joined the NSDAP in 1923, having met Röhm in Munich. His love affair with the steely romanticism of the Nazis led to his involvement in the Beer Hall Putsch.

This effort may have failed, but Himmler had found a true sense of belonging. Of these years he reflected: 'We members of the movement were constantly in danger of our lives, but we were never afraid. Adolf Hitler was our leader and he held us together. They were the most wonderful years of my life.'

Himmler's role in the putsch, plus striking organizational abilities, were noticed by the Party hierarchy, including Hitler. He became secretary to NSDAP propaganda chief Gregor Strasser, then in 1925 was appointed Deputy *Gauleiter* for Lower Bavaria. In the same year, and as part of the political office, he joined the SS, member No 168. In 1926 he extended his *Gauleiter* role to include Upper Bavaria, and also became Deputy Reich Propaganda Chief.

It was within the SS, however, that Himmler's ambitions truly lay. Convincing Hitler of his programme

REICHSFÜHRER-SS, 1925–45

Julius Schreck – 1925–26
Joseph Berchtold – 1926–27
Erhard Heiden – 1927–29
Heinrich Himmler – 1929–45
Karl Hanke – 1945

for the SS, which involved transforming it into a more powerful, racially 'pure' elite, Himmler was appointed by Hitler as Deputy *Reichsführer-SS* in 1927. Then, in January 1929, the current *Reichsführer-SS*, Erhard Heiden, resigned, and Himmler stepped into his shoes. It is hard to overstate the significance of Himmler's ascension. He would transform the SS from a marginalized bodyguard into the dominant paramilitary political force in Germany. In membership alone the results were impressive. By December 1930 the SS membership stood at 2727, nearly triple what it was the previous year. Membership applications were, admittedly, also galvanized by the onset of the Great Depression – the SS offered a smart form of employment in hard times.

The impressive discipline of SS members, however, began to attract a higher standard of recruit than the strong-arm men who gravitated to the SA. Himmler also introduced energetic elements of ritual and racial belonging that appealed to young men. For example, each SS candidate had to prove an Aryan ancestry stretching back several generations – Jewish, Polish or Slavic blood would automatically block the application. Himmler later stated, in his favoured agricultural terms:

We went about it like a nursery gardener trying to reproduce a good old strain which has been adulterated and debased; we started from the principles of plant selection and then proceeded to weed out the men whom we did not think we could use... I started with a minimum height requirement of five feet eight inches; I knew that men of a certain height must somewhere possess the blood I desired.
(Quoted in Graber, 1978)

It is unlikely that Himmler had anything other than a romantic, racist urge connecting physical height and the quality of someone's racial 'blood'. Yet at this vulnerable time in the SS's evolution, Himmler's networking and organizational skills were exactly what it needed. It also

SS-OBERABSCHNITTE (MAIN DISTRICTS), 1934–39

Oberabschnitte	Sections under control of the Oberabschnitt
Oberabschnitt Mitte	Abschnitte II, XVI, XVIII, XXVII
Oberabschnitt Nord	Abschnitte XIII, XV, XX
Oberabschnitt Nordost	Abschnitte VII, XXVI
Oberabschnitt Nordwest	Abschnitte IV, XIV
Oberabschnitt Ost	Abschnitte III, XII, XXIII
Oberabschnitt Rhein	Abschnitte XI
Oberabschnitt Süd	Abschnitte I, IX, XXVIII
Oberabschnitt Südost	Abschnitte VI, XXI, XXII
Oberabschnitt Südwest	Abschnitte X, XIX
Oberabschnitt West	Abschnitte V, XXV

OFFICES UNDER THE *REICHSFÜHRER-SS*, 1934–39

Amt für Sicherheitsaufgaben (Office for Security Roles)

Ergänzungsamt (Replacement Office)

Führungsabteilung (Management Department)

Inspekteur der Konzentrationslager und Wachverbände (Inspector of Concentration Camps and Guard Units)

Personalabteilung (Personnel Department)

Persönlicher Stab RFSS (Personal Headquarters *Reichsführer-SS*)

Rasse und Siedlungshauptamt (Race and Settlement Main Office)

Rasseamt (Race Office)

Reichsarzt SS (Reich Doctor SS)

Sanitätsamt (Medical Office)

Schulungsamt (Training Office)

SD-Hauptamt (SD Main Office)

Siedlungsamt (Settlement Office)

Sippenamt (Family Office)

SS-Gericht (SS Court)

SS-Hauptamt (SS Main Office)

Statistik und Archiv (Statistics and Archives)

Verwaltungsamt (Administration Office)

Verwaltungschef SS (Chief of SS Administration)

had to face the challenge of increasing resistance from a newly threatened SA organization.

Challenging the SA

In 1930 several changes occurred that transformed the status and fortunes of the SS in relation to the SA. First, Hitler granted the SS operational independence from the SA: SS units no longer had to accept orders from SA commanders. As if to back up the new position, the SS was given a new uniform – black breeches, black tie, black-edged swastika armband and a black kepi featuring the death's head emblem.

Structurally, the SS also underwent reorganization. At its operational level, it was organized around the *Sturm* of 70–120 men, three *Stürme* making up a *Sturmbann* (Storm Unit), and three or four *Sturmbanne* making up a *Standarte* (Regiment) of up to 3000

men. At a broader national level, the local SS territories were also reshaped. Initially, the SS was ordered according to *SS-Oberführerbereiche* (SS Regional Command Areas), of which there were three – *Ost* (East), *West* (West) and *Süd* (South).

By 1931, the *SS-Oberführerbereiche* had been redesignated as *Gruppen*

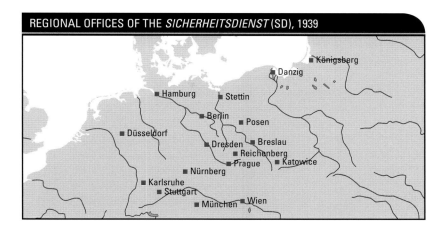

REGIONAL OFFICES OF THE *SICHERHEITSDIENST* (SD), 1939

▲ **REGIONAL OFFICES OF THE *SICHERHEITSDIENST* (SD), 1939. Each regional office dedicated much of its time to compiling security reports on potential 'enemies of the state', all these reports being filed centrally in Berlin. The SD in Poland was also integral to implementing Jewish ghetto policies.**

COMPLETE LIST OF *SS-ABSCHNITTE* (WITH HEADQUARTERS), 1933–45

Abschnitte	HQ locations*	Abschnitte	HQ locations*
SS-Abschnitt I	Munich	SS-Abschnitt XXIV	Oppeln, Neustadt, Kattowitz
SS-Abschnitt II	Chemnitz, Dresden	SS-Abschnitt XXV	Dortmund
SS-Abschnitt III	Berlin	SS-Abschnitt XXVI	Danzig
SS-Abschnitt IV	Braunschweig	SS-Abschnitt XXVII	Weimar, Gotha
SS-Abschnitt V	Essen	SS-Abschnitt XXVIII	Bayreuth, Regensburg
SS-Abschnitt VI	Breslau	SS-Abschnitt XXIX	Konstanz, Mannheim
SS-Abschnitt VII	Königsberg	SS-Abschnitt XXX	Kassel
SS-Abschnitt VIII	Linz	SS-Abschnitt XXXI	Wien
SS-Abschnitt IX	Würzberg, Kulmbach, Nuremberg	SS-Abschnitt XXXII	Augsburg
SS-Abschnitt X	Stuttgart	SS-Abschnitt XXXIII	Schwerin
SS-Abschnitt XI	Koblenz, Munich, Wiesbaden	SS-Abschnitt XXXIV	Neustadt
SS-Abschnitt XII	Frankfurt, Dühringhof, Liebenow	SS-Abschnitt XXXV	Graz
SS-Abschnitt XIII	Stettin	SS-Abschnitt XXXVI	Innsbruck
SS-Abschnitt XIV	Bremen	SS-Abschnitt XXXVII	Reichenberg
SS-Abschnitt XV	Kiel	SS-Abschnitt XXXVIII	Karlsbad
SS-Abschnitt XVI	Zoppot, Zwickau, Halle, Magdeburg, Dessau Mar	SS-Abschnitt XXXIX	Prague
SS-Abschnitt XVII	Münster	SS-Abschnitt XXXX	Bromberg
SS-Abschnitt XVIII	Halle, Weimar	SS-Abschnitt XXXXI	Thorn
SS-Abschnitt XIX	Karlsruhe	SS-Abschnitt XXXXII	Gnesen
SS-Abschnitt XX	Kiel	SS-Abschnitt XXXXIII	Litzmannstadt, Lodsch
SS-Abschnitt XXI	Hirschberg, Liegnitz, Görlitz	SS-Abschnitt XXXXIV	Gumbinnen
SS-Abschnitt XXII	Allenstein	SS-Abschnitt XXXXV	Strasburg
SS-Abschnitt XXIII	Berlin		

*Summary of all HQ locations, not occupied simultaneously

KNOWN INDIVIDUALS EXECUTED AS CONSEQUENCE OF 'NIGHT OF THE LONG KNIVES', 29/30 JUNE 1934

Name	Position held (where known)	Name	Position held (where known)
Otto Ballerstadt	Diplomat	Hans Hayn	SA-Gruppenführer, NSDAP Reichstag deputy.
Fritz Beck	Director	? Heck	SA-Standartenführer
Karl Belding	SA-Standartenführer	Edmund Heines	SA-Obergruppenführer, NSDAP Reichstag deputy
Erwald Kuppel Bergmann			
Veit Ulrich von Beulwitz	SA-Sturmführer	Oskar Heines	SA-Obersturmbannführer
Alois Bittman	SA-Scharführer	Robert Heiser	
Franz Blasner	SA-Truppführer	Hans Peter von Heydebreck	SA-Gruppenführer, NSDAP Reichstag deputy
Herbert von Bose	Secretary to Franz von Papen		
Ferdinand von Bredow	Generalmajor in Reichswehr	Anton Freiherr von Hohberg und Buchwald	SS-Reiter and Obertruppführer
A. Charig		Edgar Julius Jung	Journalist, speech writer
? von der Decken		Gustav Ritter von Kahr	Former Staatskommissar for Bavaria
Georg von Detten	SA-Gruppenführer, SA political chief,	? Kamphausen	City Engineer
NSDAP Reichstag deputy		Eugen von Kessel	Hauptman Polizei
? Ender-Schulen	SA-Sturmbannführer	? Kirschbaum	
Kurt Engelhardt	SA-Sturmbannführer	Dr Erich Klausener	Head of Preußisch Ministerie Polizei, Centre Party, Catholic Action
Werner Engels	SA-Sturmbannführer, acting Police President of Breslau		
		Willi Klemm	SA-Brigadeführer
? Enkel	SA-Standartenführer	Hans Karl Koch	SA-Brigadeführer
Karl Ernst	Freikorps Roßbach, SA-Gruppenführer, NSDAP Reichstag deputy	Heinrich Konig	SA-Oberscharführer
		Ewald Koppel	Communist
Ernst Martin Ewald	Leiter der ND Gau Sachsen	? Krause	SA-Sturmbannführer
Hans Joachim von Falkenhausen	SA-Oberführer	Fritz Ritter von Kraußer	SA-Obergruppenführer, NSDAP Reichstag deputy.
Gustav Fink	SS-Mann		
Dr Walter Förster	Lawyer	Friedrich Karl Laemmermann	HJ Führer
? Gehrt	SA-Sturmbannführer	Gotthard Langer	SA-Obertruppführer.
Fritz Gerlich	Journalist	Dr Lindemann	
Daniel Gerth	SA-Obersturmführer	Karl Lipinsky	SA-Reiter-Sturmführer
Dr Alexander Glaser		? Max	Röhm's chauffeur
Freiherr von Guttenberg		? Marcus	SA-Standartenführer
Dr Haber			

(Groups) and increased in number to five; they were then renamed *Oberabschnitte* (Main Districts). Below the *Oberabschnitte* were the *SS-Abschnitte* (SS Districts). These applied initially within the Reich, Austria and Czechoslovakia, but later were extended into occupied Poland and France. Each *Abschnitt* contained a certain number of *Standarten*. Tying the whole package together between 1929 and 1935 was the *SS-Amt* (SS Office), the main headquarters office

for the SS, under the command of Himmler. More about the structural nature of the early SS is discussed in the next section, but we now return to the ongoing saga of SA and SS relationships, which during the early 1930s took an ominous turn.

The Blood Purge
It became increasingly clear to the SA leadership that Hitler was favouring the SS over the SA, and that Himmler's remit was becoming

unacceptably broad. Indeed, the SS was no longer a mere bodyguard group – Himmler defined its role as 'carrying out police duties within the Party' and protecting the values and integrity of the 'Nordic race' against the pollution of Bolshevism. Moreover, Hitler's star was inexorably rising.

In 1933, by which time the SS numbered more than 50,000, Hitler took power as Chancellor. Röhm had by this time returned as leader of the

Name	Position held (where known)	Name	Position held (where known)
Dr Hermann Mattheis	SA-Standartenführer	August Schneidhüber	SA-Obergruppenführer, Munich Police Chief, NSDAP Reichstag deputy
Walter von Mohrenschildt		Walter Schotte	
? Muhlert		Konrad Schragmüller	SA-Gruppenführer, NSDAP Reichstag deputy
Edmund Neumeier	SA-Rottenführer		
Heinrich Nixdorf	SA-Oberst Feldjagerei	Dr Joachim Schroder	SA-Obersturmführer
Dr Ernst Oberfohren	Nationalist Reichstag deputy?	Max Walter Otto Schuldt	SA-Sturmführer
Lambeardus Ostendorp	SA-Oberst Feldjager	Walter Schulz	Stabschef der SA Gruppe Pommern
Otto Pietrzok	SA-Sturmbannführer	Max Schulze	SA-Obersturmführer
Fritz Pleines	SS-Mann	Hans Schweighardt	SA-Standartenführer
Adalbert Probst	Catholic youth leader in Munich, former Bavarian Landtag deputy	Emil Sembach	SS-Oberführer
Hans Ramshorn	SA-Brigadeführer, Police president of Gleiwitz	Hans Graf von Spreti-Weilbach	SA-Standartenführer, SA-Führer zur besonderen Verwendung
Robert Reh	Communist	Oskar Stable	Freikorps Maercker, Freikorps Roßbach, NSDAP/NSDStB
Ernst Röhm	Stabschef SA, NSDAP Reichstag deputy		
Paul Röhrbein	Frontbahn	Father Bernhard Stempfle	Catholic priest
Wilhelm Sander	SA-Stabsführer	Gregor Strasser	Gauleiter of Niederbayern-Oberpfalz; Reichsorganisationsleiter
Emil Saasbach			
Wilhelm Sander	SA-Brigadeführer	Otto Stucken	SA-Obersturmführer
Martin Schätzl	SA-Standartenführer	? Surk	SA-Standartenführer
Gaiseric Scherl	SA-Standartenführer, NS Studentenbund	? Thomas	SA-Standartenführer
		Ottmar Toifl	SS-Truppführer; Polizei kommissar
Erich Schieweck	SA-Obertruppführer	Dr Erwin Villain	SA-Standartenartzt
Elisabeth von Schleicher	Wife of General von Schleicher	Max Vogel	SA-Obersturmführer
Kurt von Schleicher	Chancellor of Germany (1932–33)	Gerd Voss	Attorney to Strasser
Hans W. Schmidt	SA-Obersturmführer	Karl Eberhard von Wechmar	SA-Gruppenführer
Theodor Schmidt	SA-Gruppenführer	Udo von Woyrsch	
Dr Wilhelm Schmidt	Music critic; mistaken for SA-Gruppenführer Schmidt	Karl Zehnter	Associate of Röhm and Heines
		Ernestine Zoref	
Wilhelm Eduard Schmidt	SA-Gruppenführer	Alex Zweig	
		Jeanette Zweig	

SA, which still dwarfed the SS in terms of numbers. The NSDAP victory brought massive membership gains to both organizations – by the end of 1933 the SS was 204,000 strong, but the SA had more than three million members. Hitler, eager to align himself with the German Army and the conservative business elite, feared the SA's revolutionary spirit. Röhm made speeches in which he proposed that the SA was the true army of National Socialism, and that the regular army should be sidelined. By implying that he would be the leader of this army, Röhm seemed to threaten a putsch, and Himmler, Göring and a new force in the SS, Reinhard Heydrich, dragged up apparent evidence that Röhm was planning such a move.

Hitler decided to act first. During June he and his Nazi officials compiled a list of key SA leaders and thinkers. Those on the list not only included Röhm, naturally, but also Gregor Strasser and the former Chancellor Kurt von Schleicher. On 30 June 1934, on Hitler's orders, Himmler unleashed his SS hit squads in a coordinated 48-hour operation to exterminate the SA leadership. Röhm was shot in a prison cell in Dachau concentration camp. In two days, up to 600 people were killed (Hitler acknowledged 77 deaths in the *Reichstag*), and the SA was effectively headless, leaving the way forward for Himmler's SS.

The Rise of an SS Army, 1933–39

With the SA emasculated by the Blood Purge of 1934, and Hitler establishing dictatorial powers over the Third Reich, the SS was set to expand into a huge force, ultimately divided into the Allgemeine *(General) SS and the* Waffen *(Armed) SS.*

The Blood Purge was a savage illustration of the power that the SS had become in Germany, a tool by which Hitler could engineer his own political ends. Within a month of the action, the SS was given fully independent status from the SA. Note, however, that the SA continued to exist. The role of *Stabschef* was taken by Viktor Lutze, previously an SA leader in Hamburg and a key internal assistant in the purge. The men aged 18–35 were called away for active military service; in 1935 Hitler conclusively demonstrated his break from the Versailles Treaty by reintroducing conscription. Those older men that remained in the SA played little part in the military life of the Third Reich, mainly delivering training services and operating *Landsturm* (Land Storm) home guard forces. Essentially, the SS no longer had a competitor for the role of NSDAP paramilitary wing.

Rapid growth
In terms of simple membership growth, the rise of Hitler to power could not have been more significant for the SS. Hitler declared himself *Führer* in August 1935 (by this time he had already fused the offices of Chancellor and President into one), and during his early years in power passed rapid-fire legislation that centred power upon himself,

including banning opposition political parties and, from 2 August 1934, changing the armed forces' oath of allegiance to him personally, not to the constitution or abstract nation.

For Himmler's SS, the triumph of Hitler brought an unfettered ability to thrive. By the end of 1933, SS membership stood at 204,000 and would more than double in the next five years. On account of both its scale and its spreading political remit, the SS had also grown into a more complicated, multifaceted organization.

Dividing the SS
In the autumn of 1934, the units of the SS were categorized according to two fundamental divisions, which would hold until 1945. On one side there was the *Allgemeine-SS* (General SS). This was essentially the SS non-combat wing, and consisted of full- or part-time members dedicated to administrative, economic, race, legal, intelligence, security and personnel issues. The *Allgemeine-SS* would become a sprawling organization encompassing everything from the concentration camp system through to administering SS business interests.

In contrast to the *Allgemeine-SS* was the *Bewaffnete-SS* (Armed SS). This title referred to those units with a focused combat capability, and it

was these units that laid the foundations of the future *Waffen-SS*. The nature and composition of both sides of the SS will be explored in depth as we progress through this book, but here it is important to explore something of their development in the pre-war years.

Allgemeine-SS, 1933–39
Although the *Waffen-SS* has captured the lion's share of the historical 'glamour' attached to the SS, it was arguably the *Allgemeine-SS* that was by far the most influential. It would be impossible here to explore the full range of bodies encompassed by the *Allgemeine-SS*, which included numerous offices dedicated to every aspect of running the SS and policing the Nazi state. Understanding the pre-war development of several key departments, however, is critical to appreciating how the SS worked and its overall agenda.

In 1933, Hitler's new regime – which doubtless expected a significant inrush of political prisoners – began establishing a new concentration camp system to house political prisoners. The first three camps were those at Dachau, Buchenwald and Sachsenhausen, and the SS was a natural, politically reliable candidate to provide their guard units. Responsibility for these guard units fell to *Brigadeführer* Theodor Eicke, a man who would become notorious even amongst the merciless standards of the SS. Eicke, who previously had been appointed the commander of Dachau, was in July 1934 promoted to the position of *Inspekteur der Konzentrationslager und SS-Wachverbände* (Inspector of Concentration Camps and SS Guard Formations). He then took the early SS guard formation known as the *Wachmannschaft* (Guard Unit), and in 1936 re-formed it into the appropriately menacing *SS-Totenkopfverbände* (SS Death's Head Formations; SS-TV). The SS-TV would become rightly feared, not only in the concentration and extermination camps of Germany and the occupied territories, but also in the form of its wartime *Waffen-SS* offshoot, the 3rd SS-Panzer Division *Totenkopf*.

RuSHA

The SS-TV would, in time, become an integral component of the Holocaust, but it was not the only *Allgemeine-SS* department created to implement racial policies. Originally established in 1931, the *SS-Rasse- und Siedlungshauptamt* (SS Race and Settlement Main Office; RuSHA) was officially founded as a Third Reich office, under the same name, in 1935, and initially came under the leadership of the mystically minded Walter Darré. The RuSHA was diligently concerned with the racial integrity of SS members, and policed issues such as genealogy, marriages and recruitment approvals. Expanding in size to 11 offices, the RuSHA indicated how important racial purity was to the SS mindset,

although as we shall see in later chapters, the strictness of its early guidelines was relaxed during the war years, by virtue of necessity.

Apart from its concentration camp duties, the *Allgemeine-SS* is also chiefly remembered for its expansive and insidious powers of policing,

REINHARD HEYDRICH

■ Reinhard Heydrich, as head of the RSHA, was in charge of the Nazi Party's security services, including the SD and the *Sicherheitspolizei* (Security Police – Sipo), which incorporated the Gestapo and *Kriminalpolizei* (Criminal Police – Kripo). He was also the administrative driving force behind the Holocaust, being chosen to lead *Die Endlosung* (The Final Solution) from January 1942, a role cut short by his assassination later in the year.

Birth:	7 March 1904
Death:	4 June 1942 (following assassination attempt on 27 May 1942)
SS ID number:	10120
Place of birth:	Halle, near Leipzig
Father:	Richard Bruno Heydrich
Mother:	Elisabeth Anna Maria Amalia Heydrich (née Kranz)
Education:	Reform-Realgymnasium; also joined the Maracker Freikorps in 1914
Military service:	Joined German Navy in 1922, forced to resign his commission in 1931 for 'conduct unbecoming an officer and a gentleman'
Nazi Party positions:	Member of the NSDAP (1931)
	Member of the SS (1931)
	Head of the SD (1932)
	Heinrich Himmler's deputy (1933)
	Head of Reich Central Office for Jewish Emigration (1939)
	Head of the Reich Security Main Office (RHSA) (1939)
	Deputy Reich Protector of Bohemia and Moravia (1941)

EXTRACTS FROM HITLER'S ORDERS TO CREATE ARMED ELEMENTS OF THE SS, 17 AUGUST 1938*

* Source of translation: *Nazi Conspiracy and Aggression*, Volume III (US Government Printing Office, District of Columbia, 1947)

A. The *SS-Verfügungstruppe*

1. The *SS-Verfügungstruppe* is neither a part of the *Wehrmacht* nor a part of the police. It is a standing armed unit, exclusively at my disposal. As such, and as a unit of the NSDAP its members are to be selected by the *Reichsführer-SS* according to the ideological and political standards which I have ordered for the NSDAP and for the *Schutzstaffeln*.

Its members are to be trained and its ranks filled with volunteers from those who are subject to serve in the army who have finished their duties in the obligatory labour service. The service period for volunteers is 4 years. It may be prolonged for *SS-Unterführer*. Special regulations are in force for SS leaders. The regular compulsory military service (paragraph 8 of the law relating to military service) is fulfilled by service of the same amount of time in the *SS-Verfügungstruppe*.

The *SS-Verfügungstruppe* receives its financial resources through the Ministry of the Interior. Its budget requires a checkup by the high command of the *Wehrmacht*.

2. The *SS-Verfügungstruppe* falls into the following parts:

    1 headquarters staff (*Leibstandarte-SS Adolf Hitler*) .
    3 regiments motorized.
    2 motorcycle battalions under a *Standarte* staff.
    1 engineer battalion motorized.
    1 signal battalion motorized.
    1 medical unit.

The complete strength, the organization, the arming, and the equipment of the *SS-Verfügungstruppe* depend on the task allocated in peace time and in case of mobilization. In case of mobilization, the *Standarten* and independent *Sturmbanne* are organized like the corresponding units of an infantry division respectively or a motorized infantry division of the army.

The engineer unit is fully motorized.

The signal unit (motorized) is organized like an infantry division signal unit (motorized).

The peacetime strength and equipment of the army are the pattern for the strength and equipment of the staffs and units of the *SS-Verfügungstruppe*. Personnel and material necessary above the peace time strength and the table of equipment will be determined in cooperation with the high command of the *Wehrmacht* and the *Reichsführer-SS* and chief of the German police.

For use in the interior, the *Standarten* are reinforced by the following special formation:

Leibstandarte-SS Adolf Hitler reinforced by:
    1 armored reconnaissance platoon.
    1 motorcycle platoon.
    1 motorized engineer platoon.

the other *Standarten* by:
each
    1 armored reconnaissance platoon.
    1 light infantry motorcycle platoon.
    and by additional telephone and radio units for the signal platoons.

the non-motorized units by:
    1 trucking platoon each.

The signal unit (motorized) with additional means of communication in order to safeguard the communication system of the *Reichsführer-SS* and chief of the German police. The necessary personnel and material will be determined in cooperation with the high-command of the *Wehrmacht* and the *Reichsführer-SS* and chief of the German police.

The final aim is the complete mobilization of all *Standarten* and independent units; in the case of mobilization, the skeleton corps of the reinforcement units of the *SS-Totenkopfverbaende*, to whom in peacetime the short training of replacements for the *SS-Totenkopfverbaende* was entrusted, are to be devoted to the task of ensuring replacements for the *SS-Verfügungstruppe* (see C 2).

The supreme commander of the army prepares the *SS-Verfügungstruppe* for their use within the wartime army. He issues the necessary orders, regulates their working with reserve army authorities, supports the training and makes inspections. He is authorized to transfer these powers to lower echelon offices and to report to me about the state of combat training, after prior consultation with the *Reichsführer-SS* and chief of the German police.

A timely exchange of officers, respectively leaders between the army and the *SS-Verfügungstruppe* is to be carried out in mutual agreement as soon as the officer situation permits it.

Any changes in the organization, the strength and the arming of the *SS-Verfügungstruppe* have to be approved by me.

3. Orders for the case of mobilization.

A. The employment of the *SS-Verfügungstruppe* in case of mobilization is a double one:

1. By the supreme commander of the army within the wartime army. In that case, it comes completely under military laws and regulation, but remains a unit of the NSDAP politically.

2. In case of necessity in the interior according to my orders. In that case, it is under the *Reichsführer-SS* and chief of the German police.
In case of mobilization, I myself will make the decision about the time, strength and manner of the incorporation of the *SS-Verfügungstruppe* into the wartime army; these things will depend on the inner political situation at that time.

During the war, the skeleton corps of the reinforcement units of the *SS-Totenkopfverbände*, to whom in peace time the short training of replacements for the *SS-Totenkopfverbände* was entrusted, are to be devoted to the task of ensuring a reserve which should meet the ideologic and political spirit of the *Verfügungstruppe*.

In case of mobilization, all members of the SS who did their compulsory military duty in the *SS-Verfügungstruppe* are generally to be used to reinforce the *SS-Verfügungstruppe*.

Older classes of the *SS-Verfügungstruppe* also may be used to fill the ranks of the reinforcement of the *SS-Totenkopfverbände* police reinforcement which will be set-up in case of mobilization in so far as they are not needed as replacements for the *SS-Verfüngungstruppe*.

In case of mobilization, the replacements for the *SS-Verfügungstruppe* also may be used to fill up the ranks of young, untrained draftees.

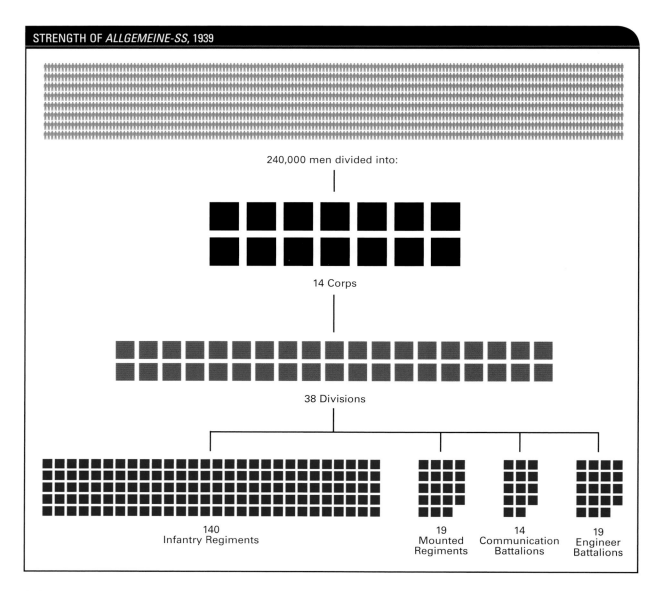

STRENGTH OF *ALLGEMEINE-SS*, 1939

240,000 men divided into:

14 Corps

38 Divisions

140
Infantry Regiments

19
Mounted
Regiments

14
Communication
Battalions

19
Engineer
Battalions

delivered principally through the talents of Reinhard Heydrich. Heydrich, a passionate Nazi who had joined the SS in 1932, was a talented and charismatic figure who caught Himmler's attention in the early 1930s. Heydrich was appointed to create the NSDAP's first security service, under SS authority. The result was the *Sicherheitsdienst* (Security Service; SD), at first a kind of Party auxiliary police force but one that became (in 1938) the state as well as the Party intelligence organization.

The SD was just the tip of the iceberg in terms of SS jurisdiction over policing. In 1936, Heydrich was placed in charge of the *Sicherheitspolizei* (Security Police; *Sipo*), an additional state/SS security organization that included the *Geheime Staatspolizei* (Secret State Police; *Gestapo*) and the detective activities of the *Kriminalpolizei*

(Criminal Police; *Kripo*). Distinct from the *Sipo* were the *Ordnungspolizei* (Order Police; *Orpo*), the regular uniformed officers patrolling the streets and fighting everything from crime to heavy traffic. Yet Himmler's ardent desire was to incorporate all policing and security structures of the Third Reich under his centralized control. In 1936 he got his way, when he extended his titular authority to *Reichsführer-SS und Chef der Deutschen Polizei im Reichsministerium des Innern* (Reich Leader SS and Chief of the German Police in the Reich Ministry of the Interior). This office placed Himmler in overall control of the police forces of the Third Reich, including the *Orpo*. Note that the *Orpo*, although technically now under the authority of the *Allgemeine-SS*, retained its civilian structure and rank system, and many of its officers were not SS or even Party members.

Nevertheless, Himmler's overall authority for German policing, and his tightening grip over the court system, meant that the processes of law and order were pulled into the SS domain, which steered them towards his own racial and political goals. (For an in-depth study of SS policing, see 'Police and Intelligence' chapter).

Armed SS

Considering its roots, it was natural that force of arms would be a key component of the growing SS. One of the earliest paramilitary bodies of the SS proper was the *SS-Stabswache Berlin*, a hand-picked bodyguard unit of 117 men commanded by Josef 'Sepp' Dietrich. In 1933 Himmler renamed this unit the *Leibstandarte*

SS Adolf Hitler (Bodyguard Regiment SS Adolf Hitler; LSSAH), and it was this unit that would eventually grow into the SS's first full combat division, the 1st SS-Panzer Division *Leibstandarte SS Adolf Hitler*, in 1942, passing through brigade strength in the meantime. In addition to units such as the LSSAH, the SS also formed *Politische Bereitschaften* (Political Readiness Detachments), principally to act as urban military reserves to combat Communist-led strikes or riots. Historian of the SS Marc J. Rikmenspoel notes of these men: 'They consisted of both dedicated party members and men who could not find semi-military service elsewhere. German Army and discharged *Reichswehr* veterans provided the leadership' (Rikmenspoel, 2004).

In October 1934, Himmler undertook a broader general restructuring that separated all armed SS elements from the *Allgemeine-SS*. The *Politische Bereitschaften* and other armed units were amalgamated under the category *SS-Verfügungstruppe* (SS Special Use Troops; SS-VT). From 1935, the SS-VT was arranged into familiar battalion then regimental structures, making it clear that it was to operate as a supplementary military force to the regular army. Hitler was at pains to reassure the Army that the SS-VT was not intended as its replacement. In 1934, Hitler himself, in conversation with Himmler, described the rationale behind the SS-VT:

In the Reich of the future, the SS and police will possess the

necessary authority in their relations with other citizens only if they have soldierly character. Through their past experience of glorious military events and their present education by the NSDAP, the German people have acquired such a warrior mentality that a fat, jovial, sock-knitting police such as we had during the Weimar era can no longer exert authority. For this reason it will be necessary for our SS and police, in their own closed units, to prove themselves at the front in the same way as the Army and to make blood sacrifices to the same degree as any other branch of the armed forces.

(Quoted in Williamson, 1994)

Hitler here presents the armed SS almost as a necessary exercise in fairness and respect – the Party's army had to show equal commitment to sacrifice. Hitler might also have added that the SS was simply there to do his dirty work, which could be very sordid indeed. By the late 1930s, Germany's Jews were suffering under a fearsome spectrum of persecution, a stream of racist legislation having made them pariahs in their own country. On the night of 9/10 November 1938, ostensibly in response to the attempted assassination of a German diplomat by a Jew in Paris, Heydrich unleashed SS teams and Nazi youths on Jewish people and property in cities throughout Germany. In *Kristallnacht* ('Night of the Broken Glass'), 91 Jews were murdered, 7500 Jewish businesses destroyed and 260 synagogues torched. Himmler's SS was clearly an instrument of terror.

KRISTALLNACHT ORDER, 8 NOVEMBER 1938

To – all headquarters and stations of the State Police. All districts and sub-districts of the SD

Urgent! For immediate attention of Chief or his deputy!

Re: Measures against Jews tonight

Following the attempt on the life of Secretary of the Legation vom Rath in Paris, protests against the Jews are expected in all parts of the Reich during the coming night, 9/10 November 1938. The instructions below are to be used for handling these events:

1. The chiefs of the State Police, or their deputies, must immediately upon receipt of this telegram contact, by telephone, the political leaders in their respective areas – *Gauleiter* or *Kreisleiter* – who have jurisdiction in their districts, and arrange a joint meeting with the inspector or commander of the *Ordnungspolizei* to discuss the arrangements for the demonstrations. At these discussions the political leaders will be informed that the German police has received instructions, detailed below, from the *Reichsführer-SS* and the Chief of the German Police, with whom the political leadership is asked to coordinate its own measures:

a) Only those measures should be taken that do not endanger German lives or property (i.e., synagogues are to be burned down only if the fire presents no danger to nearby buildings).

b) Places of business and apartments belonging to Jews may be destroyed but not looted. The police is instructed to implement this order and to arrest looters.

c) In commercial streets particular care is to be taken that non-Jewish businesses are completely undamaged.

d) Foreign citizens – even if they are Jews – are not to be molested.

2. Assuming that the guidelines detailed under para. 1 are observed, the demonstrations are not to be prevented by the police, which is only to supervise the following of the guidelines.

3. On receipt of this telegram, police will seize all archives to be found in all synagogues and offices of the Jewish communities so as to prevent their destruction during the demonstrations. This refers only to material of historical value, not to contemporary tax records, etc. The archives are to be handed over to the local officers of the SD.

4. Control of the measures of the Security Police regarding the demonstrations against the Jews is vested in the authority of the State Police, unless inspectors of the Security Police have given their own instructions. Officials of the Criminal Police, members of the SD, of the Reserves and the SS in general may be utilized to apply the measures taken by the Security Police.

5. As soon as the events of the night allow the release of the officials required, as many Jews in all districts – especially the rich – as can be accommodated in existing prisons are to be arrested. For the time being only healthy male Jews, who are not too old, are to be detained. After the detentions have been carried out the appropriate concentration camps are to be contacted immediately for the prompt accommodation of the Jews in the camps. Special care is to be taken that the Jews arrested in accordance with these instructions are not ill-treated....

Signed Heydrich,
SS *Gruppenführer*

Life in the Early SS

The SS clearly fostered a sense of elitism, which combined with attractive uniforms and a sharp identity was extremely appealing to young men. Its members felt part of a brotherhood, not just a paramilitary unit.

The SS, at least in the days before war forced it into a more emergency-oriented mindset, imposed strict standards of recruitment upon its manpower. Those wanting to join armed SS formations had to demonstrate superb levels of physical fitness, often far higher than those required for regular army service, meet minimum height requirements, be able to prove their Aryan ancestry and have no evidence of criminality in their personal histories. This last point was important to Himmler; in the stampede to join the *Allgemeine-SS* after Hitler came to power, many undesirables had slipped into the ranks of the security services or law enforcement. Known by the old guard as 'March Violets', the newcomers were stringently winnowed down by Himmler in 1934–35, resulting in thousands of explusions from the

SS RANKS, 1930–32			
SS Rank	*Translation*	*SS Rank*	*Translation*
■ Gruppenführer	Group leader	■ Sturmführer	Storm Leader
■ Oberführer	Senior leader	■ Haupttruppführer	Head Troop Leader
■ Standartenführer	Regiment leader	■ Truppführer	Troop Leader
■ Sturmbannführer	Storm Unit Leader	■ Scharführer	Squad Leader
■ Sturmhauptführer	Storm Head Leader	■ Mann	Trooper

SS RANKS, 1932–34			
SS Rank	*Translation*	*SS Rank*	*Translation*
■ Obergruppenführer	Senior Group Leader	■ Haupttruppführer	Head Troop Leader
■ Gruppenführer	Group Leader	■ Obertruppführer	Senior Troop Leader
■ Brigadeführer	Brigade Leader	■ Truppführer	Troop Leader
■ Oberführer	Senior Leader	■ Oberscharführer	Senior Squad Leader
■ Standartenführer	Regiment Leader	■ Scharführer	Squad Leader
■ Obersturmbannführer	Senior Storm Unit Leader	■ Rottenführer	Section Leader
■ Sturmbannführer	Storm Unit Leader	■ Sturmmann	Storm Trooper
■ Sturmhauptführer	Storm Head Leader	■ Mann	Trooper
■ Obersturmführer	Senior Storm Leader	■ Anwärter	Recruit
■ Sturmführer	Storm Leader		

ranks. Those that did join the ranks of the armed SS typically signed up for four years (enlisted men), 12 years (NCOs) or 25 years (officers), with the option for NCOs to apply for officer training after they had spent two years in the service.

The levels of motivation amongst SS personnel were extremely high, and the early bias for recruits from rural areas (reflecting Himmler's own veneration of rural living) meant that many of them brought excellent standards of fieldcraft. Such qualities made the *Wehrmacht* (Armed Forces) frequently jealous of the SS's ability to secure good-quality recruits, although in balance the educational background of the SS men was generally not as high as that of the *Heer* (Army) – some 50 per cent of *Waffen-SS* recruits would have only limited schooling, and officers were generally less academically inclined than *Heer* officers. Nevertheless, what the SS recruits typically brought to the table was plenty of resilience, both mental and physical, and a desire to excel.

Training

Training for the armed SS units was very much along familiar infantry lines, albeit with the emphasis placed emphatically on fast manoeuvres and a ruthless disregard for the humanity of the enemy. Most of the training was conducted at training depots close to the regimental home town.

SS RANKS, 1934–45

SS Rank	Translation	Wehrmacht equivalent
■ Reichsführer-SS	Reich Leader SS	Generalfeldmarschall
■ Oberstgruppenführer	Supreme Group Leader	Generaloberst
■ Obergruppenführer	Senior Group Leader	General
■ Gruppenführer	Group Leader	Generalleutnant
■ Brigadeführer	Brigade Leader	Generalmajor
■ Oberführer	Senior Leader	N/A
■ Standartenführer	Regiment Leader	Oberst
■ Obersturmbannführer	Senior Storm Unit Leader	Oberstleutnant
■ Sturmbannführer	Storm Unit Leader	Major
■ Haupsturmführer	Head Storm Leader	Hauptmann
■ Obersturmführer	Senior Storm Leader	Oberleutnant
■ Untersturmführer	Junior Storm Leader	Leutnant
■ Sturmscharführer	Storm Squad Leader	Stabsfeldwebel
■ Hauptscharführer	Head Squad Leader	Oberfeldwebel
■ Oberscharführer	Senior Squad Leader	Feldwebel
■ Scharführer	Squad Leader	Unterfeldwebel
■ Unterscharführer	Junior Squad Leader	Unteroffizier
■ Rottenführer	Section Leader	Obergefreiter
■ Sturmmann	Storm Trooper	Gefreiter
■ Oberschütze/Obermann	Senior Rifleman/Senior Trooper	Oberschütze
■ Schütze/Mann	Rifleman/Trooper	Schütze
■ Anwärter	Recruit	N/A
■ Beweber	Candidate	N/A

The ultimate objective of any training was to breed dispassionate, hardened men, and in that goal the SS largely succeeded. Weapons handling, particularly using small arms, was also central to the daily training regime, and vicious route marches, unarmed combat classes and boxing sessions helped inure the men to pain.

Those men who could not take such a regime were not necessarily failed; instead they might find themselves employed in less physically demanding units such as as signallers or cooks, but the overall failure rate did remain high.

A critical element in the reshaping of the SS recruit was ideological indoctrination. It has to be remembered that the SS was a specifically Nazi force, and hence its manpower had to embody Nazi values at the deepest level. At least three times every week, an early SS man would have to attend lectures on Nazi ideology and theory, with a particular focus on ingraining the men with NSDAP racial concepts. The men were left in no doubt as to whom they were to classify as *Untermenschen* (sub-humans) – Jews, Gypsies, Slavs, Communists, Freemasons and homosexuals. In a speech to SS officers at Poznan in 1943, Himmler famously spelled out his thoughts on such people:

What happens to a Russian or to a Czech does not interest me in the slightest... Whether nations live in prosperity or starve to death interests me only so far as we need them as slaves for our culture; otherwise, it is of no interest to me.

DETAILS OF SS BLACK SERVICE UNIFORM, 1932

Headgear:

Visored cap – black lacquered peak; black wool/tricot top and black band (wool/tricot for enlisted/NCO ranks, velvet for officers); white or aluminium piping to crown and edges of band; Death's Head emblem on front of band

Field cap – black wool with scalloped front portion to the flap; small silvered Death's Head badge on front of flap; silver-grey eagle and swastika emblem stitched on left side of crown

M16 or M18 German steel helmet – replaced with M35 pattern from 1934. SS runic symbols painted on helmet from 1934

Footwear:

Black shoes or black jackboots

Trousers:

Black with white piping along outer seam

Shirt:

Brown shirt with black tie (enlisted and NCO ranks); white shirt and black tie (officer ranks)

Tunic:

Single-breasted fastened by four aluminium buttons; two pleated breast patch pockets; two unpleated skirt patch pockets (all pockets button down); alloy belt support loops at waist level plus two aluminium buttons at the rear to provide additional belt support; open collar

Collar definition:

Enlisted ranks – black/white twisted cord; NCO ranks – black/silver twisted cord; officers – silver twisted cord; collar patches indicated rank on left collar and unit on right collar

Sleeve features

Regulation woollen armband – worn on left upper sleeve: black swastika set in white circle on red wool background, with black bands at top and bottom of armband.

Unit cuffband – worn on lower left sleeve above the cuff: 3cm (1.18in) black rayon material aluminium thread edging

Belt work:

Black leather waist belt featuring silver metal buckle (circular for officers, rectangular for lower ranks) with eagle and swastika motif, and bearing the SS motto *Mein Ehre Heisst Treue* (My Honour is Loyalty). Leather cross belt worn by all ranks

Whether ten thousand Russian females fall down from exhaustion while digging an antitank ditch interests me only so far as the antitank ditch for Germany is finished.

Such attitudes soaked through the ranks and fused with the ritualistic aspects of SS culture (see final chapter). These beliefs would inform SS behaviour in war, in acts of horror remembered to this day.

CHAPTER 2

The Allgemeine (General) SS

The SS became a vast administrative organization, its interests stretching from running the concentration and extermination camps through to offices dedicated to marital, legal and racial issues. To order this sprawling structure, the SS was broadly rationalized according to two main divisions.

On the one hand was the armed SS, embodied during the war years by the Waffen-SS. On the other was the Allgemeine-SS, a force that encompassed all the main administrative and policing functions of the SS. The Allgemeine-SS did not attain the same historical high profile as its combat counterpart, but its influence was widespread. Although it performed mainly administrative and home defence functions, its various race policy and state security agencies, plus its connections to the concentration camps through the SS-Totenkopfverbände, meant that the Allgemeine-SS was another insidious force within the Third Reich.

■ **SS men carrying Nazi standards take part in one of the early Nuremberg rallies, 1934. Note the SA men standing on the embankment behind.**

Command Structure

The Allgemeine-SS grew inexorably during the 1930s, its membership reaching 485,000 by the end of 1938. Although its physical strength, and in a sense its importance, declined during the war years, it still formed an integral element of SS operations.

SS-OBERABSCHNITTE AREAS & COMMANDERS, 1933–45

SS-Oberabschnitt Alpenland

SS-Gruppenführer Alfred Rodenbucher	(June 1939–May 1941)
SS-Brigadeführer Dr Gustav-Adolf Scheel	(May 1941–Nov 1941)
SS-Gruppenführer Erwin Rösener	(Nov 1941–May 1945)
SS-Brigadeführer Hermann Harm *	(Nov 1944–May 1945)

SS-Oberabschnitt Böhmen-Mähren

SS-Obergruppenführer Karl Hermann Frank	(Apr 1944–8 May 1945)
SS-Oberführer Emanuel Sladek *	(Feb 1945–May 1945)

SS-Oberabschnitt Österreich/Donau

SS-Brigadeführer Alfred Rodenbücher	(Feb 1934–Sep 1934)
SS-Obersturmbannführer Karl Taus	(Feb 1934–Jan 1937)
SS-Oberführer Ernst Kaltenbrunner	(Jan 1937–Jan 1943)
SS-Gruppenführer Rudolf Querner	(Feb 1943–Oct 1944)
SS-Gruppenführer Walter Schimana	(Oct 1944–May 1945)

SS-Oberabschnitt Elbe

SS-Brigadeführer August Heissmeyer	(Nov 1933–May 1934)
SS-Gruppenführer Friedrich Karl Freiherr von Eberstein	(May 1934–Apr 1936)
SS-Brigadeführer Theodor Berkelmann	(Apr 1936–Apr 1940)
SS-Obergruppenführer Udo von Woyrsch	(Apr 1940–Feb 1944)
SS-Gruppenführer Ludolf von Alvensleben	(Feb 1944–May 1945)

SS-Oberabschnitt Fulda-Werra

SS-Obergruppenführer Josias Erbrinz zu Waldeck-Pyrmont	(Jan 1937–1945)

SS-Oberabschnitt Main

SS-Gruppenführer Heinrich Schmauser	(Apr 1936–May 1941)
SS-Brigadeführer Dr Benno Martin	(May 1941–May 1945)

SS-Oberabschnitt Mitte

SS-Gruppenführer Friedrich Jeckeln	(Aug 1933–July 1940)
SS-Gruppenführer Günther Pancke	(July 1940–Sep 1943)
SS-Gruppenführer Hermann Höfle	(Sep 1943–Oct 1944)
SS-Obergruppenführer Rudolf Querner	(Oct 1944–May 1945)

SS-Oberabschnitt Nord

SS-Obergruppenführer Fritz Weitzel	(Apr 1940–June 1940)
SS-Gruppenführer Wilhelm Rediess	(June 1940–May 1940)

SS-Oberabschnitt Nordost

SS-Gruppenführer Werner Lorenz	(Dec 1933–Feb 1934)
SS-Brigadeführer Erich von dem Bach	(Feb 1934–Feb 1936)
SS-Gruppenführer Wilhelm Rediess	(Feb 1939–June 1940)
SS-Gruppenführer Jakob Sporrenburg	(June 1940–Apr 1941)
SS-Gruppenführer Hans-Adolf Prützmann	(Apr 1941–May 1945)
SS-Oberführer George Ebrecht *	(Dec 1941–Dec 1944)
SS-Gruppenführer Otto Hellwig *	(Dec 1944–May 1945)

SS-Oberabschnitt Nordsee

SS-Gruppenführer Josef Dietrich	(Oct 1932–Apr 1933)
SS-Oberführer Kurt Wittje	(Apr 1933–Feb 1934)
SS-Gruppenführer Werner Lorenz	(Feb 1934–Mar 1937)
SS-Gruppenführer Hans-Adolf Prützmann	(Mar 1937–Apr 1941)
SS-Gruppenführer Rudolf Querner *	(Apr 1941–Apr 1943)
SS-Gruppenführer Georg von Bassewitz-Behr *	(Apr 1943–May 1945)

SS-Oberabschnitt Nordwest

SS-Brigadeführer Hans-Alben Rauter	(June 1940–May 1945)

SS-Oberabschnitt Ost

SS-Obergruppenführer Friedrich-Wilhelm Krüger	(Sep 1942–Nov 1943)
SS-Obergruppenführer Wilhelm Koppe	(Nov 1943–May 1945)

SS-Oberabschnitt Ostland

SS-Obergruppenführer Friedrich Jeckeln	(Dec 1941–Mar 1945)

SS-Oberabschnitt Ostsee

SS-Gruppenführer Emil Mazuw	(Apr 1936–May 1945)

SS-Oberabschnitt Rhein

SS-Brigadeführer August Heissmeyer	(Jan 1934–May 1935)
SS-Gruppenführer Josias Erbinz zu Waldeck-Pyrmont	(June 1935–Dec 1936)

The *Allgemeine-SS* was officially founded in mid-1934, in an attempt to distinguish the administrative from the armed elements within the SS. In essence it was the organization that kept the wheels of SS interests turning. As the SS had its fingers in so many pies, it naturally became a huge organization, too large to explain in its entirety here. What we can do, however, is chart its major structure and function, and, in the next section, look at some of its specialist departments and purposes.

Commands

At the top of the SS tree, presiding over both *Allgemeine-SS* and

SS-Gruppenführer Richard Hildebrandt	(Jan 1937–Sep 1939)
SS-Brigadeführer Jakob Sporrenburg	(Sep 1939–June 1940)
SS-Brigadeführer Erwin Rösener	(June 1940–Nov 1941)
SS-Gruppenführer Theodor Berkelmann	(Nov 1941–Sep 1943)

SS-Oberabschnitt Rhein-Westmark

SS-Obergruppenführer Theodor Berkelmann	(Sep 1943–Nov 1943)
SS-Gruppenführer Jürgen Stroop	(Nov 1943–Mar 1945)

SS-Oberabschnitt Spree

SS-Standartenführer Kurt Wege	(Sep 1929–Dec 1930)
SS-Oberführer Kurt Daluege	(Dec 1930–Sep 1931)
SS-Oberführer Kurt Wege	(Sep 1931–July 1932)
SS-Gruppenführer Kurt Daluege	(July 1932–Oct 1933)
SS-Gruppenführer Joseph Dietrich	(Oct 1933–May 1945)
SS-Gruppenführer Paul Moder	(Nov 1938–Nov 1939)
SS-Gruppenführer Max Schneller	(Nov 1939–May 1945)

SS-Oberabschnitt Süd

SS-Obergruppenführer Rudolf Hess	(1929–Oct 1930)
SS-Oberführer Josef Dietrich	(Oct 1930–Oct 1932)
SS-Oberführer Richard Hildebrandt	(Oct 1932–Jan 1933)
SS-Oberführer Friedrich Jeckeln	(Jan 1933–July 1933)
SS-Brigadeführer Henrich Schmauser	(July 1933–Apr 1936)
SS-Obergruppenführer Friedrich Karl Freiherr von Eberstein	(Apr 1936–Apr 1945)
SS-Brigadeführer Hermann Freiherr von Schade	(June 1939–July 1939)
SS-Brigadeführer Anton Vogler	(Feb 1945–Apr 1945)
SS-Obergruppenführer Wilhelm Koppe	(Apr 1945–May 1945)

SS-Oberabschnitt Südost

SS-Gruppenführer Udo von Woyrsch	(Mar 1932–Jan 1935)
SS-Brigadeführer Wilhelm Rediess	(Jan 1935–Feb 1936)
SS-Gruppenführer Erich von dem Bach	(Feb 1936–June 1941)
SS-Obergruppenführer Heinrich Schmauser	(June 1941–Feb 1945)
SS-Brigadeführer Walter Bierkamp *	(Feb 1945–Mar 1945)
SS-Obergruppenführer Richard Hildebrandt	(Feb 1945–May 1945)

SS-Oberabschnitt Südwest

SS-Gruppenführer Hans-Adolf Prützmann	(Nov 1933–Feb 1937)
SS-Brigadeführer Paul Kaul	(Mar 1937–Apr 1943)
SS-Gruppenführer Otto Hofmann	(Apr 1943–May 1945)

SS-Oberabschnitt Ukraina

SS-Obergruppenführer Hans-Adolf Prützmann	(Dec 1941–Sep 1944)

SS-Oberabschnitt Warthe

SS-Gruppenführer Wilhelm Koppe	(Oct 1939–Nov 1943)
SS-Obergruppenführer Theodor Berkelmann	(Nov 1943–Dec 1943)
SS-Brigadeführer Heinz Reinefarth	(Dec 1943–Dec 1944)
SS-Oberführer Friedrich Gehrhardt *	(? 1944–Dec 1944)
SS-Gruppenführer Willy Schmelcher	(Dec 1944–May 1945)

SS-Oberabschnitt Weichsel

SS-Gruppenführer Richard Hildebrandt	(Nov 1939–Apr 1943)
SS-Gruppenführer Fritz Katzmann	(Apr 1943–May 1945)

SS-Oberabschnitt West

SS-Standartenführer Fritz Weitzel	(Nov 1929–Apr 1940)
SS-Gruppenführer Theodor Berkelmann	(Apr 1940–July 1940)
SS-Gruppenfu?hrer Friedrich Jeckeln	(July 1940–June 1941)
SS-Gruppenführer Karl Gutenberger	(June 1941–May 1945)

SS-Oberabschnitt Westmark

SS-Gruppenführer Theodor Berkelmann	(Oct 1940–Sep 1943)

(* Temporary or substitute commander)

35

Waffen-SS organizations, was the *Reichsführer-SS* (RFSS), Heinrich Himmler. Himmler was personally served by the *Hauptamt Persönlicher Stab Reichsführer-SS* (Headquarters Personal Staff RFSS; *Pers. Stab RFSS*). This organization had a peculiarly broad range of responsibilities to smooth the path of Himmler's governance, and included several heads of the various other SS *Hauptämter* (headquarters). The *Pers. Stab RFSS* delivered services for Himmler, such as handling correspondence, awarding decorations to SS officers and dealing with the press. It was also deeply entangled in administering Himmler's personal racial theories, both through the commissioning and execution of cultural research and also through its running of the *Lebensborn* ('Fount of Life') project, a sexually opportunistic breeding programme for SS personnel. (See the final chapter for more about what can loosely be termed SS 'cultural activities'.)

Yet there was also a certain combat command function to the *Pers. Stab RFSS*. Himmler took increased levels of combat leadership during the war, posts that typically served to illustrate his complete lack of suitability to military leadership. Within the *Pers. Stab RFSS* was the *Kommandostab RFSS* (Command HQ RFSS), which also took the operational title *Feldkommandostelle RFSS* (Field Command Staff RFSS) during the war. This agency acted as Himmler's command HQ for leading his personal combat formations, typically second-line units that were eventually

absorbed into the *Waffen-SS* anyway. It had its own combat elements, including anti-aircraft units and an infantry battalion. (Note: for the important *Allgemeine-SS* commands of *Höherer SS- und Polizeiführer* (HSSPF) and *Höchste SS- und Polizeiführer* (HöSSPF), see 'Police and Intelligence' chapter.)

SS-Hauptamt
The *SS-Hauptamt* (SS Main Office; SS-HA) was the administrative centre of the SS, in charge of files for non-commissioned personnel and also for processing recruitment applications and assignments. During the pre-war years, the SS-HA had actually been an office of confident power, initially acting as the central headquarters for the entire SS, including the *Politische Bereitschaften* (see previous chapter) and other guard units, and had jurisdiction over everything from garrison life to officer training. The demands of war meant that it had to jettison many of its responsibilities to new, dedicated-purpose departments, but its hold over SS recruitment meant that it was still a highly influential office, particularly in terms of the strength and vitality of the SS.

SS-Führungshauptamt
A purely wartime organization (it was created in August 1940), the *SS-Führungshauptamt* (SS Main Operational Office; SS-FHA) had critical powers for the functioning of both the *Allgemeine-SS* and the *Waffen-SS*. It was concerned with the operational control of SS units, its responsibilities including training, supply and logistics, controlling the

concentration camps (1940–42), mobilizing forces and deployment procedures. Historian Mark Yeger here further clarifies the SS-FHA's command relationship to the wider SS and German Army:

This main office was not responsible to the Oberkommando der Wehrmacht (Armed Forces High Command) and it had no control of Waffen-SS troops in combat areas who were led by the Army. It was also not responsible to the SS-Hauptamt, though a main part of the SS as a whole, since it served as the Armed SS Headquarters.

(Yeger, 1997)

SS-Rasse- und Siedlungshauptamt
The *SS-Rasse- und Siedlungshauptamt* (SS Race and Settlement Main Office; RuSHA) was, as its name evokes, a department concerned primarily with the racial purity and quality of the SS members. We have already observed its formation in Chapter 1 and outlined its key responsibilities for genealogy and the approval of SS marriages. Note, however, that during the war the pressures of speed-recruitment meant that it restricted its background checks to officers and their spouses or fiancées. All the other personnel, including foreigners, were admitted on the basis of signed declarations. In terms of organization, RuSHA officers were stationed in every town, city and *Oberaschnitt*, to provide support for local SS units.

Note that during the war another responsibility of the RuSHA was resettling Germans in the occupied

SS-OBERABSCHNITT REGIONS, 1941

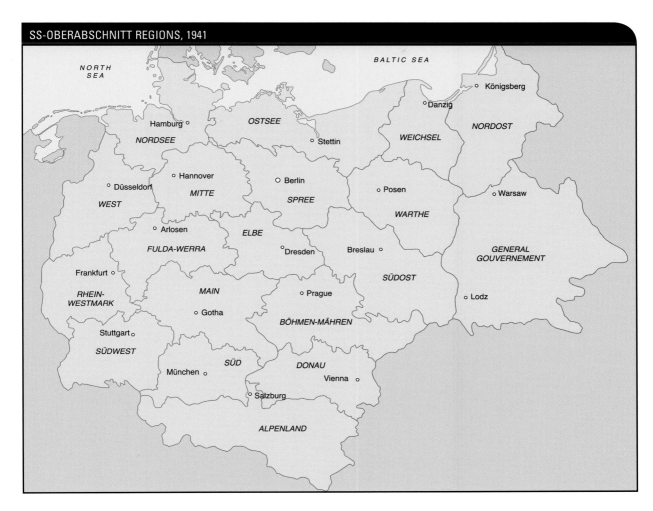

NORTH SEA

BALTIC SEA

Königsberg

Danzig

Hamburg

OSTSEE

NORDOST

NORDSEE

Stettin

WEICHSEL

Hannover

Berlin

Düsseldorf

MITTE

Posen

Warsaw

WEST

SPREE

WARTHE

Arlosen

ELBE

Dresden

Breslau

GENERAL GOUVERNEMENT

Frankfurt

FULDA-WERRA

SÜDOST

RHEIN-WESTMARK

MAIN

Prague

Lodz

Gotha

Stuttgart

BÖHMEN-MÄHREN

SÜDWEST

SÜD

DONAU

München

Vienna

Salzburg

ALPENLAND

▲ **SS-OBERABSCHNITT were the largest territorial commands within the** *Allgemeine-SS*. **The officer in charge of an** *Oberabschnitt* **was designated** *Führer der Oberschnitt*, **while the chief staff officer was the** *Stabsführer*.**The territories of the** *Oberabschnitte* **generally corresponded with the** *Wehrkreis* **(Military District) administrative system used by the German armed forces.**

Eastern territories, a task that involved implementing misery on a huge scale as families from Poland, the Baltic states and Soviet territories were simply ejected to make way for SS personnel and other Germans.

Hauptamt SS-Gericht

The *Hauptamt SS-Gericht* (Main SS Legal Office) had a fairly innocuous title, but like many of the SS offices it had some sinister undercurrents. It provided an internal legal infrastructure for the SS, conducting its own investigations and trials relating to offences by SS personnel and police. It also created SS laws and administered the penal camps that held any SS and police convicts. The SS courts could also deliver death sentences, although Himmler himself would have to approve the sentence before it was carried out.

Originally, the office had simply been titled *SS-Gericht*, and functioned as part of the *SS-Hauptamt*, but as with so many other

LIST OF *SS-STANDARTEN,* WITH HEADQUARTERS LOCATIONS

SS-Standarten

1. SS-Standarte Julius Schreck	Munich
2. SS-Standarte Hessen	Frankfurt/Main
3. SS-Standarte	Nuremberg
4. SS-Standarte Schleswig-Holstein	Altona
5. SS-Standarte Mosel	Brohl, Koblenz, Traben, Trier
6. SS-Standarte Eduard Felsen (also Charlottenburg)	Berlin
7. SS-Standarte Fritz Schlegel	Plauen
8. SS-Standarte Niederschlesien	Hirschberg
9. SS-Standarte Pommern	Stettin
10. SS-Standarte Pfalz	Neustadt, Kaiserslautern
11. SS-Standarte Planetta (also Burgenland)	Vienna
12. SS-Standarte Niedersachsen	Hanover
13. SS-Standarte Württemberg	Stuttgart
14. SS-Standarte Gothaland (also Thüringen)	Gotha
15. SS-Standarte Brandenburg	Berlin, Neuruppin
16. SS-Standarte Unterelbe	Breslau
17. SS-Standarte	Harburg-Wilhelmsburg, Celle
18. SS-Standarte Ostpreußen	Königsberg
19. SS-Standarte Westfalen-Nord	Münster
20. SS-Standarte Fritz Weitzel	Düsseldorf
21. SS-Standarte	Magdeburg
22. SS-Standarte von der Schulenburg (also Mecklenburg)	Schwerin
23. SS-Standarte Oberschlesien	Oppeln, Gleiwitz, Beuthen
24. SS-Standarte Ostfriesland	Oldenburg
25. SS-Standarte Ruhr	Essen
26. SS-Standarte Paul Berck	Halle
27. SS-Standarte Ostmark	Frankfurt/Oder
28. SS-Standarte	Hamburg
29. SS-Standarte Schwaben	Niderraunau, Munich, Augsburg, Lindau
30. SS-Standarte Adolf Höh (also Westfalen-Süd)	Bochum
31. SS-Standarte Niederbayern	Landshut, Dingolfind, Regensburg, Straubing
32. SS-Standarte Baden	Heidelberg
33. SS-Standarte Rhein-Hessen	Darmstadt, Mainz
34. SS-Standarte Oberbayern	Munich
35. SS-Standarte	Kassel
36. SS-Standarte	Danzig, Zoppot
37. SS-Standarte Ob der Enns	Linz
38. SS-Standarte	Leoben, Bruk, Graz
39. SS-Standarte Ostpommern	Kolberg, Lauenburg, Köslin
40. SS-Standarte	Kiel

41. SS-Standarte Oberfranken	Kulmbach, Hof, Coburg, Bayreuth	84. SS-Standarte Saale	Weissenfels, Chemnitz
42. SS-Standarte Fritz von Scholz	Berlin	85. SS-Standarte	Saarbrücken
43. SS-Standarte	Glatz, Frankenstein	86. SS-Standarte Hanauer Land	Offenburg
44. SS-Standarte Uckermark	Berlin, Eberswalde	87. SS-Standarte Tirol	Innsbruck
45. SS-Standarte Neisse	Neisse, Opeln	88. SS-Standarte Stedingen	Bremen
46. SS-Standarte	Dresden	89. SS-Standarte Holzweber	Vienna
47. SS-Standarte	Gera	90. SS-Standarte Franz Kutschera (also Kärnten)	Spittal, Klagenfurt
48. SS-Standarte	Leipzig	91. SS-Standarte	Torgau, Wittenberg
49. SS-Standarte Braunschweig	Braunschweig, Goslar	92. SS-Standarte Alt-Bayern	Ingolstadt
50. SS-Standarte Nordschleswig	Flensburg	93. SS-Standarte	Koblenz
51. SS-Standarte Harz	Göttingen	94. SS-Standarte Obersteiermark	Leoben
52. SS-Standarte Unter-Enns	Vienna, Amstetten, Krems	95. SS-Standarte	Trantenau
53. SS-Standarte Dithmarschen	Wesselburen, Heide	96. SS-Standarte	Brüx
54. SS-Standarte Seidel-Dittmarsh	Dühringshof, Landsberg	97. SS-Standarte	Eger
55. SS-Standarte Weser	Nienburg, Minden, Berben	98. SS-Standarte	Märisch-Schönberg
56. SS-Standarte Franken	Bamburg	99. SS-Standarte	Znaim
57. SS-Standarte Thüringer Wald	Schleusingen, Meiningen	100. SS-Standarte	Reichenberg
58. SS-Standarte	Aachen, Cologne	101. SS-Standarte	Karlsbad
59. SS-Standarte Loeper	Dessau, Strassfurt, Quedling	102. SS-Standarte	Jägerndorf
60. SS-Standarte	Insterburg	103. SS-Standarte	Aussig
61. SS-Standarte Masuren	Allenstein	104. SS-Standarte	Troppau
62. SS-Standarte	Karlsruhe	105. SS-Standarte	Memel
63. SS-Standarte Württemberg Süd	Reutlingen, Tübingen	106. SS-Standarte	Augsburg
64. SS-Standarte Marienburg	Marienwerder, Zoppot, Danzig	107. SS-Standarte	Brünn
65. SS-Standarte Schwarzwald	Lajr/Baden, Freiburg	108. SS-Standarte	Prague
66. SS-Standarte Friedland	Elbing	109. SS-Standarte	Posen
67. SS-Standarte Wartburg	Langensalza, Erfurt	110. SS-Standarte	Hohensalza
68. SS-Standarte Oberpfalz	Amberg, Regensburg	111. SS-Standarte	Kolmar
69. SS-Standarte Sauerland	Hagen	112. SS-Standarte	Litzmannstadt
70. SS-Standarte	Glogau	113. SS-Standarte	Kalisch
71. SS-Standarte Weichsel	Zoppot, Danzig	114. SS-Standarte	Lesslau
72. SS-Standarte Lippe	Detmold	115. SS-Standarte	Ziecenau
73. SS-Standarte Mittelfranken	Ansbach	116. SS-Standarte	Bromberg
74. SS-Standarte Ostsee	Griefswald	117. SS-Standarte	Konitz
75. SS-Standarte Widukind (also Tempelhof)	Berlin	118. SS-Standarte	Stargard
76. SS-Standarte	Salzburg	119. SS-Standarte	Graudenz
77. SS-Standarte	Schneidemühl	120. SS-Standarte	Kulm
78. SS-Standarte	Wiesbaden	121. SS-Standarte	Strasbourg
79. SS-Standarte	Ulm	122. SS-Standarte	Strasbourg
80. SS-Standarte Groß-Beeren	Berlin	123. SS-Standarte	Kolmar
81. SS-Standarte	Würzburg	124. SS-Standarte	Kattowitz
82. SS-Standarte	Bielefeld	125. SS-Standarte	Metz
83. SS-Standarte Oberhessen	Giessen	126. SS-Standarte	Marburg-Drau
		127. SS-Standarte	Oslo

OFFICES OF THE *PERSÖNLICHER STAB RFSS*

Chef

■ Persönliche Referent	(Personal Advisor)
■ Adjutantur	(Adjutant)
■ Feldkommandostelle des Reichsführer-SS	(Field Command Staff *Reichsführer-SS*)
■ Hauptabteilung Auziechungen und Orden	(Central Awards Department)
■ Gesellschaft Ahnenerbe	(Ancestral/Genealogical Society)
■ SS-Mannschafthäuser	(SS Housing Officer)
■ Reichsarzt SS	(SS Reich Doctor)
■ RFSS Persönlicher Stab Beaftragter	(RFSS Personal HQ)
■ Amt für Bevolkerungspolitik	(Department for Population)
■ Kulturreferat der RFSS	(Culture Unit for the RFSS)
■ Statistisch – Wissenschaftlische Institut RFSS	(Statistics – RFSS Scientific Institute)
■ Dienststelle für Kulturelle Forschungen mit SS-Schule Haus Wewelsburg	(Department for Cultural Research, SS-School Wewelsburg)
■ Chef des Protokolle	(Head of Protocol)
■ Rohestoffamt RFSS	(RFSS Raw Materials)
■ Amt L (Lebensborn)	(Department L – Lebensborn)
■ Chef Fernmeldungswesen bei RFSS	(Head of RFSS Telecommunications)
■ SS-Richter bei RFSS Persönlicher Stab	(SS Judge of the RFSS Personal HQ)
■ RFSS Persönlicher Stab für Jagd und Forstwesen	(RFSS Personal HQ for Hunters and Forestry)
■ Dienststelle Vierjahresplan	(Department for the Four-Year Plan)
■ Presstelle RFSS	(RFSS Press Office)
■ SS-Wirtschaftsring	(SS Economics Group)
■ Abteilung Wirtschaftliche Hilfe	(Department of Economic Assistance)

SS offices, the growth of SS membership necessitated its split to become an independent entity. The motivation to establish the *Hauptamt SS-Gericht* was fundamentally the desire to put the SS beyond the reach of civilian courts. An incident during the mid-1930s, when SS concentration camp guards were arrested by a local civilian magistrate for killing prisoners, alarmed the SS hierarchy, who felt that the civilian world had no business interfering in its activities.

Each *Oberabschnitt* had its own SS court and legal officials (there were 38 regional SS courts throughout the Third Reich), including a main SS court in Munich staffed by more than 600 lawyers, which even carried the authority to try SS officers of general rank. The reach of the *Hauptamt SS-Gericht* also extended over the *Waffen-SS* – each corps and division had a *Richter* (judge advocate) present on the headquarters staff to handle crimes committed in field units. (Bearing in mind the scale of SS human rights abuses, obviously the criteria for what constituted a crime were particularly skewed.) The only time legal authority would pass to non-SS jurisdiction was in the case of *Waffen-SS* personnel who committed crimes while assigned to a German Army unit.

Internally the *Hauptamt SS-Gericht* was divided into four main departmental groups, designated *Amtsgruppen* I–IV. *Amtsgruppe* I was in charge of general legal affairs, including making policy and laws and reviewing trials. *Amtsgruppe* II was tasked with matters of organization, personnel and disciplinary issues, while *Amtsgruppe* III handled pardons, reprieves and the execution of sentences. *Amtsgruppe* IV served as a liaison office.

The *Hauptamt SS-Gericht* was a highly administrative body, but its practical effect was to place the SS outside the reach of civilian law, and hence enable it to live by its own rules and conventions. Furthermore, although the department was staffed by many trained legal personnel, Himmler's frequent personal interest in verdicts and sentencing meant that the system was very much shaped along his preferred lines.

SS-Personalhauptamt
The *SS-Personalhauptamt* (SS Personnel Department) was effectively the documentation centre for the SS, holding the records of all SS enlisted men and officers. Its value lay in the fact that it not only had data on all SS personnel, but that it was also charged with maintaining and developing manpower levels in both the *Allgemeine-SS* and the *Waffen-SS*. Such a job became increasingly more testing during the

later years of the war as war losses began to bite.

Reichssicherheitshauptamt
The *Reichssicherheitshauptamt* (Reich Main Security Office; RSHA) is explored more fully in the later 'Police and Intelligence' chapter. Suffice here to say, however, that the RSHA was the most powerful of the *Allgemeine-SS* departments. Formed on 27 September 1939, it brought together all the security and intelligence organizations of the Reich under one central SS authority (initially Reinhard Heydrich, prior to his assassination in 1942). The RSHA included the *Gestapo*, *Sicherheitsdienst* (Security Service; SD) and the *Kriminalpolizei* (Criminal Police; *Kripo*) services, which together policed the ideology and political life of Hitler's Germany and the occupied territories abroad.

SS-Wirtschafts- und Verwaltungshauptamt
This office, translated as SS Economics and Administrative Department (WVHA), was the financial heart of the SS, running its vast industrial interests (as well funding the *Einsatzgruppen* and *Totenkopfverbände*) and ordering the SS accounts. It delivered its roles through five main departments:

Amt A – Finance, Law and Administration
Amt B – Supply, Administration and Equipment
Amt C – Works and Buildings
Amt D – Concentration Camps
Amt W – Economics
Funded directly by the Reich Finance

Ministry, the WVHA ended up controlling multiple interests from mining concerns through to the finances of the *Waffen-SS* divisions.

Regional structures
Below the main command offices, the *Allgemeine-SS* was arranged according to regional structures. At the top of the tree were the *Oberabschnitte*, generally matching the Reich's *Wehrkreise* (Military Districts) and commanded by a high-ranking SS officer. By 1944 there were 17 *Oberabschnitte* in Germany and six in the occupied territories. The *Oberaschnitte* were in turn broken down into *Abschnitte* (Districts), and these controlled the essential building block of the *Allgemeine-SS*, the *Fuß-Standarten* (Foot Regiments).

The *Fuß-Standarten* individually numbered anywhere between 400 and 2000 men, typically depending on the year of the war, and were composed of several *Sturmbanne* (Storm Units) plus a medical detachment. Three of the Storm Units would be active, and one would operate in reserve. In turn, the *Sturmbanne* were divided into three to five *Stürme* (Companies), each of which featured three or four *Züge* or *Trupps* (Platoons). These were themselves split down into three *Scharen* (Sections) each, and at the bottom was the *Rotte* (File), like the modern fire team or squad.

Note also that the *Allgemeine-SS* also had 22 *Reiterstandarten* (Cavalry Regiments), which were largely ceremonial formations, although as with the foot regiments they could be used for crowd control.

Special Interests

The Allgemeine-SS *was as much a major corporation as it was a political and military organization. With a totally free supply of labour in the form of concentration camp workers, it was in the ideal position to develop a business empire.*

It is undeniable that the influence of the *Allgemeine-SS* waned considerably during the war years. This decline was principally due to the rise of the *Waffen-SS*, which became the dominant slice of the SS membership (see pie chart on opposite page). What had previously been simply bodyguard units expanded to become entire regiments and then divisions (see chart below), and during the war these divisions played a naturally critical role in Germany's conquests and then its defensive retreat. Yet although the *Allgemeine-SS* became more peripheral, that did not mean it went into stagnation. One particular area of continuing energy was SS business activities, which remained lively until the end of the war.

Commercial advantage
Himmler, despite his inveterate resistance to comprehending economics or finance at any serious level, seemed determined from the outset to exploit the economic opportunities of the SS. By the late 1930s, indeed, it became clear that the SS had a range of potent commercial advantages.

First, and most important, it had an almost endless supply of free labour in the form of concentration camp inmates and, from 1941, the huge volumes of Soviet POWs shipped back into Germany from the East. Second, its authority in the Party plus its control over the police forces and much of the legal process meant it could largely develop economic policy free from inconvenient legislation. Third, Hitler's extirpation of the trade unions meant it had no concerns with worker activism, even amongst German workers. Finally, the conquests of foreign lands placed dizzying amounts of natural resources, and associated industrial plant, directly under SS control. In short, it was ideally placed to create its own monopolistic enterprises, making profit on the back of persecution and human misery. (More about the actual conditions within the concentration camps will be discussed in later chapters.)

Early enterprises
Shortly after Hitler took power in Germany in 1933, Himmler began to explore the commercial possibilities of his organization. One of its earliest businesses was Nordland-Verlag GmbH, an SS publishing house founded in December 1934 exclusively for the publishing of Nazi propaganda and for giving wider distribution to Himmler's outlandish racial theories. Himmler fancied himself as something of an aesthete, and shortly after the publishing start-up he also acquired a porcelain-manufacturing company near Munich. Despite forever being a loss-making business, and much to the frustration of SS accountants, the porcelain factory kept churning out pieces of ideologically imbued art well into the war years.

Much of the work was infused with Aryan mysticism, but the quality of production was undeniably high and there were enough non-political pieces (ranging from dogs to people in national dress) to appeal to the

FROM HITLER'S BODYGUARD TO PANZER DIVISION – 1ST SS-PANZER DIVISION *LEIBSTANDARTE SS ADOLF HITLER* (LSSAH)	
SS-Stabswache Berlin	Mar–May 1933
SS-Sonderkommando Zossen	May–Sep 1933
Leibstandarte SS Adolf Hitler	Sep 1933–Dec 1934
Leibstandarte SS Adolf Hitler (mot)	Dec 1934–July 1942
SS-Division (mot) LSSAH	July–Nov 1942
SS-Panzergrenadier Division LSSAH	Nov 1942–Oct 1943
1st SS-Panzer Division LSSAH	Oct 1943–May 1945

relevant masses. Actually, some 50 per cent of output was sold directly to Himmler's own staff. In turn, the factory was run by an artistic and architectural section within the *Stab RFSS*, under *SS-Obersturmbannführer* Professor Karl Diebitsch.

The publishing and porcelain businesses were just the tip of Himmler's commercial iceberg during the mid-1930s. Another enterprise was Anton Loibl GmbH, a company named after *SS-Hauptsturmführer* Anton Loibl who, with genuine ingenuity, invented a reflective disc that fitted to bicycle wheels, making the bicycle visible at night under vehicle headlamps. Hitler rightly thought this a sterling idea for both police and civilian use, and made them a compulsory fitment on all bicycles from June 1939.

Loibl became wealthy on the proceeds, despite the fact that Himmler siphoned off 50 per cent of the profits into racial theory projects. Other sidelines included the 'Society for the Protection and Maintenance of German Cultural Monuments', essentially a vanity project dedicated to reconstructing the Renaissance castle at Wewelsburg and turning it into a Reich SS Leadership School. This goal was never actually achieved, however, despite the employment of thousands of workers.

Financial acumen

Himmler's early attempts at entrepreneurship were largely amateurish and indulgent, but he admittedly seemed to realize that better financial brains than his own were required to run the SS. Those brains, although they were not as

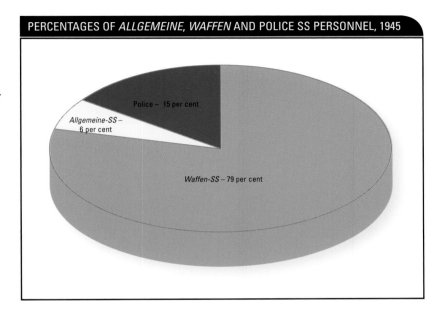

PERCENTAGES OF *ALLGEMEINE, WAFFEN* AND POLICE SS PERSONNEL, 1945

Police – 15 per cent

Allgemeine-SS –
6 per cent

Waffen-SS – 79 per cent

impressive as Himmler often believed, came in the form of Oswald Pohl, a former naval paymaster who caught Himmler's attention during the 1930s.

After testing Pohl out in some SS administrative offices, Himmler promoted him to *Reichskassenverwalter* (Chief Financial Officer) of the SS in June 1935, and on 30 April 1939 he took over responsibility for the newly formed WVHA. It was Pohl who oversaw the rise of the SS as a major economic power in its own right, although the innate brutality of the SS overlords to their workforce, plus a range of other inefficiencies, meant that the SS did not achieve its full financial promise. For example, the ideology of the SS meant that slave workers were physically abused from morn to night, meaning, from a morally suspended commercial perspective, that worker productivity

was compromised through injuries, fatigue, illness and fatalities. That being said, the SS nevertheless managed to build up some singular enterprises.

Big business

The major commercial sector of the WVHA was *Amtsgruppe* W, run by Dr Hans Hohberg. This sector was in turn divided into *Ämter* I–VIII, each with its own SS fiefdom. *Amt* I was concerned with Excavations and Quarries, and principally ran the Deutsche Erd & Steinwerke GmbH company. This company controlled some 14 stone works, brickworks and quarries, all attached to labour camps such as Buchenwald, Sachsenhausen, Gross-Rosen and Mauthausen.

Its other enterprises included various porcelain and pottery factories (including that at Allach) and an oil shale distillery.

Department	Title	Translation	Head
	HAUPTAMT VOLKSDEUTSCHE MITTELSTELLE (VOMI) ORGANIZATION, 1941		
Amt I	Amt der Dienststellenleiters	Department for Department Leaders	Walter Ellermeier
Amt II	Organisation und Personal	Organization and Personnel	Konrad Radunski
Amt III	Finanz	Finance	Heinrich Lohl
Amt IV	Presse, Berichterstattung	Press, Reporting	Waldermar Rimann
Amt V	Deutschtumerziehung	German Re-education	Dr Adolf Puls
Amt VI	Sicherung Deutschen Volkstums Reich	Protection of the Ethnic Germans of the Reich	Heinz Bruckner
Amt VII	Sicherung Deutschen Volkstums Ostgebiet	Protection of Ethnic Germans in the Eastern Territories	(not known)
Amt VIII	Kultur und Wissenschaft	Culture and Science	Horst Hoffmeyer
Amt IX	Politische Führung Deutscher Volksgruppe	German Political Leadership Group	Dr Hans Weibgen
Amt X	Führung der Wirtschaft	Leadership of the Economy	Lothar Heller
Amt XI	Umsiedlung Walter	Resettlement	Walter Ellermeier

Amt II had a similar purview with its focus on producing building materials, the financial umbrella for this activity being the Baustoffswerke und Zementfabriken (Building Materials and Cement Factories) company. A large part of this work was conducted at Auschwitz, Posen, Bielitz and Zichenau, but the occupied Eastern territories provided other opportunities in the form of captured Soviet premises.

Amt III of *Amtsgruppe* W was the food industry department. The growing of food and its health benefits were something of a personal obsession for Himmler, and to this end *Amt* III was divided into three sub-sections: mineral waters, meat, and bread. Production for the second two departments was mainly undertaken in the concentration camps, but under its mineral waters section the SS also controlled several private water firms and the Rheinglassfabrik bottling plant.

Amt IV was the German equipment office, manufacturing items principally for military use. What constituted 'German equipment' was broad: items produced or repaired by the concentration camp inmates included small arms, aircraft components, wooden furniture, webbing and police and SS uniforms.

Amt V, by contrast, was the land, forestry and fisheries department, which again plugged into Himmler's fascination with nutrition and racial health. It not only included SS-run plantations and fisheries, but also research gardens within the concentration camps that investigated herbal remedies.

Amt VI was the textiles and leatherwork office, relying mainly on workers at Dachau and Ravensbruck camps to rework uniform items for reissue to the *Wehrmacht* or SS. *Amt* VII, meanwhile, was the books and publishing office. This office was responsible for the production of SS literature under its Nordland-Verlag company, but also ran the Bauer und Cie art restoration company, touching up artworks looted from the great galleries of occupied Europe, and often destined to hang in Himmler's

personal residences. Finally, the cultural buildings office looked after the maintenance and restoration of those historic buildings in which the SS was interested. It also contained a company dedicated to the manufacture of ceremonial Damascus steel swords, works of genuine fine quality typically presented as gifts to long-serving or decorated officers.

The combined economic output of the SS industries was considerable. The Deutsche Erd & Steinwerke GmbH, for example, had a turnover equivalent to $3 million by 1943, and the textiles and leatherwork office ran at $2 million per annum in the same year. Yet it should be recognized that the SS businesses were not solely dedicated to maximizing profit. Graber here quotes Oswald Pohl in a memo of 11 July 1944:

I repeat here what I emphasize at every opportunity; the purpose of our economic undertakings is not the pursuit of profit, but the establishment of things which are of concern to us in the spirit of the SS, thus in accordance with the pronouncements of the Reichsführer-SS.

(Graber, 1978)

As Pohl points out, the SS commercial activities were more about expressing Himmler's will than genuinely serving the best interests of the Third Reich.

Resettlement

The occupation of lands in the East, as we have seen, provided real opportunities for SS nest-feathering. Hans Frank, for example, an *SS-Obergruppenführer* and ruler of the General Government in Poland, virtually had his own personal kingdom of slave labour, to do with as he pleased.

The SS was also involved in resettlement activities through two main offices. The *Hauptamt des Reichskommissar für die Festigung des Deutschen Volkstums* (Main Office of the Reich Commissioner for the Strengthening of the German Nation; RKFDV) worked towards turning portions of conquered territories into German colonies, while also reintegrating *Volksdeutsche* (ethnic German) communities back into the life of the Reich. The *Hauptamt Volksdeutsche Mittelstelle* (Ethnic German Main Assistance Office; VOMI) had a narrower focus, mainly looking at ways of moving *Volksdeutsche* descendants in the East back to Germany. These two offices were parts of the broader SS project – that of socially re-engineering Germany and the occupied territories.

HANS FRANK – ESSENTIAL FACTS

■ Hans Frank joined the DAP in 1919, and passed the Munich state Bar exam in 1926. His legal talents and Nazi affiliations eventually made Frank Hitler's personal lawyer, and he went on to take high legal office in the Reich government. He is most remembered, however, for his role as leader of the General-Government in Poland, the population of which he treated with utter cruelty.

Birth:	23 May 1900
Death:	16 October 1946 (hanging), following sentencing at Nuremberg War Crimes Trials
Place of birth:	Karlsruhe, Germany
Father:	Karl Frank
Mother:	Magdelana Frank (née Buchmaier)
Siblings:	Karl Jr (older) and Elisabeth (younger)
Wife:	Brigitte Herbst-Frank
Children:	Sigrid, Norman, Brigitte, Michael, Niklas
Military service:	Served in German Army, 1917–18
	Joined Freikorps in 1919
Education:	Studied law after World War I, passing his state examination in 1926
Political positions:	Director of NSDAP HQ Legal Department (1929)
	Elected to Reichstag (1930)
	Appointed a Reichsleiter (1931)
	Minister of Justice in Bavaria (1933)
	Reichsminister without Portfolio (1934)
	President of German Academy of Law (1939)
	Chief of Administration to Gerd von Rundstedt in the General Government (1939)
	Governor General of the General Government (1939)

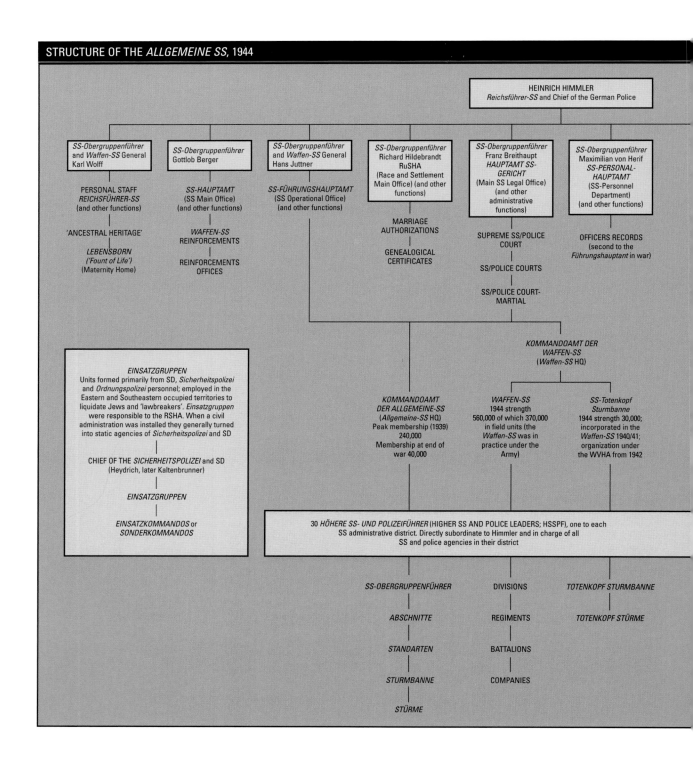

STRUCTURE OF THE *ALLGEMEINE SS*, 1944

HEINRICH HIMMLER
Reichsführer-SS and Chief of the German Police

SS-Obergruppenführer and *Waffen-SS* General Karl Wolff

PERSONAL STAFF
REICHSFÜHRER-SS
(and other functions)

'ANCESTRAL HERITAGE'

LEBENSBORN
('Fount of Life')
(Maternity Home)

SS-Obergruppenführer Gottlob Berger

SS-HAUPTAMT
(SS Main Office)
(and other functions)

WAFFEN-SS
REINFORCEMENTS

REINFORCEMENTS
OFFICES

SS-Obergruppenführer and *Waffen-SS* General Hans Juttner

SS-FÜHRUNGSHAUPTAMT
(SS Operational Office)
(and other functions)

SS-Obergruppenführer Richard Hildebrandt RuSHA
(Race and Settlement Main Office) (and other functions)

MARRIAGE
AUTHORIZATIONS

GENEALOGICAL
CERTIFICATES

SS-Obergruppenführer Franz Breithaupt
HAUPTAMT SS-GERICHT
(Main SS Legal Office)
(and other administrative functions)

SUPREME SS/POLICE
COURT

SS/POLICE COURTS

SS/POLICE COURT-
MARTIAL

SS-Obergruppenführer Maximilian von Herif
SS-PERSONAL-HAUPTAMT
(SS-Personnel Department)
(and other functions)

OFFICERS RECORDS
(second to the
Führungshauptant in war)

KOMMANDOAMT DER WAFFEN-SS
(*Waffen-SS* HQ)

EINSATZGRUPPEN
Units formed primarily from SD, *Sicherheitspolizei* and *Ordnungspolizei* personnel; employed in the Eastern and Southeastern occupied territories to liquidate Jews and 'lawbreakers'. *Einsatzgruppen* were responsible to the RSHA. When a civil administration was installed they generally turned into static agencies of *Sicherheitspolizei* and SD

CHIEF OF THE *SICHERHEITSPOLIZEI* and SD
(Heydrich, later Kaltenbrunner)

EINSATZGRUPPEN

EINSATZKOMMANDOS or
SONDERKOMMANDOS

KOMMANDOAMT DER ALLGEMEINE-SS
(*Allgemeine-SS* HQ)
Peak membership (1939)
240,000
Membership at end of war 40,000

WAFFEN-SS
1944 strength
560,000 of which 370,000 in field units (the *Waffen-SS* was in practice under the Army)

SS-Totenkopf Sturmbanne
1944 strength 30,000; incorporated in the *Waffen-SS* 1940/41; organization under the WVHA from 1942

30 *HÖHERE SS- UND POLIZEIFÜHRER* (HIGHER SS AND POLICE LEADERS; HSSPF), one to each SS administrative district. Directly subordinate to Himmler and in charge of all SS and police agencies in their district

SS-OBERGRUPPENFÜHRER

ABSCHNITTE

STANDARTEN

STURMBANNE

STÜRME

DIVISIONS

REGIMENTS

BATTALIONS

COMPANIES

TOTENKOPF STURMBANNE

TOTENKOPF STÜRME

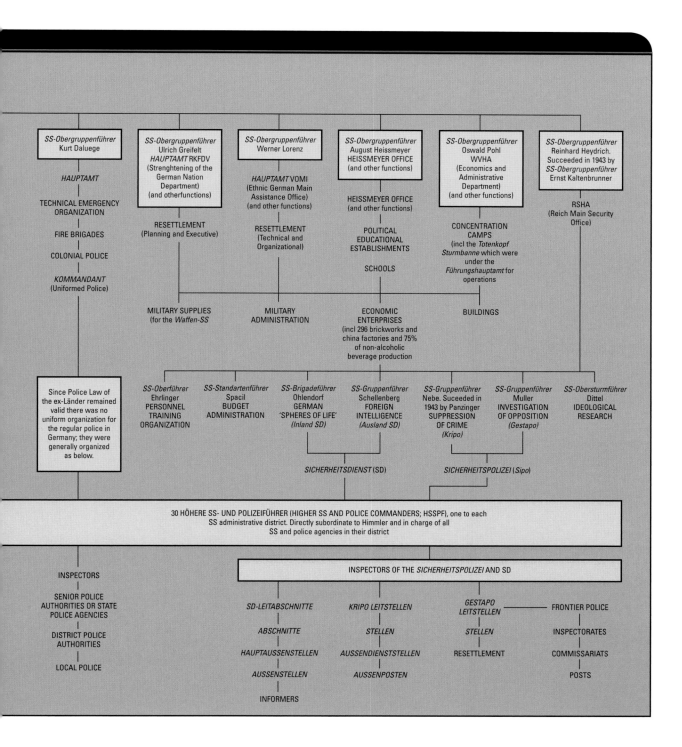

SS-Obergruppenführer Kurt Daluege
HAUPTAMT
TECHNICAL EMERGENCY ORGANIZATION
FIRE BRIGADES
COLONIAL POLICE
KOMMANDANT (Uniformed Police)

SS-Obergruppenführer Ulrich Greifelt
HAUPTAMT RKFDV (Strenghtening of the German Nation Department) (and otherfunctions)
RESETTLEMENT (Planning and Executive)
MILITARY SUPPLIES (for the Waffen-SS

SS-Obergruppenführer Werner Lorenz
HAUPTAMT VOMI (Ethnic German Main Assistance Office) (and other functions)
RESETTLEMENT (Technical and Organizational)
MILITARY ADMINISTRATION

SS-Obergruppenführer August Heissmeyer HEISSMEYER OFFICE (and other functions)
HEISSMEYER OFFICE (and other functions)
POLITICAL EDUCATIONAL ESTABLISHMENTS
SCHOOLS
ECONOMIC ENTERPRISES (incl 296 brickworks and china factories and 75% of non-alcoholic beverage production

SS-Obergruppenführer Oswald Pohl WVHA (Economics and Administrative Department) (and other functions)
CONCENTRATION CAMPS (incl the Totenkopf Sturmbanne which were under the Führungshauptamt for operations
BUILDINGS

SS-Obergruppenführer Reinhard Heydrich. Succeeded in 1943 by SS-Obergruppenführer Ernst Kaltenbrunner
RSHA (Reich Main Security Office)

Since Police Law of the ex-Länder remained valid there was no uniform organization for the regular police in Germany; they were generally organized as below.

SS-Oberführer Ehrlinger PERSONNEL TRAINING ORGANIZATION

SS-Standartenführer Spacil BUDGET ADMINISTRATION

SS-Brigadeführer Ohlendorf GERMAN 'SPHERES OF LIFE' (Inland SD)

SS-Gruppenführer Schellenberg FOREIGN INTELLIGENCE (Ausland SD)

SS-Gruppenführer Nebe. Succeeded in 1943 by Panzinger SUPPRESSION OF CRIME (Kripo)

SS-Gruppenführer Muller INVESTIGATION OF OPPOSITION (Gestapo)

SS-Obersturmführer Dittel IDEOLOGICAL RESEARCH

SICHERHEITSDIENST (SD)

SICHERHEITSPOLIZEI (Sipo)

30 HÖHERE SS- UND POLIZEIFÜHRER (HIGHER SS AND POLICE COMMANDERS; HSSPF), one to each SS administrative district. Directly subordinate to Himmler and in charge of all SS and police agencies in their district

INSPECTORS
SENIOR POLICE AUTHORITIES OR STATE POLICE AGENCIES
DISTRICT POLICE AUTHORITIES
LOCAL POLICE

INSPECTORS OF THE SICHERHEITSPOLIZEI AND SD

SD-LEITABSCHNITTE
ABSCHNITTE
HAUPTAUSSENSTELLEN
AUSSENSTELLEN
INFORMERS

KRIPO LEITSTELLEN
STELLEN
AUSSENDIENSTSTELLEN
AUSSENPOSTEN

GESTAPO LEITSTELLEN
STELLEN
RESETTLEMENT

FRONTIER POLICE
INSPECTORATES
COMMISSARIATS
POSTS

CHAPTER 3

The Waffen-SS

The Waffen-SS *is arguably the most notorious military organization in the history of the twentieth century. It is rightly remembered for its involvement in numerous war crimes in both the Western and Eastern theatres of war, crimes that were the products of its dark racial perspectives and brutalizing experience of war.*

The Waffen-SS *differed from the regular army in its allegiance. Whereas the* Wehrmacht *was the military expression of the state, the* Waffen-SS *was in a sense Hitler's 'private army' that, according to official policy from 1938, was 'exclusively at the disposal of the Führer'. Yet there is no denying that the native German soldiers of the* Waffen-SS *were, in the main, superb general combatants, known for their high levels of motivation. Thus they were often applied in 'firefighting' roles, sent to critical areas of a front line to restore offensive momentum or defend against an enemy attack.*

◼ SS men in a *Schwimmwagen* amphibious car examine road signs during the Ardennes Offensive, December 1944. The Sixth Panzer Army under 'Sepp' Dietrich spearheaded a campaign that Hitler hoped would push the Western Allies back to the Channel coast.

Command and Control

The Waffen-SS *was a Nazi army that, although separate to the* Wehrmacht, *nonetheless had a close command relationship to the Army hierarchy, plus its own parallel levels of command and control.*

We have already looked into the origins of the armed element of the SS, which by the late 1930s had evolved into the SS-VT formation. The official birth date of the *Waffen-SS* proper is arguably 7 November 1939, when an official SS document instructed *Allgemeine-SS* officers to apply as reserve officers in the *Waffen-SS* and police. From that date onwards, the combat wing of the SS would take the *Waffen-SS* title.

Command network

The *Waffen-SS* swelled its ranks during the war years, its expansion fuelled by Hitler and Himmler's desire to have a politically reliable but combat-oriented force in the field. At the beginning of the war, the *Waffen-SS* consisted of four operational field regiments, plus a handful of specialist regiments and battalions, but by the end of the conflict it had fielded 38 divisions. Such growth naturally led to issues of command between the far larger German Army and its *Waffen-SS* counterpart. In fact, the operational relationship between Army and armed SS was being thrashed out back in the mid-1930s. At first, the SS-VT was theoretically governed by the *Inspektion der SS-VT* (Inspectorate of SS-VT), which was in turn subject to the *SS-Hauptamt*. Yet as Gordon Williamson points out, the command picture for the early

armed SS was a generally confused one:

...commanders of the various SS-Oberabschnitte were entitled to take command of SS-VT units in emergencies and could even commandeer SS-VT units to assist in the military training of the Hitler Youth and Allgemeine-SS. *Even within the SS-VT itself, the inspectorate did not exercise full control. The Leibstandarte SS Adolf Hitler (LSSAH), the premier armed unit of the SS, was under the direct control of Himmler himself.*

(Williamson, 2005)

Complicating this picture was how the SS related to the *Wehrmacht*. During the second half of the 1930s, the *Wehrmacht* and the SS viewed each other with mutual suspicion and even antipathy. The *Wehrmacht* saw the SS as political interlopers, pulling away good manpower from the traditional armed forces, while the SS considered themselves an elite apart from the general mass of German soldiery.

In the late 1930s, however, Hitler realized that an independent SS nevertheless needed to be part of the overall command network of the German armed forces, of which the *Heer* was the dominant part. In August 1938, Hitler issued a series of

directives spelling out the status of the wartime SS-VT. The combat units would be subordinate to the *Oberbefehlshaber des Heeres* (Commander-in-Chief of the Army) as part of his available resources. This structuring was sharpened by an *Oberkommmando der Wehrmacht* (Armed Forces High Command; OKW) directive on 17 September 1938, which placed SS units that were incorporated into *Wehrmacht* command under the same 'rights and duties' as soldiers serving in the regular army. Note, however, that SS units deployed to deal with threats inside Germany itself were controlled by Himmler, not the Army.

Formations and units

The *Waffen-SS* in the field was ordered in much the same way as any army, although the generic names for its units and formations sometimes differed from those of the regular forces. At the higher levels of command, however, there were some notable distinctions. An important layer of SS high command was provided by the *Höhere SS- und Polizeiführer* (Higher SS and Police Leaders; HSSPF), a regional command position with similar powers over SS interests as a *Gauleiter* (District Leader; in Germany) and a *Reichskommissar* (Reich Commissioner; in the occupied

WAFFEN-SS AREA COMMANDS

Area command	Known Commanders	Notes
Befehlshaber der Waffen-SS West	SS-Brigadeführer Kurt Knoblauch (Oct 1940–Jan 1941)	Redesignated Befehlshaber der Waffen-SS Nordwest in January 1941
Befehlshaber der Waffen-SS Nord	SS-Brigadeführer Karl Hermann (Nov 1940–Apr 1941)	Befehlshaber der Waffen-SS Nordwegen
Befehlshaber der Waffen-SS Nordost	SS-Brigadeführer Kurt Knoblauch (c. Nov 1940–Apr 1941) SS-Brigadeführer Karl von Treuenfeld (Apr 1941) SS-Brigadeführer Kurt Knoblauch (Jan–Apr 1941)	
Befehlshaber der Waffen-SS Ost	SS-Brigadeführer Karl-Maria Demelhuber (Nov 1940–Apr 1941)	
Befehlshaber der Waffen-SS Nordwest	SS-Brigadeführer Kurt Knoblauch (Dec 1940–Jan 1941) SS-Brigadeführer Karl von Treuenfeld (Jan–Apr 1941) SS-Oberführer Karl Heinrich Brenner (Dec 1941–Feb 1942) SS-Standartenführer Alfred Karrasch (Feb–June 1942)	Redesignated as Befehlshaber der Waffen-SS Niederlande in June 1942
Befehlshaber der Waffen-SS Südost	SS-Brigadeführer Karl-Maria Demelhuber (Apr 1941)	
Befehlshaber der Waffen SS in den Protektorat	SS-Brigadeführer Karl von Treuenfeld (Dec 1941–Sep 1942) SS-Brigadeführer Carl Graf von Puckler-Burghaus (Sep 1942–Apr 1943) SS-Standartenführer Alfred Karrasch (Apr–July 1943) SS-Gruppenführer Georg Keppler (July 1943–Mar 1944) SS-Brigadeführer Carl Graf von Puckler Burghaus (Mar 1944–May 1945)	Redesignated as Befehlshaber der Waffen-SS Böhmen-Mähren in March 1942
Befehlshaber der Waffen-SS Serbien	SS-Brigadeführer Arthur Phelps (Feb–Mar 1942)	
Befehlshaber der Waffen-SS Niederlande	SS-Obergruppenführer Karl-Maria Demelhuber (June 1942–July 1944) SS-Oberführer Martin Kohlroser (Nov 1944–May 1945)	
Befehlshaber der Waffen-SS Rußland-Süd	SS-Brigadeführer Karl von Treuenfeld (July–Nov 1943)	
Befehlshaber der Waffen-SS Ost	SS-Obergruppenführer Walter Krüger (Mar–July 1944) SS-Oberführer Gustav Krukenberg (July–Aug 1944)	
Befehlshaber der Waffen-SS Ostland	SS-Obergruppenführer Walter Krüger (Mar–July 1944) SS-Oberführer Gustav Krukenberg (July–Aug 1944)	
Befehlshaber der Waffen-SS Ostland und Rußland-Nord	SS-Obergruppenführer Walter Krüger (Mar–July 1944) SS-Oberführer Gustav Krukenberg (July–c. Sep 1944)	
Befehlshaber der Waffen-SS Ungarn	SS-Gruppenführer Georg Keppler (Mar–Sep 1944) SS-Obergruppenführer Karl von Pfeffer-Wildenbruch (Sep–Nov 1944) SS-Obergruppenführer Georg Keppler (Nov 1944–Feb 1945)	
Befehlshaber der Waffen-SS Italien	SS-Gruppenführer Karl von Treuenfeld (June 1944) SS-Gruppenführer Lothar Debes (June 1944–May 1945)	
Befehlshaber der Waffen-SS Slowakei	SS-Obergruppenführer Karl von Pfeffer-Wildenbruch (from Aug 1944)	

ORGANIZATION OF THE *SS-FÜHRUNGSHAUPTAMT*

Amtsgruppe A
Organisation, Personal, Versorgung
(Organization, Personnel and Supply)

- **Amt I** *Kommandoamt der Allgemeinen-SS* (HQ of the *Allgemeine-SS*)
- **Amt II** *Kommandoamt der Waffen-SS* (HQ of the *Waffen-SS*)
- **Amt III** *Zentralkanzlei* (Central Chancellery)
- **Amt IV** *Verwaltungsamt* (Administration Department)
- **Amt V** *Personalamt* (Personnel Department)
- **Amt VI** *Reit- und Fahrwesen* (Horsemanship and Driver Training)
- **Amt VII** *Nachschubwesen* (Logistics Planning)
- **Amt VIII** *Waffenamt* (Weapons Office)
- **Amt IX** *Technische Ausrüstung und Maschinen* (Technical and Mechanical Development)
- **Amt X** *Kraftfahrzeugwesen* (Motor Vehicle Organization)

Amtsgruppe B
Ausbildung (Training)

- **Amt XI** *Führer-Ausbildung und SS-Junkerschulen* (Officer Training and Officer Cadet Schools)
- **Amt XII** *Unterführer-Ausbildung und SS-Unterführerschulen* (NCO Training and NCO Training Schools)

Amtsgruppe C
Inspektionen (Inspectorates)

- **Inspektion 2** *Infanterie- und Gebirgstruppen* (Infantry and Mountain Troops)
- **Inspektion 3** *Kavallerie* (Cavalry)
- **Inspektion 4** *Artillerie* (Artillery)
- **Inspektion 5** *Pioniere/Techniker* (Engineers/Technicians)
- **Inspektion 6** *Panzertruppen* (Armoured Troops)
- **Inspektion 7** *Nachrichtentruppen* (Signals Troops)
- **Inspektion 8** *Feldzeug- und Instandsetzungstruppen* (Field Maintenance Troops)
- **Inspektion 9** *Versorgungstruppen* (Service and Support Troops)
- **Inspektion 10** *Kraftfahrparktruppen* (Motor Pool Troops)
- **Inspektion 11** Not known
- **Inspektion 12** *Technische Lehrgänge* (Technical Training)
- **Inspektion 13** *Flakartillerie* (Anti-Aircraft Artillery)

■

Amtsgruppe D
Sanitätswesen der Waffen-SS
(Waffen-SS Medical Services)

└─■ **Amt XIII** *Verwaltung*
(Administration)

└─■ **Amt XIV** *Zahnwesen*
(Dental)

└─■ **Amt XV** *Versorgung*
(Supply)

└─■ **Amt XVI** *Ärztliche*
Behandlung
(Medical Treatment)

territories. HSSPF was largely an *Allgemeine-SS* position, but the commander could organize *Kampfgruppen* (Battle Groups) for special purposes, these consisting of armed police or *Waffen-SS* units and tasked with roles such as anti-Partisan operations. Specific *Waffen-SS* area commands were also in place, however, these being governed by multiple *Befehlshaber der Waffen-SS* (Chiefs of the Waffen-SS; BdWSS). A US Army intelligence document from 1945 spells out the command relationships of the BdWSS:

In certain selected areas the SS High Command has installed territorial commanders of the Waffen-SS *(Befehlshaber der* Waffen-SS*—Bfh.d.W-SS). These represent the regional echelon of the SS High Command for the* Waffen-SS *only. They execute its directives and are in complete command of all units of the* Waffen-SS *in their areas. The commander of the* Waffen-SS *shares with the HSSPf control of the static installations of the* Waffen-SS*, but is otherwise completely independent of him.*

(TM-E 30-451, March 1945)

Organizing the combat units along more regular lines, the largest formation was the *Armee* (Army), of which there were two during the course of the war – Sixth SS-Panzer Army, created in autumn 1944, and the ragged 11th SS-Panzer Army, formed in February 1945 from whatever personnel could be scraped together from a collapsing Eastern Front. Smaller than the SS

armies were the 13 SS corps formed during the war, these being composed of a fluid arrangement of divisions, rather than being fixed entities. The SS corps were in place between 1942 and 1945.

Divisions (*Divisionen*) and regiments (*Standarten*) were the principal upper level structures of the *Waffen-SS*. As mentioned earlier, there were a total of 38 *Waffen-SS* divisions formed during the war, including the foreign divisions (see the next chapter), but some of the later divisions were essentially understrength or on-paper formations only. The indigenous German divisions were generally denoted by a divisional number, a descriptive title, and an honorific title, e.g. *1.SS-Panzer-Division Leibstandarte SS Adolf Hitler* and *6.SS-Gebirgs-Division Nord*, a mountain formation. The bedrock types of *Waffen-SS* division were the Panzer, Panzergrenadier, mountain, cavalry and grenadier (infantry) divisions. Each division was broken down into regimental- and battalion-sized units and so on, the whole comprising a mixed structure of infantry, vehicular, artillery and support arms. (More about the structure of individual combat units is described in the 'War Service' section below.)

In terms of the broader auxiliary support arms, the *Waffen-SS* had a wide range of organizations acting in assistance. These included the *SS-Feldgendarmerie* (SS Field Police), the *SS-Kriegsberichter* (SS 'War Correspondents' – actually a mobile propaganga unit) and the all-female administrative unit known as the *SS-Helferinnen* (SS Helpers).

Recruitment and Training

The recruitment and training policies of the Waffen-SS *were integral to its developing reputation as an elite within the German armed forces. Only from the mid-war years, and with the inclusion of foreign personnel, did standards decline.*

Recruitment to the SS-VT was initially a highly choosy process, as the SS naturally sought out the best personnel to distinguish their identity from the *Wehrmacht*. Interestingly, during the early days of the armed SS the recruiters sought or obtained much of their human material from rural rather than urban communities; the country dwellers were deemed to have greater natural fieldcraft skills and toughness, and were seen as less corruptible characters than the city folk. A glance at the SS-VT recruiting criteria on the opposite page shows how particular the armed SS was to obtain someone of the right physical, social, racial and

familial characteristics. If an individual felt he met the criteria, and wished to join the armed SS, he simply had to present himself at the local SS recruiting office (there was usually one recruiting office serving several military districts) with all the correct paperwork. (More about the recruitment standards and procedures for foreign personnel is dealt with in the next chapter.)

Officer candidates

Unlike the *Wehrmacht*, the *Waffen-SS* had a relatively strict 'bottom up' approach to rank progression. Rather than step straight into an officer training school, officer candidates

typically joined as enlisted men and served for one year in the ranks before they could be considered for the *SS-Junkerschulen* (SS Officer Cadet Schools). An SS enlisted man who had reached the rank of *Rottenführer* (Section Leader) was also able to make a choice whether to continue onwards through the non-commissioned ranks, or apply for officer training.

Soldiers who showed leadership capabilities were recommended for officer training by their company commander. This process sounds meritocratic, but it could also have its failings. Combined with the low educational standards of many of the candidates, the favouritism of the company commander could lead to unsuitable characters being forwarded to officer training school. Indeed, an abiding myth of the *Waffen-SS* is that they had poor leadership, with officers more motivated by political enthusiasm than by genuine military skill.

History has shown this accusation to be largely false. Any military organization, especially one on the scale of the *Waffen-SS*, will have its fair share of command incompetence, but around 80 per cent of high-ranking SS officers had service experience from World War I, and many had built on that experience with continuing service in

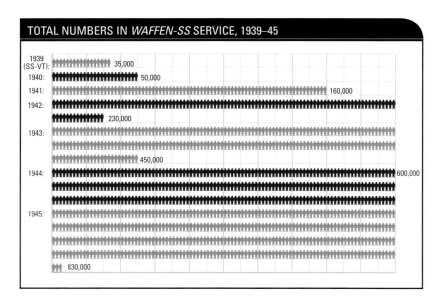

TOTAL NUMBERS IN *WAFFEN-SS* SERVICE, 1939–45

1939 (SS-VT): 35,000
1940: 50,000
1941: 160,000
1942: 230,000
1943: 450,000
1944: 600,000
1945: 830,000

the *Reichswehr* or *Wehrmacht* in the post-war period. The *Waffen-SS* had a particularly strong body of corps and divisional commanders, and Rikmenspoel notes that the many highly decorated *Waffen-SS* officers received their decorations 'almost always through the recommendation of impressed *Heer* corps and army commanders'. For those individuals who did opt for officer training, the training programme usually lasted between 18 and 24 months, although the pressures of war later shortened the training period to around six months. During this period they would progress through a series of officer candidate ranks – *Junker*, *Oberjunker*, *Standartenjunker*, and *Standartenoberjunker*. When the candidate achieved the final rank in that list he was regarded as a probationary officer and sent to a field unit for operational appraisal. If he passed through this period and a final exam with no problems, then he formally became an SS officer, taking the rank of *SS-Untersturmführer* (equivalent to a second-lieutenant in the Allied rank systems).

Much of the SS officer training was conducted at the *SS-Junkerschulen* at Bad Tölz and Braunschweig, with a platoon leader's course school at Dachau. Note that there were certain exceptions to the typical officer candidate route. A *Wehrmacht* officer who transferred into the *Waffen-SS* was often able to take the direct SS equivalent of his Army rank. Furthermore, later in the war it was not uncommon for *Waffen-SS* soldiers to receive field commissions, being promoted to officer rank without having ever passed through a

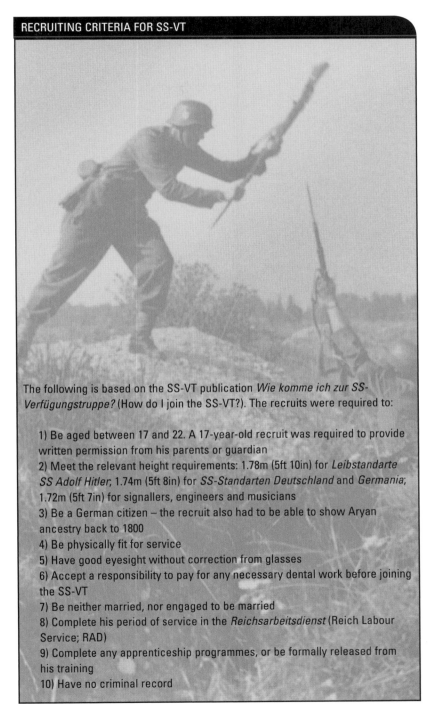

RECRUITING CRITERIA FOR SS-VT

The following is based on the SS-VT publication *Wie komme ich zur SS-Verfügungstruppe?* (How do I join the SS-VT?). The recruits were required to:

1) Be aged between 17 and 22. A 17-year-old recruit was required to provide written permission from his parents or guardian
2) Meet the relevant height requirements: 1.78m (5ft 10in) for *Leibstandarte SS Adolf Hitler*; 1.74m (5ft 8in) for *SS-Standarten Deutschland* and *Germania*; 1.72m (5ft 7in) for signallers, engineers and musicians
3) Be a German citizen – the recruit also had to be able to show Aryan ancestry back to 1800
4) Be physically fit for service
5) Have good eyesight without correction from glasses
6) Accept a responsibility to pay for any necessary dental work before joining the SS-VT
7) Be neither married, nor engaged to be married
8) Complete his period of service in the *Reichsarbeitsdienst* (Reich Labour Service; RAD)
9) Complete any apprenticeship programmes, or be formally released from his training
10) Have no criminal record

WAFFEN-SS DIVISIONS, 1938–45

Divisional Insignia	Type/Title of Division	Years in Operation	Divisional Insignia	Type/Title of Division	Years in Operation
	1st SS-Panzer Division *Leibstandarte SS Adolf Hitler*	1933–45		11th SS-Volunteer Panzergrenadier Division *Nordland*	1943–45
	2nd SS-Panzer Division *Das Reich*	1939–45		12th SS-Panzer Division *Hitlerjugend*	1943–45
	3rd SS-Panzer Division *Totenkopf*	1939–45		13th *Waffen* Mountain Division of the SS *Handschar* (Croatian No 1)	1943–45
	4th SS-Police Panzergrenadier Division	1940–45		14th *Waffen* Grenadier Division of the SS *Galizien* (Ukrainian No 1)	1944–45
	5th SS-Panzer Division *Wiking*	1940–45		15th *Waffen* Grenadier Division of the SS (Latvian No 1)	1942–45
	6th SS-Mountain Division *Nord*	1941–45		16th SS-Panzergrenadier Division *Reichsführer-SS*	1943–45
	7th SS-Volunteer Mountain Division *Prinz Eugen*	1942–45		17th SS-Panzergrenadier Division *Götz von Berlichingen*	1943–45
	8th SS-Cavalry Division *Florian Geyer*	1942–45		18th SS-Volunteer Panzergrenadier Division *Horst Wessel*	1944–45
	9th SS-Panzer Division *Hohenstaufen*	1943–45		19th Waffen Grenadier Division of the SS (Latvian No 2)	1944–45
	10th SS-Panzer Division *Frundsberg*	1943–45		20th Waffen Grenadier Division of the SS (Estonian No 1)	1944–45

Divisional Insignia	Type/Title of Division	Years in Operation
	21st *Waffen* Mountain Division of the SS *Skanderbeg* (Albanian No 1)	1944–45
	22nd *Waffen* Mountain Division of the SS *Maria Theresia*	1944–45
	23rd *Waffen* Mountain Division of the SS *Kama* (Croatian No 2)	1944
	23rd SS-Volunteer Panzergrenadier Division *Nederland* (Netherlands No 1)	1945
	24th *Waffen* Mountain Division of the SS *Karstjäger*	1944–45
	25th *Waffen* Grenadier Division of the SS *Hunyadi* (Hungarian No 1)	1944–45
	26th *Waffen* Grenadier Division of the SS *Hungaria* (Hungarian No 2)	1944–45
	27th SS-Volunteer Grenadier Division *Langemarck* (Flemish No 1)	1944–45
	28th SS-Volunteer Grenadier Division *Wallonien* (Walloon No 1)	1944–45
	29th *Waffen* Grenadier Division of the SS *Italien* (Italian No 1)	1945
	29th *Waffen* Grenadier Division of the SS (Russian No 1)	1944
	30th *Waffen* Grenadier Division of the SS (Russian No 2)	1944

Divisional Insignia	Type/Title of Division	Years in Operation
	31st SS-Volunteer Grenadier Division	1945
	31st *Waffen* Grenadier Division of the SS *Böhmen-Mähren*	1945
	32nd SS-Volunteer Grenadier Division *30. Januar*	1944–45
	33rd *Waffen* Grenadier Division of the SS *Charlemagne* (French No 1)	1945
	33rd SS-Volunteer Grenadier Division (Hungarian No 3)	1945
	34th SS-Volunteer Grenadier Division *Landstorm Nederland* (Netherlands No 2)	1945
	35th SS-Police Grenadier Division	1945
	36th *Waffen* Grenadier Division of the SS *Dirlewanger*	1945
	37th SS-Volunteer Cavalry Division *Lützow*	1945
	38th SS-Panzergrenadier Division *Nibelungen*	1945

JOSEF 'SEPP' DIETRICH – ESSENTIAL FACTS

■ Josef 'Sepp' Dietrich rose rapidly through the ranks of the SS during the 1920s and 1930s, and was a noted *Waffen-SS* combat commander. The failed Ardennes offensive in 1944–45 resulted in Hitler renouncing his loyal servant.

Birth:	28 May 1892
Death:	1966 (of a heart attack in Ludwigsburg at age 73)
SS ID number:	1177
Place of birth:	Hawangen, Bavaria
Parents:	Pelagius and Kreszentia Dietrich
Military career:	World War I – Served in German Army with artillery and early armoured forces
	1919 – Joined *Freikorps Oberland*
	5 May 1928 – Joined the SS
	17 March 1933 – 4 June 1943 – Commander of 1st SS-Panzer Division *Leibstandarte SS Adolf Hitler*
	27 July 1943 – 9 August 1944 – Commander of I SS-Panzer Corps
	September 1944 – May 1945 – Commander of Sixth SS-Panzer Army
Dates of rank:	SS-Sturmbannführer (1 August 1928)
	SS-Standartenführer (18 September 1929)
	SS-Oberführer (10 October 1930)
	SS-Gruppenführer (18 December 1931)
	SS-Obergruppenführer (1 July 1934)
	General der Waffen-SS (19 November 1940)
	SS-Oberstgruppenführer und Panzer-Generaloberst der Waffen-SS (1 August 1944)
Major decorations:	Iron Cross second (1917) and first (1918) classes
	Cross of Honour (1934)
	Clasp to the Iron Cross second (1939) and first (1939) classes
	Knight's Cross (1940), with Oak Leaves (1941), Swords (1943), Diamonds (1944)

Junkerschule. Indeed, the general recruiting standards for *Waffen-SS* soldiers softened or were modified as the war went on and ate into existing manpower, with physical 'imperfections' increasingly overlooked to get men into the ranks.

Combat training

The training for any man joining the *Waffen-SS* was both intimidating and arduous in its nature. The SS instructors sought to reshape the raw human material into physically and emotionally hardened men capable of total battlefield commitment and a disdain for the value of human life, at least in terms of the enemy. It should be noted that some one in three men who attempted SS training failed the course and had to leave the SS. The *Waffen-SS* being a pure combat wing, its training was naturally focused on developing core infantry skills, particularly in handling small arms and also in close-quarter combat, which was meant to foster the right sort of martial aggression. Physical fitness training was also high on the agenda. (Each SS soldier was expected to have obtained the State Sports Badge and the SA Sports Badge.) An hour of PT was completed every morning before breakfast, the recruits having to present themselves for training within minutes of their 6 a.m. rise time. Long route marches in full kit were naturally par for the course, but the soldier was still expected to keep his rain- and mud-splattered uniform in top condition.

Realism was a key ingredient of *Waffen-SS* training, which aimed to inoculate the soldier to the realities of combat before he actually found himself on the front line. One classic training exercise (admittedly one also used by some of the more elite regiments of the *Wehrmacht*) was to have the recruits hunker down in a slit trench while a tank drove over the top of them. The exercise required real nerve – panicking and attempting to flee the approaching vehicle was liable to result in death or serious injury. Many other exercises involved the expenditure of large amounts of live ammunition, often over the heads of recruits.

As with many other aspects of the *Waffen-SS*, the combat training became a little less rigorous as the war years progressed, partly to reduce the failure rate and partly because of the need to conserve weapons and ammunition for front-line use.

Mutual respect

A key feature of the *Waffen-SS* capability was the frequently powerful bonds between the SS officers and their men. The *Waffen-SS* leaders tended to be hard individuals, but as a whole the formation avoided simple dictatorialism, and instead fostered

command relationships based upon mutal respect. This respect and understanding was helped considerably by the fact that the officers had themselves progressed through basic training with the enlisted men, sometimes with the very men whom they would later command. Furthermore, although the *Waffen-SS* was a very disciplined organization, it was not excessively insistent upon formalities. Enlisted men and NCOs were not required to salute the officer, instead using an abbreviated version of the Nazi salute (raising the forearm from the lowered elbow) as an acknowledgement of respect. The officers were not

addressed with the deferential 'Sir', but always with the rank. The result of this relationship between officers and men was excellent battlefield cohesion, and a desire to impress superiors.

All *Waffen-SS* soldiers also received ideological training, inculcating the SS outlooks on race and martial destiny. We should not overemphasize this part of training – any classroom lessons were likely to have been tedious for physically fidgety soldiers – but for the officers it was undoubtedly important for informing their overall leadership outlook, and for creating the motivation behind later war crimes.

SS-TRUPPENÜBUNGSPLÄTZE (SS TROOP TRAINING AREAS)

- Danzig-Mariensee
- Seelager
- Westpreußen
- Kurmark/Guben
- Ostpolen
- Moorlager
- Beneschau/Böhmen-Mähren
- Debica/Heidelager
- Konitz

▲ **SS TROOP TRAINING AREAS: The *SS-Truppenübungsplätze* were self-contained centres for handling recruits and bringing them up to physical and tactical standards. Each training area featured a guard battalion, an SS field gendarmerie unit, an SS hospital and a recruiting depot. Many of the camps were built by slave labour from the concentration camps.**

SS UNIT ORGANIZATION TERMS & DEFINITIONS

German term	English equivalent
Abteilungen/Bataillone	**Battalions**
SS-Bataillone	SS Battalions
SS-Panzergrenadier-Bataillone	SS Armoured Infantry Battalions
SS-Gebirgsjäger-Bataillone	SS Mountain Battalions
SS-Schi-Bataillone	SS Ski Battalions
SS-Jäger-Bataillone	SS 'Hunter' Battalions
SS-Fallschirmjäger-Bataillone	SS Paratroop Battalions
SS-Flak-MG-Bataillone	SS Anti-Aircraft Machine Gun Battalions
SS-Jagdverbände	SS 'Hunter' Groups
SS-Sonderverbände	SS Special Units
SS-Begleit-Bataillon 'RFSS'	SS Escort Battalion 'RFSS'
SS-Legionen	SS Legions
SS-Freikorps	SS Free Corps
SS-Waffengruppen	SS Combat Group
SS-Waffenverbände	SS Combat Group
SS-Kampfgruppen	SS (Ad hoc) Battle Groups

ARMOURED AND MOTORIZED TROOPS

German term	English equivalent
Divisionen	**Divisions**
SS-Panzer-Divisionen	SS Armoured Divisions
SS-Kavallerie-Divisionen	SS Cavalry Divisions
SS-Kosaken-Kavallerie-Divisionen	SS Cossack Cavalry Divisions
Brigaden	**Brigades**
SS-Panzer-Brigaden	SS Armoured Brigades
Regimenter	**Regiments**
SS-Panzer-Regimenter	SS Armoured Regiments
SS-Schützen-Regimenter	SS Mot Rifle Infantry Regiments
SS-Kradschützen-Regimenter	SS Motorcycle Regiments
SS-Kavallerie-Regimenter	SS Cavalry Regiments
SS-Kosaken-Reiter-Regimenter	SS Cossack Rider Regiments
Abteilungen/Bataillone	**Battalions**
SS-Panzer-Abteilungen	SS Armoured Battalions
SS-Panzerabwehr-Abteilungen	SS Tank Destroyer Battalions
SS-Panzerjäger-Abteilungen	SS Anti-Tank Battalions
SS-Panzer-Aufklärungs-Abteilungen	SS Armoured Reconnaissance Battalions
SS-Aufklärungs-Abteilungen	SS Reconnaissance Battalions
SS-Radfahr-Aufklärungs-Abteilungen	SS Bicycle Reconnaissance Battalions
SS-Radfahr-Bataillone	SS Bicycle Battalions

German term	English equivalent
INFANTRY	
Divisionen	**Divisions**
SS-Divisionen	SS Divisions
SS-Panzergrenadier-Divisionen	SS Armoured Infantry Divisions
SS-Grenadier-Divisionen	SS Grenadier Divisions
SS-Gebirgs-Divisionen	SS Mountain Divisions
Brigaden	**Brigades**
SS-Brigaden	SS Brigades
SS-Panzergrenadier-Brigaden	SS Armoured Infantry Brigades
SS-Grenadier-Brigaden	SS Grenadier Brigades
SS-Gebirgs-Brigaden	SS Mountain Brigades
SS-Sturm-Brigaden	SS Assault Brigades
Regimenter	**Regiments**
SS-Standarten	SS Regiments
SS-Regimenter	SS Regiments
SS-Infanterie-Regimenter	SS Infantry Regiments
SS-Polizei-Regimenter	SS Police Regiments
SS-Panzergrenadier-Regimenter	SS Armoured Infantry Regiments
SS-Grenadier-Regimenter	SS Grenadier Regiments
SS-Gebirgsjäger-Regimenter	SS Mountain Regiments

War Service

The war record of the Waffen-SS *is deeply controversial. The combat performance of its elite divisions was unquestionably high, but this is set against a record of landmark war crimes and the limited abilities of its foreign divisions.*

Describing the German war against the Soviet Union, Heinrich Himmler outlined with chilling clarity the racial and ideological baggage that the *Waffen-SS* was to bring to World War II:

This is a battle of ideology and a struggle of races. National Socialism is based on the value of our Germanic, and Nordic, blood – a beautiful, upstanding and equitable society. On the other side stands a population of 180 million people, a mixture of races whose very names are unpronounceable, and whose nature means that we can shoot

them down without pity or compassion. These animals have been welded by the Jews into one religion, an ideology that is called Bolshevism.

The *Waffen-SS* took such a perspective into a conflict the like of which the world had never witnessed. True to Himmler's sentiments, they burned their way across the Soviet Union in both advance and retreat, showing the formal enemy no mercy in combat (and little in capture) and often treating civilian lives with equal contempt. War crimes in the West,

such as the destruction of Oradour-sur-Glane in France on 10 June 1944, and the killing of US POWs at Malmédy in December of the same year, simply confirmed to the wider world that the *Waffen-SS* were Nazi monsters. The war crimes of the *Waffen-SS* are undeniable, yet they are far from the entirety of the *Waffen-SS* contribution to Germany's military campaigns. Instead, the *Waffen-SS* largely fought and died as ordinary soldiers in distant lands.

Organized for battle
Before exploring the combat history of the *Waffen-SS*, it is worth

PEAK STRENGTH FIGURES OF *WAFFEN-SS* DIVISIONS 1–12

Division	Peak strength
1st SS-Panzer Division *Leibstandarte SS Adolf Hitler*	22,100 (Dec 1944)
2nd SS-Panzer Division *Das Reich*	20,100 (June 1944)
3rd SS-Panzer Division *Totenkopf*	21,115 (June 1944)
4th SS-Police Panzergrenadier Division	16,100 (June 1944)
5th SS-Panzer Division *Wiking*	19,300 (June 1941)
6th SS-Mountain Division *Nord*	21,300 (Dec 1942)
7th SS-Volunteer Mountain Division *Prinz Eugen*	21,100 (Dec 1943)
8th SS-Cavalry Division *Florian Geyer*	12,900 (June 1944)
9th SS-Panzer Division *Hohenstaufen*	19,611 (Dec 1943)
10th SS-Panzer Division *Frundsberg*	19,300 (Dec 1943)
11th SS-Volunteer Panzergrenadier Division *Nordland*	11,740 (June 1944)
12th SS-Panzer Division *Hitlerjugend*	21,500 (Dec 1943)

DEPLOYMENTS OF 1ST SS-PANZER DIVISION *LEIBSTANDARTE SS ADOLF HITLER*, 1939–45*

1. September 1939   Poland
2. May–June 1940   Netherlands, northern France (Dunkirk perimeter)
3. October 1940–June 1941   Balkans (Yugoslavia and Greece)
4. June 1941–July 1942   Operation *Barbarossa* (Kiev and Rostov)
5. July 1942–January 1943   Normandy – refitting and re-forming as a
                              Panzergrenadier division
6. January–July 1943   Ukraine (Kharkov and at Belgorod)
7. July–October 1943   Italy
8. October 1943–April 1944   Ukraine (Kiev) and Galicia
9. April–October 1944   Normandy (Caen, Mortain, Falaise Pocket)
10. December 1944–January 1945 Ardennes offensive
11. January–March 1945   Hungary (Budapest)
12. March–May 1945   Withdraws into Austria

* Shows 1939 borders

◀ **1ST SS-PANZER DIVISION LSSAH DEPLOYMENT: The 1st SS-Panzer Division** *Leibstandarte Schutzstaffel Adolf Hitler* **(LSSAH), to use its full title, only received divisional status in 1942, by which time (in its regimental and brigade forms) it had already seen combat in Poland, the Netherlands, France and the Soviet Union. As the map shows, the LSSAH had an extremely busy deployment record, and its fighting in 1943–44 in southern Russia, the Ukraine, Normandy and the Ardennes resulted in extremely high casualty rates.**

clarifying a little more about the composition and make-up of the *Waffen-SS* formations and units that went to war. (Note that the structure of *Waffen-SS* units naturally changed over time and according to the respective campaign – the descriptions here are general principles only, and apply mainly to the mid-years of the war.)

The vanguard of the *Waffen-SS* combat formations consisted of the Panzer and Panzergrenadier divisions. The core of the former was four regiments – an armoured infantry regiment, a motorized infantry regiment, a tank regiment plus a regiment of artillery in support. The tank regiment was split into two battalions, each battalion usually operating different tank types, such as Panzer IVs in one battalion and Panthers in the other. The on-paper strength of each battalion was 70–80 tanks, although the operational reality could be extremely different. The infantry regiments were split into three battalions each, and were transported by either soft-skinned vehicles or armoured halftracks. The artillery regiment contained three or four battalions, which between them provided a mix of howitzers (light and heavy), rocket launchers and self-propelled guns.

In addition to the Panzer division's main regiments, a series of battalion-strength units provided support functions. These included a Panzerjäger tank-hunting battalion featuring self-propelled and towed anti-tank guns, an engineer battalion, an armoured signals battalion, an anti-aircraft battalion, as well as an administrative services battalion.

The Panzergrenadier divisions were formed from motorized/ mechanized infantry regiments. (The term 'Panzergrenadier' was actually introduced in 1942, and it could be applied both to a division and to a mechanized regiment or battalion within a division.) A typical *Waffen-SS* Panzergrenadier division consisted of two motorized infantry regiments and one motorized artillery regiment, plus a tank battalion, anti-tank battalion, armoured reconnaissance battalion, anti-aircraft battalion, combat engineer battalion and signals battalion.

The *Waffen-SS* also included six *Gebirgs* (Mountain) divisions during its lifetime. As we would expect from the terrain focus of these formations, the emphasis in the mountain divisions was on light, manoeuvrable

SOME SPECIALIST SS BATTALIONS

Unit	Purpose	Commanders
SS-Fallschirmjäger Bataillon 500	Airborne assault battalion; anti-Partisan warfare	*SS-Sturmbannführer* Herbert Gilhofer *SS-Hauptsturmführer* Kurt Rybka *SS-Hauptsturmführer* Siegfried Milius
SS-Fallschirmjäger-Bataillon 600	Airborne assault battalion; anti-Partisan warfare; covert operations	*SS-Sturmbannführer* Siegfried Milius
Funkschutz-Bataillon	Protection for German radio stations	*SS-Hauptsturmführer* Leopold Swoboda *SS-Sturmbannführer* Franz Voss
SS-Schijäger Bataillon Norwegen	Norway-based ski troops	Gust Jonassen Richard Benner Frode Halle Egil Hoel
Karstwehr Bataillon	Specialist anti-Partisan mountain unit for operations in the Karst area of the Julian Alps	*SS-Standartenführer* Dr Hans Brand *SS-Sturmbannführer* Josef Berschneider
Wachbataillone	There were 15 of these 'guard battalions', used to perform police-like functions, such as maintaining order in areas that had suffered from heavy bombing	Various

forces and equipment. The artillery, for example, included mule-packed 75mm (2.95in) or 105mm (4.1in) howitzers, and mountain divisions sometimes featured ski-trained battalions of troops. Each mountain division had a distinct composition of its own, but roughly speaking it had two infantry regiments, each divided into three battalions, plus a three-battalion artillery regiment and the typical range of support battalions, including a Panzerjäger battalion.

Cavalry and grenadiers

The remaining two types of Waffen-SS division were the cavalry divisions and the grenadier divisions. As much as the German armed forces appeared to be a mechanized entity in the propaganda images, it remained acutely dependent upon horse power throughout the war period, primarily for logistics but also with some reconnaissance applications. The Allgemeine-SS had formed cavalry detachments in late 1939, making them part of the SS-Totenkopf Standarten, using them as vehicles to teach horse handling and care with particular relevance to policing duties.

In 1941, the cavalry detachments were combined into the two SS-Kavallerie Standarten, which together became a brigade in July of that year. The brigade then achieved divisional status in June 1942, subsequently taking its final title – 8th SS-Cavalry Division Florian Geyer – the following year. The Florian Geyer honorific was given after the Franconian knight Florian Geyer (1490–1525), who was a leader of the German peasants during the Peasant's War of 1522–25.

By the end of the war, two more cavalry divisions had been formed – the 22nd SS-Volunteer Cavalry Division Maria Theresia and the 37th SS-Volunteer Cavalry Division Lützow, although as the latter was formed in February 1945 it was far from combat capable.

Cavalry divisions were primarily used in anti-Partisan operations in the occupied territories, and in performing those duties they gained a justified reputation for committing war crimes. In terms of their organization, the cavalry divisions were ideally divided into three battalion-sized cavalry regiments, plus an artillery regiment of three

battalions and the usual range of support arms.

The Waffen-SS grenadier regiments were no more than traditional infantry regiments, the 'grenadier' title adding a touch of panache and tradition to the divisional name. As such, the typical composition was three three-battalion infantry regiments, a four-battalion artillery regiment (three battalions of light howitzers and one of heavy howitzers) plus an assortment of specialist battalions: fusilier, anti-aircraft, anti-tank, combat engineer and signals.

Early war

A full war history of the Waffen-SS is not possible here – indeed the subject has filled entire volumes. Yet an overview of how the Waffen-SS evolved and fought during World War II is instructive, and assists us in making a judgment as to whether the men of the Waffen-SS were 'just soldiers', or outright war criminals.

For an organization that would eventually be given elite status, the armed SS had relatively unpromising beginnings. At the time of the Poland invasion, there were only four SS-VT

NOTABLE WAR CRIMES OF 2ND SS-PANZER DIVISION DAS REICH		
Location	Date	Incident
Lahoysk, Belorussia	September 1941	Assists in the killing of 920 Jews, alongside Einsatzgruppen B
Frayssinet-le-Gélat, France	21 May 1944	15 civilians killed in reprisal for killing of German officer
Rouffillac and Carsac-Aillac, France	8 June 1944	29 civilians, including women and children, killed at the two separate locations
Tulle, France	9 June 1944	97 civilians executed in reprisal attacks
Argenton-sur-Creuse, France	9 June 1944	67 civilians executed in reprisal for Resistance sabotage attacks
Marsoulas, France	10 June 1944	27 civilians killed in a reprisal action
Oradour-sur-Glane, France	10 June 1944	642 civilians killed during the destruction in a reprisal raid

2ND PANZER DIVISION *DAS REICH* ORGANIZATION, 1944

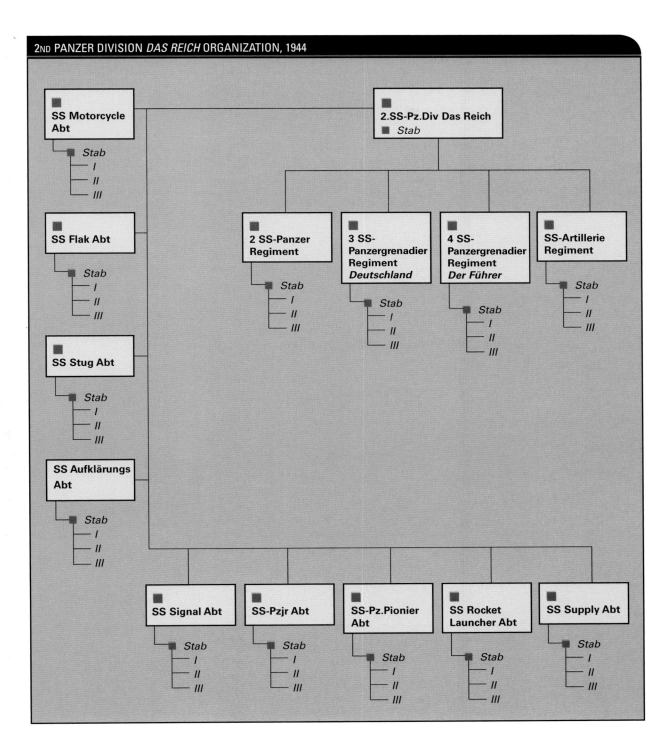

regiments in existence – *Leibstandarte*, *Deutschland*, *Germania* and *Der Führer*, the first on the list operating independently under the command of the infamous Josef 'Sepp' Dietrich, while the other three were in the process of being formed up into a division, the *SS-Verfügungstruppe* (SS-V) Division. (This division would evolve to form the 2nd SS-Panzer Division *Das Reich* by May 1942.) Himmler hoped that these units would blaze a trail during the Polish campaign, but the results were less than satisfactory. Committed in a piecemeal fashion, the armed SS units displayed courage and commitment, but, according to *Wehrmacht* observers, of a reckless rather than intelligent variety. OKW leaders claimed that the SS field commanders were rash and inexperienced, leading to incidents such as the *Leibstandarte* having to be rescued by *Heer* forces after being surrounded at Pabianica.

It was the post-Poland analysis that led to Hitler's decision to allow the SS to form its own divisions, but that those divisions were under OKW command. Such was a compromise

between Himmler's desire that his SS be independent, and the OKW's belief that the armed SS would best be disbanded. It would take some time before the *Waffen-SS* and the *Wehrmacht* came to a position of grudging mutal respect.

Late 1939 brought some expansion with the addition of the *Totenkopf* and *Polizei* (Police) divisions, which now pushed the total strength of the armed SS to an appreciable 100,000 men. The *Waffen-SS* now secured control over its recruiting, support and supply systems, but faced a significant challenge in equipping its formations, particularly in terms of heavy weaponry such as artillery. Ultimately, the SS was forced to go directly to the armaments minister, Fritz Todt, and request all the necessary weapons and pieces of kit. Surprisingly, the request was granted without too much fuss – the SS had to supply 20,000 Polish workers in return. Yet when the OKW heard that the SS was also dealing directly with the arms factories themselves, Himmler's private supply arrangements were brought to an acrimonious end.

▶ **3rd SS-PANZER DIVISION *TOTENKOPF* DEPLOYMENT**
The infamous *Totenkopf* division was raised from police, reservists and concentration camp guards, and despite its fearsome name was at first badly armed and plagued by indiscipline. Improved training and recruits from late 1940, however, transformed the division into a more coherent and effective outfit, which went on to prove itself on the Eastern Front. Its defence of the Demyansk Pocket in February–October 1942 was of near legendary status, and it fought in most of the fall-back Ukrainian engagements of the later war years. It ended its days battling in Hungary and Austria, desperately weakened by losses.

MAJOR UNITS OF THE 3RD SS-PANZER DIVISION *TOTENKOPF*
2.SS-Totenkopf-Infanterie-Regiment
3.SS-Panzer-Regiment
3.SS-(Panzer-) Artillerie-Regiment
5.SS-Panzergrenadier-Regiment *Thule*
6.SS-Panzergrenadier-Regiment *Theodor Eicke*
3.SS-Panzerjäger-Abteilung
3.SS-Sturmgeschutz-Abteilung
3.SS-Flak-Abteilung
3.SS-Werfer-Abteilung
3.SS-(Panzer-) Nachrichten-Abteilung
3.SS-Feldlazarett, etc
3.SS-Panzer-Aufklärungs-Abteilung
3.SS-Panzer-Pionier-Bataillon
3.SS-Dina
3.SS-Feldgendarmerie-Trupp
3.SS-Kriegsberichter-Zug
3.SS-Feldersatz-Bataillon
SS-Heimwehr-Danzig
Freikorps Danmark

COMMANDERS OF THE 3RD SS-PANZER DIVISION *TOTENKOPF*, 1939–45	
SS-Obergruppenführer Theodor Eicke	Nov 1939–July 1941
SS-Obergruppenführer Matthias Kleinheisterkamp	7 July 1941–18 July 1941
SS-Obergruppenführer Georg Keppler	18 July 1941–19 Sep 1941
SS-Obergruppenführer Theodor Eicke	19 Sep 1941–26 Feb 1943
SS-Gruppenführer Max Simon	26 Feb 1943–27 Apr 1943
SS-Gruppenführer Heinz Lammerding	27 Apr 1943–1 May 1943*
SS-Obergruppenführer Hermann Priess	1 May 1943–10 Oct 1943*
SS-Obergruppenführer Hermann Priess	10 Oct 1943–20 June 1944
SS-Oberführer Karl Ullrich	20 June 1944–13 July 1944
SS-Brigadeführer Helmuth Becker	13 July 1944–8 May 1945
* Both officers acting commanders for Max Simon	

DEPLOYMENTS OF 3RD SS-PANZER DIVISION *TOTENKOPF*, 1939–45*

1. Nov 1939–May 1940	Germany
2. May 1940–June 1941	Belgium & France (La Bassée Canal)
3. June 1941–Oct 1942	Baltic states and Leningrad Front (Lake Ilmen, Demyansk Pocket)
4. Oct 1942–Feb 1943	France (re-forming)
5. Feb 1943–Apr 1944	Eastern Front, southern sector (area southwest of Kharkov; Kursk, Mius Bridgehead; Krivoi Rog, Korsun, Kirovgrad), retreat across Dnieper
6. Apr 1944	Romania
7. July–Dec 1944	Poland (fighting around Warsaw, Modlin)
8. Dec 1944–Apr 1945	Hungary (fighting around Budapest)
9. Apr 1945	Austria (Vienna)

NORWAY

ESTONIA

LATVIA

LITHUANIA

SOVIET UNION

GERMANY

POLAND

FRANCE

AUSTRIA   HUNGARY

ROMANIA

ITALY

YUGOSLAVIA

GREECE

* Shows 1939 borders

Meanwhile, the *Waffen-SS* was about to embark on another major campaign. The performance of the *Waffen-SS* in the Netherlands, Belgium and France in 1940 was a signal improvement on its track record in Poland, and included a heroic defence by the *Deutschland* Regiment against a British armoured counter-attack around Merville on the River Lys.

But the action in France also brought a notorious atrocity, when some 100 men of the 2nd Royal Norfolk Regiment were machine-gunned and bayoneted to death by soldiers of the *Totenkopf* Division after the British soldiers had delayed the German advance for almost an hour around Merville.

MAJOR UNITS OF THE 12TH SS-PANZER DIVISION *HITLERJUGEND*
12.SS-Panzer-Regiment
12.SS-Panzer-Artillerie-Regiment
12.SS-Kradschützen-Regiment
12.SS-Aufklärungs-Abteilung
25.SS-Panzergrenadier-Regiment
26.SS-Panzergrenadier-Regiment
12.SS-Panzerjäger-Abteilung
12.SS-Werfer-Abteilung
12.SS-Flak-Abteilung
12.SS-Pionier-Abteilung
12.SS-Panzer-Nachrichten-Abteilung
12.SS-Instandsetzungs
12.SS-Nachschub-Truppen
12.SS-Wirtschafts-Bataillon
12.SS-SS-Führerbewerber-Lehrgang
12.SS-Kriegsberichter-Zug (mot)
12.SS-Feldgendarmerie-Kompanie/Trupp
12.SS-Feldpostamt (mot)
12.SS-Sanitäts-Abteilung
12.SS-Werfer-Abteilung

Notwithstanding the brutality, the *Waffen-SS* felt more justified in its existence following the campaign in the West, and Hitler in particular singled his warriors out for praise. Yet as Hitler's ambitions now switched to the Soviet Union, it became clear that the *Waffen-SS* was still too small to have a central battlefield influence. All that would soon change as the SS underwent a major period of expansion and an influx of new blood.

The Balkans

The *Waffen-SS* foreign contingents are discussed in full in the next chapter, but suffice here to say that in the later months of 1940 Himmler, aided by his recruiting chief, Gottlob Berger, persuaded Hitler to open the doors of the SS to suitably Aryan foreign recruits. Danes, Norwegians and Belgians were channelled into two new regiments, *Nordland* and *Westland*, which would eventually form the bedrock of a new division, the 5th SS-Panzer Division *Wiking*. Through its expansion and reorderings, the *Waffen-SS* had expanded to six divisions in strength by the beginning of 1941, all of which were destined to shed much blood on the Eastern Front.

Before the launch of Operation *Barbarossa* on 22 June 1941, however, the *Waffen-SS* was involved in the bloody 'Balkan interlude' – Operation *Marita*, Hitler's invasion of Greece and Yugoslavia on 6 April. The performance of the *Waffen-SS* during the hard campaign southwards through Greece won the respect of even the *Wehrmacht*, who particularly acknowledged the

Leibstandarte's tortuous capture of Height 997 from the Australian 6th Division, and the advance through the Klisura Pass under the startling leadership of Major Kurt Meyer, later to become a legend in the SS pantheon of leaders.

Facing east

Although the *Waffen-SS* had significantly expanded since the days of the Poland campaign, it still formed just a small part of the three million German soldiers that surged across the Soviet border in June 1941. The *Totenkopf* and *Polizei* divisions advanced towards Leningrad with Army Group North, the *Reich* (later *Das Reich*) Division was part of Army Group Centre's drive towards Moscow, while Army Group South benefited from the presence of *Wiking* and *Leibstandarte*.

As history has revealed, and as Himmler encouraged, the war against the Soviet Union was one in which the SS's brutal racial outlook could have free rein. Although in December 1941 the German offensive ground to a halt under appalling winter conditions, the *Waffen-SS* was nevertheless heralded for its exceptional vigour in both attack and defence. Yet while the casualties inflicted upon the Soviets were horrifying, the *Waffen-SS* soldiers were also suffering under a war of unimaginable scale. By the end of the year, the *Waffen-SS* had lost 43,000 men, with some divisions suffering a 60 per cent reduction in strength, and selected regiments taking even greater losses. Such major losses not only affected the combat performance of the *Waffen-SS* divisions, but they

WAFFEN-SS CORPS, 1943–45

Corps	Date formed	Commanders
I SS-Panzer Corps *Leibstandarte SS Adolf Hitler*	27 July 1943	*SS-Oberstgruppenführer* Josef Dietrich (July 1943–Aug 1944) *SS-Brigadeführer* Fritz Krämer (Aug 1944) *SS-Obergruppenführer* Georg Keppler (Aug–Oct 1944) *SS-Obergruppenführer* Hermann Priess (Oct 1944–May 1945)
II SS-Panzer Corps (first as SS-Corps Command)	14 September 1942	*SS-Oberstgruppenführer* Paul Hausser (June 1942–June 1944) *SS-Obergruppenführer* Willi Bittrich (June 1944–May 1945)
III (Germanic) SS-Panzer Corps	15 April 1943	*SS-Obergruppenführer* Felix Steiner (May1943–Oct 1944) *SS-Obergruppenführer* Georg Keppler (Nov 1944–Feb 1945) *SS-Obergruppenführer* Matthias Kleinheisterkamp (Feb 1945) *Generalleutnant* Martin Unrein (Feb–Mar 1945) *SS-Brigadeführer* Joachim Ziegler (Mar–May 1945)
IV SS-Panzer Corps	1 June 1943	*SS-Obergruppenführer* Alfred Wünnenburg (June–Oct 1943) *SS-Obergruppenführer* Walter Krüger (Oct 1943–Mar 1944) *SS-Obergruppenführer* Matthias Kleinheisterkamp (July 1944) *SS-Brigadeführer* Nikolaus Heilmann (July–Aug 1944) *SS-Obergruppenführer* Herbert Otto Gille (Aug 1944–May 1945)
V SS-Volunteer Mountain Corps	1 July 1943	*SS-Obergruppenführer* Arthur Phleps (July 1943–Sep 1944) *SS-Obergruppenführer* Friedrich-Wilhelm Krüger (Sep 1944–Mar 1945) *SS-Obergruppenführer* Friedrich Jeckeln (Mar–May 1945
VI *Waffen* Army Corps of the SS (Latvian)	8 October 1943	*SS-Obergruppenführer* Karl von Pfeffer-Wildenbruch (Oct 1943–June 1944) *SS-Obergruppenführer* Friedrich Jeckeln (June–July 1944) *SS-Gruppenführer* Karl Fischer von Treuenfeld (July 1944) *SS-Obergruppenführer* Walter Krüger (July 1944–May 1945)
VII SS-Panzer Corps	24 June 1943	*SS-Obergruppenführer* Matthias Kleinheisterkamp (May–June 1944) (staff formed well after official formation)
VIII SS-Cavalry Corps	Never formed	
IX *Waffen* Alpine Corps of the SS (Croatian)	June 1944	*SS-Gruppenführer* Karl-Gustav Sauberzeig (June 1944–Dec 1944) *SS-Obergruppenführer* Karl von Pfeffer-Wildenbruch (Dec 1944–Feb 1945)
X SS-Army Corps	January 1945	*SS-Obergruppenführer* Erich von dem Bach-Zelewski (Jan–Feb 1945) *Generalleutnant* Günther Krappe (Feb–Mar 1945) *SS-Standartenführer* Herbert Golz (Mar 1945)
XI SS-Army Corps	1 August 1944	*SS-Obergruppenführer* Matthias Kleinheisterkamp (Aug 1944–May 1945)
XII SS-Army Corps	August 1944	*SS-Obergruppenführer* Matthias Kleinheisterkamp (Aug 1944) *SS-Obergruppenführer* Curt von Gottberg (Aug–Oct 1944) *SS-Obergruppenführer* Karl-Maria Demelhuber (Oct 1944) *General der Infanterie* Günther Blumentritt (Oct 1944–Jan 1945) *Generalleutnant* Fritz Bayerlein (Jan 1945) *Generalleutnant* Eduard Crasemann (Jan–Apr 1945)
XIII SS-Army Corps	1 August 1944	*SS-Obergruppenführer* Hermann Priess (Aug–Oct 1944) *SS-Gruppenführer* Max Simon (Oct 1944–May 1945)
XV SS-Cossack Cavalry Corps	February 1945	*Generalleutnant* Helmuth von Pannwitz (Feb–May 1945)
XVI SS-Army Corps	January 1945	*SS-Obergruppenführer* Karl-Maria Demelhuber (Jan–Feb 1945)
XVII *Waffen* Army Corps of the SS (Hungarian)	January 1945	*Waffen-General der Waffen-SS* Franz Zeidner (Jan–Mar 1945) *Waffen-General der Waffen-SS* Eugen Ranzenberger (Mar–May 1945)
XVIII SS-Army Corps	December 1944	*SS-Gruppenführer* Heinz Reinfarth (Dec 1944–Feb 1945) *SS-Obergruppenführer* Georg Keppler (Feb–May 1945)

also placed intense pressure on SS recruitment policies. It is little wonder that in this environment the *Waffen-SS* would take its reputation for brutality to new levels.

Fighting on

The gaping holes that opened up in *Waffen-SS* ranks had to be filled as far as possible. As we shall see in the next chapter, a broadening policy towards accepting foreign recruits became the primary recruitment vehicle from 1942. Back in the Reich, however, the qualifications for acceptance into the *Waffen-SS* were critically slackened:

> *Members of the Reich's Labor Corps were conscripted without choice, and the boys of the Hitler Youth organization were intimidated into volunteering. Press gangs rounded up ethnic Germans for service. Obergruppenführer Hans Jüttner, head of the SS high command,*

complained as early as 1942 that many so-called volunteers had actually been lured into the Waffen-SS through trickery; he cited the case of Hungarian nationals who joined up thinking that they were going for 'short sports training.' Worse, the recruiters tended to take anyone they could get, regardless of qualifications. According to Jüttner, some of the recruits were suffering from 'epilepsy, severe tuberculosis, and other serious physical disabilities.'

(Flaherty, 2004)

Bearing in mind that some of these disabilities would almost qualify a child for euthanasia back in the late 1930s, it is evident that the SS's recruitment philosophy had made a marked shift. Divisional expansion was alarming. Eight new divisions were founded in 1943, 13 divisions in 1944 and 11 divisions in 1945, making 38 divisions in total by the end of the

war and giving the illusion of deep structural strength.

Despite the fact that many of the newer *Waffen-SS* units were of suspect quality, the steel of the original formations could not be doubted. In March 1943, following the German disaster at Stalingrad, II SS-Panzer Corps recaptured Kharkov in a bloody street battle, and then took Belgorod, in the process suffering more than 40 per cent losses. Such critical losses were starting to tell, not helped by further decimation during the failed battle of Kursk, and it was not long before the *Waffen-SS* was in retreat alongside its *Wehrmacht* comrades across the whole Eastern Front.

By the end of 1943, it was evident that the war had turned emphatically against Germany. During 1944, furthermore, the *Waffen-SS* would be spread even thinner as a new front opened in the West and Germany spiralled to destruction.

Final Acts, 1944–45

The years 1944–45 saw the final collapse of the Third Reich and the virtual obliteration of many Waffen-SS *divisions. By this time, furthermore, the reputation of the SS amongst the Allies often ensured a general reluctance to take SS men prisoner.*

The final years of *Waffen-SS* service were ones of chaos and death. With the Allied opening of a second front in Normandy in June 1944, plus the continuing slaughter in Italy and on the Eastern Front, many *Waffen-SS* formations undertook multiple theatre deployments in the space of months. The mortally taxed *Leibstandarte*

Division, for example, found itself fighting for its life in the Falaise Pocket in Normandy in August 1944, then (after re-forming in Germany) acting as a spearhead in the Ardennes offensive of December 1944, before slugging out the rest of the war in Slovakia, Hungary and finally Austria, where it surrendered

to US forces. As a general point, at the end of the war, those *Waffen-SS* divisions in Eastern Europe often made desparate attempts to surrender to the Western Allies, as they correctly expected little mercy from the Soviets. The fact that the native German *Waffen-SS* personnel usually had their blood group tattooed on the inside of the left arm, up near the armpit, meant they struggled to disguise their service identity. Some attempted to burn off the tattoo with a cigarette, but the scar this left remained an identifying mark to savvy Allied interrogators, and those who claimed that the scar was the result of a bullet wound would sometimes be X-rayed to see if there was any corresponding internal damage.

Heroism and defeat

The ultimate fate of all the *Waffen-SS* units was either death or surrender. This destiny, however, did not mean that the *Waffen-SS* went down meekly. The fortuitous deployment of the 9th and 10th SS-Panzer Divisions for rest and refitting to the area around Arnhem in early September 1944 was a critical factor in the failure of the Allied *Market Garden* operation, despite the fact that the war-ravaged corps formed by the two divisions was at only 30 per cent of its original strength. A further operation that showed the mettle of the late-war *Waffen-SS* was the Ardennes offensive of late 1944, Hitler's attempt to split the US and British forces in northern Europe and advance to capture the critical Allied port of Antwerp.

At the head of the German offensive was the Sixth SS-Panzer Army, composed of I SS-Panzer Corps (the *Leibstandarte* and *Hitlerjugend* Divisions and the 101st SS-Heavy Panzer Battalion) and II SS-Panzer Corps (the *Das Reich* and *Hohenstaufen* Divisons and the 102nd SS-Heavy Panzer Battalion).

In addition, the 150th SS-Panzer

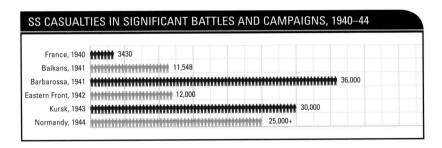

SS CASUALTIES IN SIGNIFICANT BATTLES AND CAMPAIGNS, 1940–44

France, 1940	3430
Balkans, 1941	11,548
Barbarossa, 1941	36,000
Eastern Front, 1942	12,000
Kursk, 1943	30,000
Normandy, 1944	25,000+

Brigade was created specially for the operation. It was a mixed brigade, comprising SS, *Heer* and *Luftwaffe* personnel, under SS command, and included as many English-speaking men as possible. Tasked with the capture of vital bridges, the brigade was meant to use its linguistic skills along with captured US equipment to infiltrate enemy lines, causing mayhem in the US ranks.

Ardennes offensive

The Ardennes offensive included some of the great, or at least most notorious, commanders of the *Waffen-SS*. Josef 'Sepp' Dietrich commanded the Sixth SS-Panzer Army. The skilled combat leader Joachim Peiper, who became the youngest *SS-Standartenführer* in the history of the SS, headed *Kampfgruppe Peiper*, an armoured battle group within the *Leibstandarte* Division. The leader of the 150th SS-Panzer Brigade, Otto Skorzeny, was already famous for having led the successful raid to free Mussolini from his mountain-top prison on the Gran Sasso in September 1943.

Having been rekitted with as much available equipment as Germany could give, the *Waffen-SS* formations initially made good progress in the northern sector of the offensive, but

soon ran aground against fierce opposition from the US 2nd and 99th Infantry Divisions. *Kampfgruppe Peiper* drove its Panzers almost 60km (37 miles) into the Allied lines, and on the way committed the atrocity for which Peiper is principally remembered – the massacre of more than 80 US prisoners at Malmédy. Although Peiper's men managed to inflict severe combat casualties on the US forces, eventually their own casualties mounted to unacceptable levels, and fuel shortages caused them to abandon their vehicles – around 800 men had to trek back to friendly lines on foot.

Skorzeny's men had mixed results. The presence of English-speaking German soldiers in the Allied lines did indeed cause widespread disruption, as much through paranoia as through genuine effects. Yet the vital bridges remained uncaptured, and in the end many of the SS 'spies' (as the Allies classified them) were captured and executed. Despite making a major dent in both the Allied lines and the Allies' confidence, the Ardennes offensive was finally crushed by January of the new year.

Last days

Following the Ardennes offensive, and with the addition of the massive

WAFFEN-SS GENERAL SERVICE AND CAMPAIGN AWARDS

Award	Description	Notes
General Wehrmacht *Awards*		
■ *Infanterie Sturmabzeichen* (Infantry Assault Badge)	Silver-coloured oak leaves wreath, crossed by Kar 98 rifle motif, topped by eagle and swastika; worn on left breast pocket	Awarded to soldier who had participated in at least three combat actions
■ *Panzer Kampfabzeichen* (Panzer Assault Badge)	Silver-coloured oak leaves wreath (bronze for Panzergrenadiers and armoured recon crews after June 1940) with tank representation, topped by eagle and swastika	Awarded to soldier who had participated in at least three armoured actions. From 1943, two additional patterns were introduced to reflect 25–50 actions or 75–100 actions
■ *Flak Abzeichen* (Flak Badge)	Silver-coloured oak leaves wreath featuring heavy flak gun representation, topped by eagle	Badge awarded for aircraft shot down, based on a points system
■ *Allgemeines Sturmabzeichen* (General Assault Badge)	Oak leaves wreath with central eagle and swastika, atop a crossed bayonet and stick grenades; number panel at bottom	Awarded for combat experience, in the following engagement categories: 25, 50, 75, 100
■ *Nahkampfspange* (Close Combat Clasp)	Horizontal oak leaves frame with crossed bayonet and hand grenade in the centre; topped by eagle and swastika	Awarded for hand-to-hand fighting; subsequent bronze, silver and gold clasps could be added based on duration of the fighting
■ *Panzervernichtungsabzeichen* (Tank Destruction Badge)	Strip of aluminium braid with black edging, with a tank motif in the centre	Awarded for single-handedly knocking out an enemy tank; various upgraded awards could be given based on the number of tanks destroyed
SS Awards		
■ *Ostmedaille* (Eastern Front Medal)	Circular design featuring stick grenade motif, with helmet motif balanced on top; obverse centre field with eagle and swastika design; reverse field with inscription: *Winterschlacht im Osten 1941/42*; ribbon suspension	Awarded to soldiers who had served on the Eastern Front during the first winter of campaign, and had served in a minimum of 14 days of combat operations or had been wounded
■ *Bandenkampf Abzeichen* (Anti-Partisan Badge)	Oak leaves wreath with skull and crossbones at base, with central sword around which is wrapped a hydra	Awarded in three grades (bronze, silver, gold) for days spent on anti-Partisan operations
■ Demyansk Shield	Shield featuring crossed swords framing a head-on aircraft, topped by eagle and swastika, the swastika flanked by bunkers	Awarded to SS soldiers who participated in the defence of the Demyansk Pocket, February 1941–April 1942

Soviet offensives of early 1945, the future of Germany was now set in stone. The *Waffen-SS* divisions, although seriously depleted across the board, nevertheless remained formidable, if only in delaying the inevitable and imposing horrifying casualties on less well-trained Allied units.

War crimes

The battle for Budapest between December 1944 and February 1945 saw the IX *Waffen* Alpine Corps of the SS and the IV SS-Panzer Corps help inflict more than 500,000 casualties on the Soviets before the city finally surrendered. In March 1945, the Second and Sixth SS-Panzer Armies were hurled at the Soviets in *Unternehmen Frühlingserwachen* (Operation Spring Awakening), the last great German offensive of the war, which at first made good progress until the sheer weight of Soviet armour and artillery

crushed it. Hitler's private army could, finally, do nothing to prevent their *Führer*'s downfall.

Furthermore, by the end of the war the reputation of the *Waffen-SS* was soiled by some of the well-publicized war crimes. A quick glance at the non-exhaustive list below indicates some of the worst atrocities committed by the *Waffen-SS* in the field, including the destruction of Oradour-sur-Glane in June 1944, in which 642 men, women and children were shot or burnt to death.

An ideology of barbarity

Racial indoctrination (something often received prior to *Waffen-SS* membership, within Hitler Youth organizations) and military brutalization account for much of the motivation behind such atrocities; also a fanatical loyalty to officers meant that reprisal actions were savage should an officer die from Partisan or Resistance attack.

Indeed, and without excusing the behaviour, unlike the systematic execution programmes of the *Einsatzgruppen*, the atrocities of the *Waffen-SS* rarely happened in a vacuum, and tended to occur in the context of reprisal or 'anti-Partisan' operations.

Of course, such labels often masked a simple desire for violence and vengeance, and the general treatment of Soviet civilians on the Eastern Front by all German forces, *Waffen-SS* and *Wehrmacht*, was often an exercise in barbarity.

When judging the actions of the *Waffen-SS*, it is worth remembering that there were many Allied actions that took a heavy toll on civilian lives, not least the Allied strategic bombing campaign. The difference seems to be that the *Waffen-SS* was periodically capable of looking women and children in the eye before killing them, and consequently their memory is darkened.

NOTABLE MASSACRES IN THE WEST BY *WAFFEN-SS* UNITS

Location	Date	Units involved	Details
Worhoudt, France	28 May 1940	1st SS-Panzer Division *Leibstandarte SS Adolf Hitler*	80 British and French POWs killed; there were 15 survivors
Le Paradis, France	27 May 1940	3rd SS-Panzer Division *Totenkopf*	97 British POWs machine-gunned and bayoneted; 2 were injured and survived
Ardeatine, Italy	March 1944	German police under SS leadership	335 Italian and Jewish prisoners executed
Ardenne Abbey, France	7 June 1944	12th SS-Panzer Division *Hitlerjugend*	18 Canadian soldiers executed in the abbey grounds
Tulle, France	9 June 1944	2nd SS-Panzer Division *Das Reich*	97 civilians executed in a reprisal operation
Oradour-sur-Glane, France	10 June 1944	2nd SS-Panzer Division *Das Reich*	642 men, women and children murdered and the town destroyed in reprisal operation
Distomo, Greece	10 June 1944	4th SS-Police Panzergrenadier Division	218 men, women and children killed in a reprisal attack
Sant'Anna di Stazzema, Italy	12 August 1944	16th SS-Panzergrenadier Division *Reichsführer-SS*	Retreating SS soldiers kill 560 civilians
Marzabotto, Grizzana Morandi and Monzuno, Italy	29 September– 5 October 1944	16th SS-Panzergrenadier Division *Reichsführer-SS*	c.770 civilians murdered in terror operation
Malmédy, Belgium	17 December 1944	*Kampfgruppe Peiper*	SS unit opens fire on 129 US POWs, killing 86

WAFFEN-SS SOLDIERS AWARDED THE KNIGHT'S CROSS WITH OAK LEAVES AND SWORDS

Name	Rank	Unit	Date of Award
Josef Dietrich	SS-Obergruppenführer	1st SS-Panzergrenadier Division	14 March 1943
August Dieckmann	SS-Obersturmbannführer	10th SS-Panzergrenadier Regiment	10 October 1943
Herbert-Otto Gille	SS-Gruppenführer	5th SS-Panzergrenadier Division	20 February 1944
Heinrich Schuldt	SS-Oberführer	19th Waffen Grenadier Division of the SS	25 March 1944
Hermann Priess	SS-Brigadeführer	3rd SS-Panzer Division	24 April 1944
Michael Wittmann	SS-Hauptsturmführer	101st SS-Panzer Battalion	22 June 1944
Hans Dorr	SS-Sturmbannführer	9th SS-Panzergrenadier Regiment	9 July 1944
Hermann Fegelein	SS-Gruppenführer	8th SS-Cavalry Division	30 July 1944
Fritz von Scholz Edler von Rarancze	SS-Gruppenführer	11th SS-Volunteer Panzergrenadier Division	8 August 1944
Felix Steiner	SS-Obergruppenführer	III SS-Panzer Corps	10 August 1944
Paul Hausser	SS-Oberstgruppenführer	II SS-Panzer Corps	28 August 1944
Kurt Meyer	SS-Standartenführer	12th SS-Panzer Division	27 August 1944
Theodor Wisch	SS-Brigadeführer	1st SS-Panzer Division	30 August 1944
Otto Baum	SS-Standartenführer	2nd SS-Panzer Division	2 September 1944
Heinz Harmel	SS-Brigadeführer	10th SS-Panzer Division	15 December 1944
Joachim Peiper	SS-Obersturmbannführer	1st SS-Panzer Regiment	11 January 1945
Walter Krüger	SS-Obergruppenführer	VI Waffen Army Corps of the SS	11 January 1945
Helmut Dörner	SS-Oberführer	4th SS-Police Panzergrenadier Division	1 February 1945
Otto Kumm	SS-Brigadeführer	7th SS-Volunteer Mountain Division	17 March 1945
Georg Bochmann	SS-Standartenführer	18th SS-Volunteer Panzergrenadier Division	26 March 1945
Otto Weidinger	SS-Obersturmbannführer	4th SS-Panzergrenadier Regiment	6 May 1945
Günther-Eberhardt Wisliceny	SS-Obersturmbannführer	3rd SS-Panzergrenadier Regiment	6 May 1945
Sylvester Stadler	SS-Oberführer	9th SS-Panzer Division	6 May 1945
Wilhelm Bittrich	SS-Obergruppenführer	II SS-Panzer Corps	6 May 1945

Equipment

In its early days, the Waffen-SS *struggled to gain modern equipment in sufficient quantities. These problems were largely overcome in the war years, but the quality of weapons and kit could vary significantly between divisions.*

An abiding myth of the *Waffen-SS* was that it was armed and equipped to far higher levels than equivalent *Heer* formations. There is a grain of truth to this argument, but only when focusing on specific SS divisions. The SS-V and *Leibstandarte* Divisions, because of their position in SS history and their elite status, did indeed tend to receive the best that German war production could offer. SS Panzer battalions also each had four authorized tank companies rather than the three tank companies in *Heer* battalions, so at least in terms of quantity they tended to have more tanks than the Army's Panzer units.

Yet the picture changes considerably when we factor in all the *Waffen-SS* divisions, many of which held less prestigious positions than the *Leibstandarte*. Mark Rikmenspoel points out that 'when the SS-Totenkopf division was formed during the winter of 1939–40, it had to make do with largely-captured Czech heavy weapons'. The *Prinz Eugen* Division had to rely on captured French and Yugoslav equipment, and was generally poorly equipped even when compared with *Heer* mountain divisions. Foreign divisions could fare even worse, going into battle with captured small arms such as the British Sten or the Soviet PPSh-41. Of course, utilizing captured weapons was far from uncommon in the *Heer*

either – especially in terms of artillery – but this situation should give us caution about claiming any special status for the *Waffen-SS*.

Infantry weapons
In terms of the actual tools of war, the *Waffen-SS* was of course armed with largely the same weapons as the rest of the German armed forces, with some occasional variations in distribution patterns. Looking at small arms, the *Waffen-SS* was kitted out with the typical range of firearms – Luger P08 or Walther P38 pistols, Kar 98k bolt-action rifles (plus some Gewehr 43 semi-automatic rifles from 1943), MP38 and MP40 submachine guns, MG 34 and MG42 machine guns. In addition, however, the *Waffen-SS* received the bulk of the new Sturmgewehr 44 (also known as the MP44) assault rifles. Issued in 1945, the Sturmgewehr 44, an automatic weapon, was essentially the first operationally effective assault rifle, which fired a rifle-calibre 7.92mm (0.31in) round from a *kurz* (short) cartridge. Automatic weapons such as submachine guns tended to go into the hands of squad and platoon leaders.

Looking at artillery, anti-tank weapons used by the *Waffen-SS* included the Pak 36, Pak 38, Pak 40 and Pak 43, plus self-propelled tank destroyers such as the Marder II,

Marder III, Jagdpanzer IV and Sturmgeschütz III. For personal tank hunting, the late-war *Waffen-SS* often relied upon hand-held shaped-charge rocket launchers – the Panzerfaust and the Raketenpanzerbüchse (literally 'rocket tank rifle'), both of which gave decent results at close ranges.

Waffen-SS field artillery was extremely varied, partly because of the troublesome German over-diversification in types, and also because of the tendency to acquire and use captured artillery stocks. The *Waffen-SS* also made use of rocket launchers such as the Nebelwerfer, these being used by rocket detachments of SS Panzer or infantry divisions.

The tanks of the *Waffen-SS* varied across the full range of types issued during the war, from the Czech-made Panzer 38(t), first used by *Totenkopf* in 1940, through to the Tigers and Panthers, which are popularly most associated with the *Waffen-SS* armoured force. The mainstays of the early *Waffen-SS* Panzer regiments were the Panzer III and Panzer IV, with Tigers being issued to selected regiments from 1942. In 1943, the new Panzer V Panther entered service, and from 1944, the *Waffen-SS* also took deliveries of the Tiger II 'King Tiger' plus its Jagdtiger tank-destroying variant.

ARMOURED VEHICLES USED BY THE *WAFFEN-SS*

VEHICLE	*NOTES*
Tanks	
Panzerkampfwagen (PzKpfw) II	Ausf IIF version saw *Waffen-SS* service; withdrawn within 12 months
PzKpfw III	Principally the Ausf J model
PzKpfw IV	Principally the Ausf D, F2, G, H and J models
PzKpfw V (Panther)	Principally Ausf D, A and G models. *Leibstandarte, Totenkopf, Wiking* and *Das Reich* used Panthers from July/August 1943
PzKpfw VI (Tiger)	Heavy tank companies then heavy tank battalions created with Tigers in *Leibstandarte, Das Reich* and *Totenkopf*. The battalions were designated *SS-schwere Panzer Abteilung* 101 (later 501), 102 (502) and 103 (503)
PzKpfw VI B (King Tiger)	Issued in small numbers to heavy tank battalions
Tank Destroyers and SP Guns	
Panzerjäger Marder II	Used by *Waffen-SS* from 1942
Panzerjäger Marder III	Used in infantry-support role
schweres Infanteriegeschutz (sIG) 33	Used in infantry-support role from 1939
Sturmgeschütz III	Used from 1940 in *Waffen-SS* Panzer divisions and artillery regiments
Sturmgeschütz IV	Little used by *Waffen-SS*
Sturmhaubitze Wespe	Saw service with SP artillery units of *Leibstandarte, Das Reich* and *Totenkopf*
Hummel	One battery of Hummels to each Panzer division artillery regiment

VEHICLE	NOTES
Tank Destroyers and SP Guns	
Jagdpanzer 38(t) Hetzer	Entered *Waffen-SS* service in 1944
Jagdpanzer IV	Service with *Leibstandarte, Das Reich, Polizei, Hitlerjugend, Wiking, Totenkopf, Frundsberg* and *Hohenstaufen* Divisions
Jagdpanzer V Jagdpanther	Limited late-war use with *Das Reich, Hohenstaufen* and *Frundsberg* Divisions
Flakpanzer IV Möbelwagen	Limited *Waffen-SS* use
Flakpanzer IV Wirbelwind	Limited *Waffen-SS* use
Armoured Cars/Reconnaissance Vehicles	
SdKfz 221	Used by recce platoons of SS regiments
SdKfz 222	Used by recce platoons of SS regiments
SdKfz 231/232	Recce/radio vehicle used by *Waffen-SS* on Eastern Front
SdKfz 233	Infantry-support vehicle
SdKfz 234/2 Puma	Heavy armoured car issued to *Waffen-SS* from 1943
SdKfz 234/4	Anti-tank gun armed recce vehicle
Halftracks	
SdKfz 250 leichte Schützenpanzerwagen	Used mainly in command vehicle roles
SdKfz 251 mittler Schützenpanzerwagen	Issued to the *Waffen-SS* from 1942

UNARMOURED VEHICLES USED BY THE *WAFFEN-SS*

VEHICLE		NOTES
	Halftracks (soft-skinned)	
	SdKfz 6	Used as prime mover and for towing artillery
	SdKfz 7	Used for towing artillery, although there were some Flak variants
	SdKfz 9	Heavy prime mover or engineering vehicle
	SdKfz 10	Used as armoured personnel carrier, for anti-aircraft and/or for towing artillery
	schwere Wehrmacht Schlepper (Büssing-NAG)	Transportation and towing
	Opel Maultier	General transportation, but also a Nebelwerfer variant

VEHICLE		NOTES
Trucks		
	LKW (Lastkraftwagen) Opel Blitz	Numerous variants – command vehicles, ambulances, engineering vehicles, Flak trucks etc
	LKW Mercedes L3000A	Similar functions and capabilities asOpel Blitz
	LKW Büssing-NAG 4500	Heavy truck
	LKW Kfz 70, Krupp Protze	Also used by *Waffen-SS* as Flak vehicle
Cars		
	Volkswagen VW Type 82 Kübelwagen	General-purpose vehicle
	Volkswagen VW Type 166 Schwimmwagen	Amphibious field car
	PKW (Personenkraftwagen) Steyr 1500A	Used as troop vehicle or command car
	PKW Stoewer R200 Type 40	Four-wheel drive field car
	Mercedes Benz 1500A	Troop and general-purpose vehicle
Motorcycles		
	BMW R75	Heavy motorcycle, often with sidecar combination
	Zundapp KS750	Entered service in 1941
	DKW-NZ350	Communications, recce and dispatch bike

CHAPTER 4

The Foreign SS

*It is a challenging irony that the Waffen-SS,
an organization that initially prided itself on its 'pure'
German racial heritage, would eventually be so
diluted by foreign personnel.*

*By performing some contorted racial logic,
Himmler and his recruitment chief, often under the
sceptical gaze of Hitler, at first allowed select Western
European 'Germanic' recruits to join the ranks, but
gradually widened the net to include Slavs, Armenians,
Cossacks, Latvians, Romanians, Hungarians and
Serbians amongst many other ethnicities;
there was even an Indian legion.*

*The use of foreign recruits certainly helped
the Waffen-SS fill out its ranks, but as loyal combatants
their quality was shifting and variable according to the
formation in question or the changing tides of war. They
were also treated with suspicion and often disdain by
the 'old guard' formations of the Waffen-SS.*

◼ SS men from the Narva Battalion hitch a ride on a tank. The Narva Battalion
was made up of Estonian volunteers and served as part of 5th SS Panzer

Western European Volunteers

With the German conquest of Western Europe in 1940, a new pool of potential recruits opened up to the Waffen-SS. *Although it was principally focused upon Nordic peoples, recruitment policy also included French, Belgians and even some Britons.*

Although the Nazis demonstrated a clear superiority mindset when it came to international relations, we must not think that Hitler was axiomatically hostile to all non-Germans. For a start, the Nazis' ancestral preoccupations with 'Nordic blood' meant an automatically favourable predisposition towards the Scandinavian and northern European countries, whose peoples fell into the 'Germanic' category.

Even outside these nations, however, Hitler and Himmler both had a broader racial acceptance than is generally credited, although it remained a long way from egalitarianism. Hitler showed a certain empathy with the British people, for example, at least in the days prior to defeat during the Battle of Britain. The Nazis' leanings towards eulogizing the worker meant that the industrial classes of Britain were roughly acceptable to the German mindset, and Nazi propaganda occasionally presented British workers more as victims of an acutely class-based society than as natural foes.

The magazine *Signal*, published by the *Wehrmacht* under the guidance of the Ministry of Propaganda, often featured articles depicting various races and peoples coming to a Damascene revelation of the goodness of the Germans. One article, published during the German operations in the Balkans, featured the following account from a captured British soldier:

Before the war I was a policeman in London... I volunteered for police service in the army for a period of 12 years. I have not been in any large-scale engagements. We all thought that in Greece the RAF was much stronger than the German Air Force. That is what we had been told in England. The Germans are fine fellows. We thought they were barbarians; that is what we had read in the papers. But my pals and I agree that we are treated here in the camp better than we have been by our own officers. Above all, the German officers are friendly towards us. I only hope that the war will soon be over, so that I can return to my wife who lives on the Isle of Wight.

(Mayer, 1976)

Acknowledging the fact that the account may have been embellished, or simply invented, by the *Signal* writers, what we see is both an ennobling of the German character plus a subtle attempt at showing the underlying compatibility between British and Germans. The same article features Sudanese, Greek, Czech, Cypriot, Indian and Australian POWs, all with similar treatment. The message of such articles is not open racial hostility, but the possibility of *accepted* races living peaceably (although in subjection and defeat) under German overlords. Yet that was in the future. In the meantime, there was a war to be fought, and the *Waffen-SS* had to grow rapidly if it was to develop its stature within the German armed forces.

Germanic recruits

The idea of recruiting Germanic volunteers into the SS actually pre-dated the war. In 1938, Himmler had stated that 'Nordic' foreigners could join the ranks of the *Allgemeine-SS* if they showed the right racial and ideological credentials. Himmler had greater dreams of Nordic unity than did Hitler, and envisaged a collaborationist Nordic empire (Norway, Denmark, Holland and Belgium all had fascist parties) leading to a vast multinational SS to rival or even exceed the power of the *Wehrmacht*. So it was that following the successful conclusion of the Western campaign in 1940, Himmler set Berger, his recruitment chief, to the task of bringing foreign Nordic blood into the ranks of the SS, and forming *Waffen-SS Freiwilligen* (Volunteer) legions and divisions.

In terms of the West, certain

FOREIGN *WAFFEN-SS* COLLAR TABS

Sig runes

13th Division
Handschar

15th Division
(Latvian No 1)

23rd Division
Nederland (early)

Sig runes

30th Division
(Russian No 2)

5th Division
Wiking

14th Division
Galizien

18th Division
Horst Wessel

23rd Division
Nederland (late)

28th Division
Wallonien

33rd Division
Charlemagne

France

Ukraine
(issue doubtful)

20th Division
(Estonian No 1)

23rd Division
Kama

29th Division
Italien

Indian Legion

7th Division
Prinz Eugen

19th Division
(Latvian No 2)

21st Division
Skanderbeg

25th Division
Hunyadi

29th Division
(Russian No 1)

British Legion

11th Division
Nordland

Estonian
(alternative)

22nd *Maria Theresia*
Division
(Hungarian)

27th Division
Langemarck

30th Division
(Russian No 2)

Foreign volunteer units in the Waffen-SS did not wear the standard 'Sig rune' collar tabs. Instead, they wore tabs bearing emblems indicating their national or ethnic origins. Foreign units also wore a sleeve shield with their national colours. This helped create a sense of national identity within the wider 'family' of the SS.

WESTERN EUROPEAN CONTRIBUTIONS TO *WAFFEN-SS*

Nation	Date occupied by Germans	Number of volunteers
Belgium	June 1940	40,000
Denmark	April 1940	10,000
Finland	–	3000
France	June 1940	20,000
Italy	1943	15,000
Luxembourg	May 1940	2000
Netherlands	May 1940	50,000
Norway	May 1940	6000
Spain	–	1000
Sweden	–	300
Switzerland	–	300

nations fell into the Germanic category and were therefore suitable for recruitment efforts. These nations were: Denmark, Flemish Belgium (Flanders), Great Britain, Iceland, Lichtenstein, Luxembourg, the Netherlands, Norway, Sweden and Switzerland. Italy, as an actual ally, and Spain, as a practical ally, provided more recruits. France (and also French-speaking Belgium – Wallonia) was far more suspect, for long-standing political, social and cultural reasons. Nevertheless, some 20,000 French volunteers went into the ranks of the *Waffen-SS*, mainly motivated by fervent anti-Communism. Taking each

of these recruiting regions in turn, we can see how important the Western European contribution was to a growing *Waffen-SS*.

The Netherlands
In total during the war years, the Netherlands provided 50,000 recruits for *Waffen-SS* service, more than any other Western European nation. The influx was aided not only by the close cultural and linguistic connections between the Netherlands and Germany, but also by a sizeable *Nationaal Socialistische Beweging* (National Socialist Movement; NSB) led by Anton Mussert. Although the

NSB never managed to achieve the political power it desired, its members were more inclined to warm to Berger's recruitment overtures. (In September 1940, Mussert formed the *Nederlansche-SS* – Netherlands SS – to show his fidelity.) The Dutch volunteers were initially channelled into the SS *Westland* Regiment, and from May 1941 more than 1000 also went into the *Wiking* Division and a mixed Dutch, Flemish and Danish *Nordwest* Regiment. The latter was eventually absorbed into a Dutch fighting legion, the *SS-Freiwilligen-Legion Niederlande*, in September 1941. (Note that in June 1941, Hitler had officially, albeit reluctantly, authorized the recruitment of foreigners for foreign legions, the legions to be run between the SS and the *Wehrmacht*.)

Mussert had ambitions for division-sized Dutch formations, but this would not be realized until early 1945, when 4th SS-Volunteer Panzergrenadier Brigade *Nederland* was expanded and became 23rd SS-Volunteer Panzergrenadier Division *Nederland* (Netherlands No 1). One other Dutch division was formed before war's end – 34th SS-Volunteer Grenadier Division *Landstorm Nederland* (Netherlands No 2) in February 1945, but this formation was actually smaller than a brigade.

Belgium
Belgium yielded 40,000 volunteers for SS service, principally provided by the Dutch-speaking Flemish region, which had a lively right-wing political scene. At first the Flemish volunteers went into the *Nordwest* Regiment,

COMMANDERS OF 6TH SS-MOUNTAIN DIVISION *NORD*

SS-Brigadeführer Karl Herrmann	(Feb–May 1941)
SS-Obergruppenführer Karl-Maria Demelhuber	(May 1941–Apr 1942)
SS-Obergruppenführer Matthias Kleinheisterkamp	(Apr 1942)
SS-Oberführer Hans Scheider	(Apr–June 1942)
SS-Obergruppenführer Matthias Kleinheisterkamp	(June 1942–Jan 1943)
SS-Gruppenführer Lothar Debes	(Jan 1943–June 1944)
SS-Obergruppenführer Friedrich-Wilhelm Krüger	(June–Aug 1944)
SS-Brigadeführer Gustav Lombard	(Aug–Sep 1944)
SS-Gruppenführer Karl Brenner	(Sep 1944–Apr 1945)

but tensions with the Dutch elements of that unit led to the creation of a separate *SS-Freiwilligen-Legion Flandern* in September 1941. The French-speaking Walloons responded by forming their own legion – the *Légion Wallonie* – although this was initially part of the German Army rather than the *Waffen-SS*. Having proved itself in combat, however, the legion was transferred to SS authority in 1943, and eventually grew to become the 28th SS-Volunteer Grenadier Division *Wallonien* (Walloon No 1).

France

Despite Germany's reservations about France noted above, the country nonetheless provided 45,000 volunteers for German military service, 20,000 of whom went into the SS. Himmler expressed to Hitler a notion that France could eventually be 'Germanized' through extracting and re-educating its 'Germanic' young, but Hitler, who had a long-standing antipathy towards French people and culture, was resistant to the idea. In April 1942, during a discussion with Himmler, Hitler stated that :

The mass of the French people has petit bourgeois *inclinations, so much so that it would be a triumph to succeed in removing the elements of Germanic origin from the grasp of the country's ruling class.*
(Quoted in Trevor-Roper, 2000)

Nevertheless, French volunteers began entering *Wehrmacht* service in 1941, but it would not be until 30 January 1943 that Hitler gave permission for Frenchmen to serve in

the ranks of the *Waffen-SS*. By the end of the year, the SS Frenchmen had coalesced into the 8th French SS-Volunteer Grenadier Regiment, which eventually became a *Sturmbrigade*. After heavy losses in combat, the surviving French warriors were taken into the 33rd *Waffen* Grenadier Division of the SS *Charlemagne* (French No 1).

Italy

Despite (or because of) being an ally of Germany until September 1943, Italy's *Waffen-SS* contribution was fairly modest – around 15,000 volunteers. Following the Italian armistice, the Germans nonetheless controlled major parts of the country, in which there were hundreds of thousands of disarmed or interned Italian soldiers, as well as many Italian Army divisions that were directly incorporated under *Wehrmacht* control.

The prevalent fascist elements amongst the Italian soldiery produced the thousands of volunteers sufficient to form the *Italienische SS-Freiwilligen-Legion*, renamed the 1st *Sturmbrigade* Italian Volunteer Legion in January 1944. Note that the Italian volunteers fought as part of the SS, but were technically independent, wearing their own (similar) uniform and having their own title – *Prima Brigata d'Assalto della Legione SS Italiana* (First Assault Brigade of the Italian SS Legion). Following their robust performance fighting around Anzio in spring 1944, however, Himmler awarded them the right to wear SS uniform and insignia.

Eventually the Italian contribution was given divisional status when it became 29th *Waffen* Grenadier Division of the SS (Italian No. 1) in May 1945, although it was well below divisional strength.

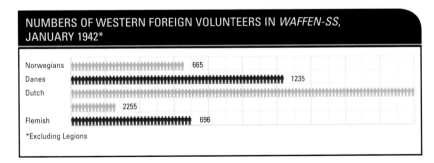

NUMBERS OF WESTERN FOREIGN VOLUNTEERS IN *WAFFEN-SS*, JANUARY 1942*

Norwegians — 665
Danes — 1235
Dutch — 2255
Flemish — 696
*Excluding Legions

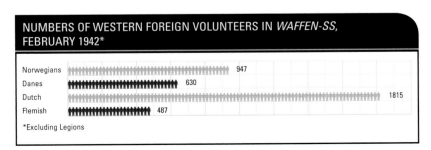

NUMBERS OF WESTERN FOREIGN VOLUNTEERS IN *WAFFEN-SS*, FEBRUARY 1942*

Norwegians — 947
Danes — 630
Dutch — 1815
Flemish — 487
*Excluding Legions

Denmark

Denmark, like Norway, was seen as a racially pure hunting ground for *Waffen-SS* recruits, and in total the country provided some 10,000 soldiers for Himmler's service. They were encouraged to enlist for two years, enticed by the promise of having simultaneous German and Danish citizenship.

Despite the expectations of Nazi racial profiling, the initial influx of recruits was disappointingly small (just 200), but combined with *Volksdeutsche* from the border territories there were soon enough to form the *Nordland* Regiment, which in turn formed part of the *Wiking* Division. Other Danes went off to service in the *Totenkopf* Division.

Greater shape was given to the Danish *Waffen-SS* contribution in June 1941. With official backing from the Danish government, Danish volunteers established the *SS-Freiwilligen-Verband Danemark* (SS Volunteer Group Denmark), also known as the *Freikorps Danmark*. By the end of 1941, the unit was two battalions and 1200 men strong, although those numbers would be slashed significantly fighting in the bloody engagements on the Eastern Front in spring 1942.

The *Freikorps Danmark* transmuted into the 24th SS-Panzergrenadier Regiment *Danemark*, although this regiment was less than 50 per cent Danish, the remainder being *Volksdeutsche* and German nationals. This unit fought on until the end of the war, while other Danes served in formations such as the 5th SS-Panzer Division *Wiking*.

Norway

Norway's contribution to SS ranks was about 6000 men, a number that disappointed the Norwegian collaborationist Vidkun Quisling, who hoped for tens of thousands of his countrymen fighting on the German side. The initial batches of recruits went into the *Nordland* Regiment, which in turn would go on to form part of the later *Wiking* Division.

Following the invasion of Russia, an event that in itself increased the numbers of foreigners generally who volunteered for *Waffen-SS* service, the Norwegian *Reichskommissar* (Reich Commissioner) Josef Terboven announced the formation of the *Freiwilligen-Legion Norwegen* (Norwegian Legion), a 1100-strong unit that went into action on the Eastern Front around Leningrad in 1942. Such was the bad experience of the legion in action that many of its survivors did not re-enlist once their period of service was over, and their stories (plus the unpopular German war against the United States) also dissuaded many fresh recruits. The Norwegians who served during the rest of the war were channelled into the 23rd SS-Panzergrenadier

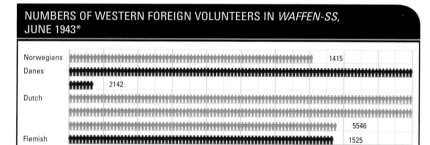

NUMBERS OF WESTERN FOREIGN VOLUNTEERS IN *WAFFEN-SS*, JUNE 1943*

Norwegians 1415
Danes
2142
Dutch
5546
Flemish 1525

*Excluding Legions. French and Walloon figures not available

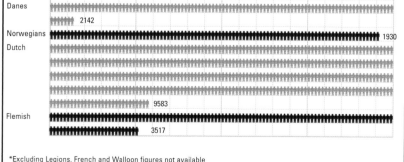

NUMBERS OF WESTERN FOREIGN VOLUNTEERS IN *WAFFEN-SS*, AUGUST 1943*

Danes
2142
Norwegians 1930
Dutch
9583
Flemish
3517

*Excluding Legions. French and Walloon figures not available

Regiment *Norge*, an element of 11th SS-Volunteer Panzergrenadier Division *Nordland*.

Finland

In mid-1941, approximately 1000 Finns joined the *Waffen-SS* to fight in Operation *Barbarossa* on the Eastern Front, most of these serving in the *Wiking* Division. The extensive combat experience gained by the Finns against the Soviets during the Winter War of 1939–40 meant that their small contribution to the division was nonetheless initially appreciated. Inexperienced Finnish recruits, by contrast, undertook training in Austria and were used to form the *SS-Freiwilligen-Bataillon Nordost* (SS Volunteer Battalion 'Northeast'), later renamed *Finnisches Freiwilligen-Bataillon der Waffen-SS*. The Finns' independent spirit meant that they never really settled under German leadership, and in July 1943 the Finnish battalion was disbanded.

Luxembourg

The precise number of Luxembourgers who went into the *Waffen-SS* is not known, but is likely to number around 2000. In total, just over 12,000 of Luxembourg's 290,000 citizens served in the German armed forces. Luxembourg itself was classed as part of Greater Germany, and was absorbed into Germany's system of *Gaue* (Districts) following the country's occupation in May 1940. For this reason, Luxembourg did not form one of the foreign legions produced by many other occupied nations, and those individuals who did serve in the *Waffen-SS* did so on an individual basis rather than as a

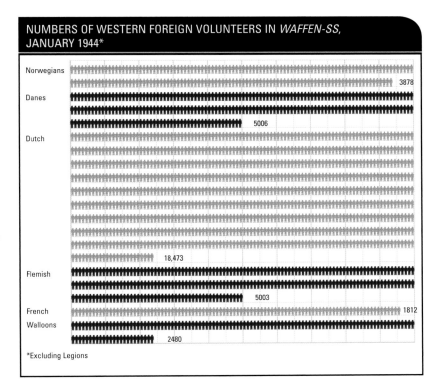

NUMBERS OF WESTERN FOREIGN VOLUNTEERS IN *WAFFEN-SS*, JANUARY 1944*

Norwegians 3878
Danes 5006
Dutch 18,473
Flemish 5003
French 1812
Walloons 2480

*Excluding Legions

recruited national block. As they were regarded as German citizens, there is little record of the units in which they served.

Spain

Spain is a particularly interesting case in terms of *Waffen-SS* foreign recruits, as technically it was not a combatant. Hitler had tried to persuade its leader, Francisco Franco, to become otherwise, an act that would have made dominating the entrance to the Mediterranean that much easier for the Axis forces. He was unsuccessful in his efforts, even though Franco had received direct military assistance from the Germans, including from the armed SS, during the Spanish Civil War of 1936–39.

In 1941, however, the Spanish government bypassed diplomatic awkwardness by allowing Spanish volunteers to offer themselves for service alongside the Germans in the war against the Soviets, a conflict that had deep resonance with many of Franco's fascists. The response was enthusiastic, and a four-regiment division was assembled (later reduced to three regiments by the Germans).

The new Spanish division belonged to the *Wehrmacht*, and was officially named the 250th Infantry Division, but was known to the Spaniards as the 'Blue Division', after the blue shirts worn by Falange fascist party members. Deployed to the Eastern Front, the division was used as a

MAIN DESTINATION UNITS OF WESTERN EUROPEAN VOLUNTEERS TO WAFFEN-SS

Nationality of volunteers	Main Waffen-SS Formation
Belgium	27th SS-Volunteer Grenadier Division *Langemarck* (Flemish No 1); 28th SS-Volunteer Grenadier Division *Wallonien* (Walloon No 1)
Denmark	5th SS-Panzer Division *Wiking*; 11th SS-Volunteer Panzergrenadier Division *Nordland*
Finland	5th SS-Panzer Division *Wiking*; 11th SS-Volunteer Panzergrenadier Division *Nordland*; Finnish Volunteer Battalion of the *Waffen-SS*
France	8th French SS-Volunteer Storm Brigade; 33rd *Waffen* Grenadier Division of the SS *Charlemagne* (French No 1)
Italy	*Waffen* Grenadier Brigade of the SS (Italian No 1); 29th *Waffen* Grenadier Division of the SS *Italien* (Italian No 1)
Luxembourg	Unknown
Netherlands	23rd SS-Volunteer Panzergrenadier Division *Nederland* (Netherlands No 1); 34th SS-Volunteer Grenadier Division *Landstorm Nederland* (Netherlands No 2)
Norway	5th SS-Panzer Division *Wiking*; *Freiwilligen-Legion Norwegen*
Spain	Spanish Volunteer Companies of the SS 101 and 102; 3rd Company of the 28th SS-Volunteer Grenadier Division *Wallonien* (Walloon No 1)
Sweden	5th SS-Panzer Division *Wiking*; 11th SS-Volunteer Panzergrenadier Division *Nordland*
Switzerland	5th SS-Panzer Division *Wiking*; SS-Standarte *Kurt Eggers*

second-line formation, and proved its ability to fight on several occasions. German appreciation of its qualities was low, however, and relations between the two sides iced over. When Spain shifted its stance from non-belligerence to total neutrality in 1943, the division was withdrawn from service.

Yet even as the Spanish division officially dispersed, the *Waffen-SS* received an influx of new Spanish volunteers, enough to form two Spanish volunteer companies, the 101st and 102nd. Another 100-plus Spaniards also went into the 28th SS-Volunteer Panzergrenadier Division *Wallonien*.

Sweden and Switzerland
Between them, Sweden and Switzerland provided less than 1000

recruits for the *Waffen-SS*. The contribution is admittedly small, but it must be remembered that both countries were strictly neutral during the war, a condition of which was a prohibition on allowing a combatant nation to recruit amongst neutral citizens.

In Sweden, however, any individuals wishing to fight for Germany could surreptitiously apply to the *Waffen-SS* through the German embassy in Stockholm. In total, around 300 Swedes made their way into the *Waffen-SS* through this route. Known units in which they served were the 5th SS-Panzer Division *Wiking*; the 11th SS-Volunteer Panzergrenadier Division *Nordland*; and the 23rd SS-Volunteer Panzergrenadier Division *Nederland*. One company of the *Nordland*

division had so many Swedes in it that it was called the *Swedenzug*.

Switzerland yielded similar numbers as Sweden for the *Waffen-SS*, although the *Wehrmacht* received up to 800 Swiss citizens. Those Swiss that did enter SS ranks mainly went to the *Wiking* Division, that most multinational of *Waffen-SS* formations.

Mixed formations
The effects of incorporating Western European foreign recruits into the *Waffen-SS* were mixed. Although the results were generally better than those experienced with Eastern Europeans, discipline problems were still endemic, and there was often an instinctive resistance to German authoritarianism. Furthermore, most Western European recruits were sent to fight on the Eastern Front, where the terrible realities of existence were enough to challenge even the most passionate anti-Communist thinker.

▶ **5th SS-PANZER DIVISION *WIKING* DEPLOYMENT**
Wiking's baptism of fire came with Operation *Barbarossa* in June 1941, and it was in action on the Eastern Front until April 1944, its time mostly spend fighting in the Ukraine. In April it was deployed to Poland. (The division had previously undergone periods of rebuilding in Poland, to help plug the extremely high levels of casualties suffered in the fighting.) It was spared final, complete destruction through a withdrawal into Austria, where it was finally able to surrender to the US forces in May 1945.

DEPLOYMENTS OF 5TH SS-PANZER DIVISION *WIKING*, 1940–45*

1. Dec 1940–June 1941	Germany	
2. June 1941–Apr 1944	Eastern Front, southern sector	
3. Apr 1944–Jan 1945	Poland	
4. Jan–Apr 1945	Hungary	
5. Apr –May 1945	Austria	

FINLAND

NORWAY

ESTONIA

LATVIA

LITHUANIA

SOVIET UNION

GERMANY

POLAND

CZECHOSLOVAKIA

FRANCE

AUSTRIA

HUNGARY

ROMANIA

ITALY

YUGOSLAVIA

* Shows 1939 borders

Eastern European Volunteers

The emptiness of Nazi racial theory is exposed by the use of Soviet and Eastern European personnel in the Waffen-SS. *Peoples previously derided as* Untermenschen *(sub-humans) suddenly found themselves serving in Himmler's army.*

In April 1942, during an evening talk between Hitler and Himmler, Hitler raised concerns over expanding policies of filling out the ranks of the German Army with foreigners, particularly those from the East:

In any case, we must not commit the mistake of enlisting in the German Army foreigners who seem to us to be worthwhile fellows, unless they can prove that they're utterly steeped in the idea of the German Reich. While we're on the subject, I'm sceptical about the participation of all these foreign legions in our struggle on the Eastern front. One mustn't forget that, unless he is convinced of his racial membership of the Germanic Reich, the foreign

legionary is bound to feel that he's betraying his country.
(Trevor-Roper, 2000)

For once, Hitler's views on race actually seem reasonably coherent. For although Himmler eventually

EASTERN EUROPEAN CONTRIBUTIONS TO *WAFFEN-SS*

Nation	Date occupied by Germans	Number of volunteers
Albania	1943	7000
Bulgaria	–	600
Croatia	April 1941	20,000
Estonia	July 1941	25,000
Hungary	–	20,000
Latvia	July 1941	80,000
Lithuania	June 1941	50,000*
Romania	–	50,000
Serbia	April 1941	10,000
Soviet Union	from June 1941	60,000+
* Principally non-SS police units		

MAIN DESTINATION UNITS OF EASTERN EUROPEAN VOLUNTEERS

Nationality of volunteers	Waffen-SS *Destinations*
Albania	21st *Waffen* Mountain Division of the SS *Skanderbeg* (Albanian No 1)
Bulgaria	*Waffen* Grenadier Regiment of the SS (Bulgarian No 1); SS-Panzer *Zerstörer* Regiment (Bulgarian)
Croatia	13th *Waffen* Mountain Division of the SS *Handschar* (Croatian No 1); 23rd *Waffen* Mountain Division of the SS *Kama* (Croatian No 2)
Estonia	Estonian SS Legion; 20th *Waffen* Grenadier Division of the SS (Estonian No 1)
Hungary	25th *Waffen* Grenadier Division of the SS *Hunyadi* (Hungarian No 1); 26th *Waffen* Grenadier Division of the SS *Hungaria* (Hungarian No 2)
Latvia	15th *Waffen* Grenadier Division of the SS (Latvian No 1); 19th *Waffen* Grenadier Division of the SS (Latvian No 2)
Lithuania	–
Romania	7th SS-Volunteer Mountain Division *Prinz Eugen*; 8th SS-Cavalry Division *Florian Geyer*
Serbia	Serbian Volunteer Corps
Soviet Union	14th *Waffen* Grenadier Division of the SS *Galizien* (Ukrainian No 1); 29th *Waffen* Grenadier Division of the SS (Russian No 1); 30th *Waffen* Grenadier Division of the SS (Russian No 2); XV Cossack Cavalry Corps

▶ **13th *WAFFEN* MOUNTAIN DIVISION OF THE SS *HANDSCHAR* (CROATIAN NO 1) DEPLOYMENT:** **Although it did not receive its *Handschar* divisional title until May 1944, a Croatian *Waffen-SS* division was in formation from May 1943. Its principal battlegrounds were Bosnia and Serbia, where it fought a reasonably effective anti-Partisan war. Against the Soviets, however, the division was totally outclassed, and during 1945 desertions reached epidemic rates as soldiers saw the writing on the wall, and fled to protect their families back home.**

DEPLOYMENTS OF 13TH *WAFFEN* MOUNTAIN DIVISION OF THE SS *HANDSCHAR* (CROATIAN NO 1), 1943–45*

1. Mar 1943–July 1943	Yugoslavia
2. July 1943–Jan 1944	France
3. Jan 1944–Mar 1944	Germany
4. Mar 1944–Dec 1944	Yugoslavia
5. Jan 1945–Apr 1945	Hungary
6. Apr 1945–May 1945	Austria

* Shows 1939 borders

DEPLOYMENTS OF 14TH *WAFFEN* GRENADIER DIVISION OF THE SS *GALIZIEN* (UKRAINIAN NO 1), 1943–45*

1. June 1943–Mar 1944   Yugoslavia
2. Mar–Oct 1944   Eastern Front, central sector
3. Oct 1944–Feb 1945   Poland & Czechoslovakia
4. Feb–Mar 1945   Yugoslavia (Slovenia)
5. Mar–May 1945   Austria

* Shows 1939 borders

accommodated more than 300,000 Eastern Europeans and Soviet citizens into his *Waffen-SS*, dwarfing the contributions from Western Europe, they proved to be a largely unreliable addition, and one that dragged down the elite reputation of the *Waffen-SS*.

Barbarossa's yield

The German invasion of the Soviet Union opened up seemingly endless manpower resources for the Third Reich. Millions of civilians and POWs were suddenly under German servitude. While hundreds of thousands of the POWs would simply rot to death in horrifying open-air camps, and equal numbers of civilians were killed in 'anti-Partisan' reprisals or *Einsatzgruppen* operations, the Germans steadily realized that they must also put the Soviets to work. The massive logistical demands of the Eastern Front led the *Wehrmacht* to form *Hilfswillige* (Volunteer Assistant, or

◀ **14th *WAFFEN* GRENADIER DIVISION OF THE SS *GALIZIEN* (UKRAINIAN NO 1) DEPLOYMENT:** Formed from July 1943, the Ukrainian No. 1 Division (also known as the Galician Division) began its combat career with anti-Partisan operations in early 1944, but entered front-line combat in July. Its losses in the central sector of the Eastern Front were severe, and it was eventually withdrawn further west to perform rear-area security duties, and like so many other *Waffen-SS* units ended the war in Austria, where it rebranded itself as the 1st Division of the Ukrainian National Army.

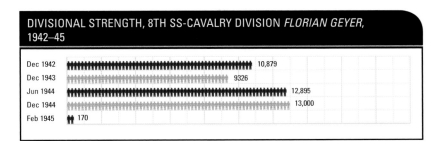

DIVISIONAL STRENGTH, 8TH SS-CAVALRY DIVISION *FLORIAN GEYER*, 1942–45	
Dec 1942	10,879
Dec 1943	9326
Jun 1944	12,895
Dec 1944	13,000
Feb 1945	170

EASTERN LEGIONS – DATES OF FORMATION	
Legion	*Date of Formation*
Armenische Legion	4 July 1942
Aserbeidschanische Legion	22 July 1942
Georgische Legion	24 February 1942
Kaukasisch-Mohammedanische Legion	24 March 1942
Nordkaukasische Legion	5 August 1942
Turkestanische-Kaukasisch-Mohammedanische Legion	13 January 1942
Turkestanische Legion	24 March 1942
Wolgatatarische Legion	January 1942

'Hiwi') auxiliary support units made up of Soviet deserters, civilians or volunteer POWs. In the Baltic states and Soviet territories, indigenous police units and additional volunteers were formed into police battalions, often used to commit horrors upon the Jews and citizens of their own countries. Eventually, entire battalions of indigenous Soviets were armed and used for anti-Partisan operations. Known as *Osttruppen* (East Troops), they tended to come from those ethnic minorities persecuted by Stalin, such as Cossacks or Kalmyks, and by the end of 1942 up to one million Soviet citizens were working directly for the German armed forces.

SS volunteers

It would be natural to think that the sharper racial ideologies of the SS would preclude Himmler's

acceptance of Slavs and other Soviet ethnicities into the *Waffen-SS*. Seeing the German Army expand itself so dramatically, however, doubtless acted as a spur to Himmler, so from 1943 the *Waffen-SS* began to create formal Soviet-origin units.

Note that by this time wider Eastern Europe was already yielding several divisions for the SS. Albania, Bulgaria, Croatia, Estonia, Hungary, Latvia, Lithuania, Romania and Serbia would all contribute manpower for the *Waffen-SS* at some stage in the war, all except Albania and Bulgaria supplying troops numbering in the tens of thousands. They included formations such as 21st *Waffen* Mountain Division of the SS *Skanderbeg* (Albanian No 1), 25th *Waffen* Grenadier Division of the SS *Hunyadi* (Hungarian No 1), 19th *Waffen* Grenadier Division of the SS (Latvian No 2) and 20th *Waffen*

SOVIET REPUBLICS LEGION SHIELDS

The Soviet territories yielded a good number of legions for either Wehrmacht *or* Waffen-SS *service. Most of the shields here indicate territories that had been roughly handled by Stalin, such as those of the Cossacks and the Tatars; these more easily shifted their loyalties to the Germans.*

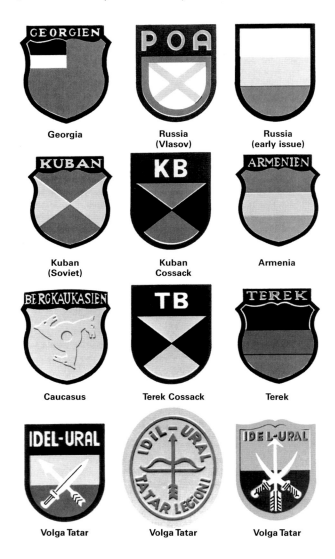

Georgia

Russia (Vlasov)

Russia (early issue)

Kuban (Soviet)

Kuban Cossack

Armenia

Caucasus

Terek Cossack

Terek

Volga Tatar

Volga Tatar

Volga Tatar

Grenadier Division of the SS (Estonian No 1).

The 14th *Waffen* Grenadier Division of the SS *Galizien* (Ukrainian No 1) was the first *Waffen-SS* division to be formed out of Soviet citizens, but it would not be the last. Of the 32 *Waffen-SS* divisions formed, either realistically or theoretically, between 1943 and 1945, one was Ukrainian and two were Russian, and the majority of the others were based around other foreign ethnic groups, particularly Latvians, Estonians, Lithuanians and Hungarians.

Serving the Reich?

The performance of the Eastern *Waffen-SS* units was, on the whole, less than sparkling. While often ruthless and committed when employed in anti-Partisan actions, their resilience against the full might of the Soviet war machine was sporadic. Indeed, the collapse in German fortunes on the Eastern Front in the autumn of 1943 led to a furious Hitler ordering that the Soviet volunteers be sent to France for manual labour, until it became apparant that Germany could not do without their manpower. The Eastern units would have to fight alongside the Germans until their defeat.

▶ FOREIGN VOLUNTEER NUMBERS
Foreign volunteers serving in the *Wehrmacht*, the *Kriegsmarine* and the *Waffen-SS* came from almost every country in occupied Europe, as well as from Allied nations and from neutrals like Sweden and Switzerland. By the end of the war over half of the *Waffen-SS* was non-German.

FOREIGN RECRUITS TO *WAFFEN-SS* BY COUNTRY

FINLAND
c.3000

NORWAY
c.6000

ESTONIA
c.25,000

LATVIA
c.80,000

SWEDEN
c.300

SOVIET UNION
c.60,000+

DENMARK
c.10,000

GREAT
BRITAIN
c.50

NETHERLANDS
c.50,000

GERMANY

BELGIUM
c.40,000

LUX.
c.2000

FRANCE
c.20,000

SWITZ.
c.300?

HUNGARY
c.20,000

ROMANIA
c.50,000

ITALY
c.15,000

YUGOSLAVIA
c.30,000

BULGARIA
c.600

SPAIN
c.1000

ALBANIA
c.7000

Loyalties and Motivation

The foreign volunteers for the Waffen-SS *joined the Germans through mixed motives. Some were inspired by a fervent anti-Communism, some by misguided adventurism, while others were essentially forced into the uniform.*

A fascinating study of the motivation behind foreigners joining the German armed forces comes from the Dutch psychologist A.F.G. van Hoesel, who in the post-war late 1940s conducted a 432-person study of 'political offenders', people who had actively collaborated with the Germans in providing military service, including in the *Waffen-SS*. (For details of this study, see Kenneth Estes' excellent *A European Anabasis – Western European Volunteers in the German Army and SS, 1940–1945*.)

Van Hoesel sub-divided the sample into 'politically reliable' and 'politically unreliable' categories, the latter being those who had shown clear political loyalties to the National Socialist ideal. He then mapped out the various motivations for joining the German armed forces. The results have their ambiguities, but they do show that the majority of the sample belonged to the 'politically unreliable' category. Yet from the total sample, political

motivation only constituted 40 per cent of those who volunteered.

A simple desire for adventure propelled 65 men into German service, but this was exceeded by combined negative factors such as food shortages, poor home life and family pressure. The picture is not one of uniform convincing commitment to Hitler's 'idea of the German Reich'. Van Hoesel also divided his data by arm of service

(see the pie charts above and below), which further revealed *Waffen-SS* samples essentially split between 'reliable' and 'unreliable' elements. Thus it is not surprising that so many Dutchmen attempted to quit the *Waffen-SS* by 1943.

Eastern Volunteers
Similar data for the Eastern volunteers is not readily available, but ethnic antipathy towards the

23RD SS-FREIWILLIGEN PANZERGRENADIER DIVISION *NEDERLAND*

Commanders

SS-Brigadeführer Jürgen Wagner	(Feb–May 1945)

Divisional Strength

January 1945	6000

Order of Battle

SS-Freiwilligen–Panzergrenadier-Regiment 48	SS-Panzerjäger-Abteilung 23
SS-Freiwilligen–Panzergrenadier-Regiment 49	SS-Pionier-Bataillon 23
SS-Artillerie-Regiment 23	SS-Flak-Abteilung 23
SS-Nachrichten-Abteilung 23	

MUTINIES WITHIN FOREIGN *WAFFEN-SS* DIVISIONS

Date	Unit involved	Details
16–17 September 1943	13th *Waffen* Mountain Division of the SS *Handschar* (Croatian No 1)	Elements of SS-Geb.Pi.Btl.13 revolted and killed five SS officers; revolt quickly suppressed
27 August 1944	30th *Waffen* Grenadier Division of the SS (Russian No 2)	Russians, Ukrainians and Poles killed over 200 Germans; switched sides to French forces
17 October 1944	23rd *Waffen* Mountain Division of the SS *Kama* (Croatian No 2)	Minor revolt cost one SS officer his life before it was quickly suppressed
December 1944	36th *Waffen* Grenadier Division *Dirlewanger*	Mass desertion from the ranks

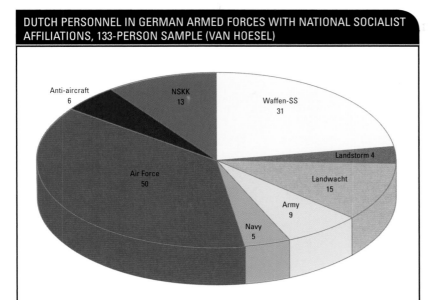

DUTCH PERSONNEL IN GERMAN ARMED FORCES WITH NATIONAL SOCIALIST AFFILIATIONS, 133-PERSON SAMPLE (VAN HOESEL)

Anti-aircraft 6
NSKK 13
Waffen-SS 31
Landstorm 4
Air Force 50
Landwacht 15
Army 9
Navy 5

As the war turned against Germany, the consequences of its integrationist policy became clearer. There were several mutinies, and desertions became rife – in two months in late 1944, for example, more than 3000 men of the Albanian *Skanderbeg* Division deserted. It was clear that the *Waffen-SS* could recruit men, but not loyalty.

◀ ▼ RELIABILITY OF FOREIGN SS RECRUITS

These two charts suggest that the Dutch Waffen-SS recruits were essentially split between those motivated by political ideals, and those driven by other sentiments. Note also how the *Waffen-SS* was only one draw on foreign recruits, the Army, Navy and Air Force also pulling many volunteers into German military service, especially in the later years of the war.

Communists, plus a virulent anti-Semitism in many communities, doubtless oiled the wheels of recruitment. Yet there were also many instances of coercion or trickery in *Waffen-SS* recruitment, such as telling the recruit he was destined for a supply unit, only to find himself thrust into the armed SS.

Mistrust and unease

Even as the *Waffen-SS* fleshed out its ranks with foreigners, there generally remained a deep-seated unease between the ethnic soldiers and the German authorities. Infamous SS officer Theodor Eicke once remarked: 'A large number of the racial Germans can only be described as intellectually substandard. They don't understand the words of command and are inclined towards insubordination and malingering.' In return, the

foreign *Waffen-SS* soldiers often looked upon their commanders as temporary masters.

DUTCH PERSONNEL IN GERMAN ARMED FORCES WITHOUT NATIONAL SOCIALIST AFFILIATIONS, 134-PERSON SAMPLE (VAN HOESEL)

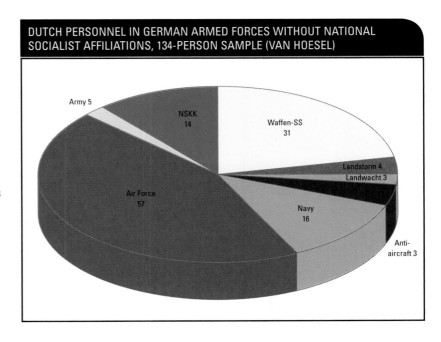

Army 5
NSKK 14
Waffen-SS 31
Landstorm 4
Landwacht 3
Air Force 57
Navy 16
Anti-aircraft 3

Broadening Diversity

The Waffen-SS *foreign legions were a mixed bag in terms of loyalty, combat performance, composition and history. Although they added significant numbers to Himmler's force, the value of their contribution was questionable.*

The policy of forming non-German legions was, as we have seen, actually in development from 1940, but it was not officially approved by Hitler until 29 June 1941. Hitler was brought round to the idea of foreign legions by the general concept of an international 'crusade against Bolshevism'. Indeed, an important point is that the foreign legions and divisions established within the *Waffen-SS* and *Wehrmacht* were not intended to be permanent fixtures of

the German armed forces. Instead, they were purposed for the defeat of Bolshevism alone, and once that was achieved then Germany would have had no more role for them. Just how international that crusade became is quite surprising.

European recruits
As we have seen, the Germans recruited widely from Western European stock to create new *Waffen-SS* formations. Although

Himmler had his own particular vision of a 'Nordic' army, ultimately his recruitment policy spread out from northern Europe and incorporated some rather unexpected nations.

Two marginal oddities of *Waffen-SS* recruitment were Britain and Greece. The former had a minor fascist presence in the form of Oswald Mosley's British Union of Fascists (BUF). A few British nationals, typically with German connections, had joined the

SS LEGIONS

Name of Legion	Date formed	Commanders	
Estnische SS-Legion	August 1942	SS-Obersturmbannführer Franz Augsberger	(Oct 1942–May 1943)
SS-Freiwilligen-Legion Flandern	September 1941	SS-Sturmbannführer Michael Lippert	(Sep 1941–Apr 1942)
		SS-Obersturmbannführer Hans Albert von Lettow-Vorbeck	(Apr–June 1942)
		SS-Hauptsturmführer Hallmann	(June 1942)
		SS-Obersturmbannführer Josef Fitzthum	(June–July 1942)
		SS-Sturmbannführer Conrad Schellong	(July 1942–May 1943)
SS-Freiwilligen-Legion Niederlande	September 1941	SS-Sturmbannführer Herbert Garthe	(Nov 1941–Feb 1942)
		SS-Oberführer Otto Reich	(Feb–Apr 1942)
		SS-Obersturmbannführer Arved Theuermann	(Apr 1942–?)
		SS-Standartenführer Josef Fitzthum (unknown)	
Freiwilligen-Legion Norwegen	June 1941	Finn Hanibal Kjelstrup	(June–Dec 1941)
		Jorgen Bakke	(Dec 1941)
		Arthur Quist	(Dec 1941–Mar 1943)
SS-Freiwilligen-Verband Flandern	July 1941	SS-Oberführer Otto Reich	(July 1941)
		SS-Sturmbannführer Michael Lippert	(July–Sep 1941)
SS-Freiwilligen-Verband Niederlande	July 1941	?	
Indische Freiwilligen-Legion der Waffen-SS	August 1944	SS-Oberführer Heinz Bertling	(Aug 1944–May 1945)
Italienische SS-Freiwilligen-Legion	March 1944	SS-Obergruppenführer Karl Wolff	(Mar–June 1944)
Lettische SS-Freiwilligen-Legion	February 1943	SS-Brigadeführer Peter Hansen	(Feb–May 1943)
		SS-Gruppenführer Carl Graf von Pückler-Burghauss	(May 1943–Feb 1944)
		SS-Brigadeführer Nikolas Heilmann	(Feb–July 1944)
		SS-Brigadeführer Herbert von Obwurzer	(July 1944–Jan 1945)
		SS-Oberführer Arthur Ax	(Jan 1945–Feb 1945)
		SS-Oberführer Karl Burk	(Feb 1945)

Waffen-SS before the war, but the attempts to recruit on a larger scale from British POWs met with little success. Recruiting was naturally made more difficult by the fact that Britain was still an obstinate combatant, hence the *Waffen-SS* recruiters assured their potential troopers that they would only be used to fight on the Eastern Front.

Even with this angle, the British soldiers were reluctant to join en masse. The Germans nevertheless remained optimistic, and in April 1943 they formed the Legion of St George, a so-far empty *Waffen-SS* legion with a tub-thumping name intended to rouse the British soldiers. It was meant to receive up to 1500 recruits, but in the end, and as far as we know, only some 40–50 British soldiers signed up for Nazi service. The Legion of St George evolved into the British Free Corps (BFC) in January 1944, practically led by a half-German pre-war British recruit, Thomas Haller Cooper.

The British volunteers were a motley bunch, some motivated by a base desire to avoid POW life after capture, while others were inspired by a passionate anti-Communism, or even anger at the Allied strategic bombing against civilian areas. For the Germans, the British force was too small to be practically useful, but it was wheeled out for the cameras as a photogenic unit for propaganda purposes. As to the men within the British force, most would come to regret their decision to join the *Waffen-SS*, either being killed in action, executed following capture, or destined to spend long periods in Allied POW camps.

OPERATIONAL STRENGTH OF NORWEGIANS IN SS VOLUNTEER UNITS

15 Aug 1941	1218
6 Feb 1943	612
30 June 1943	1314

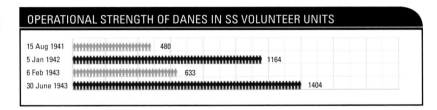

OPERATIONAL STRENGTH OF DANES IN SS VOLUNTEER UNITS

15 Aug 1941	480
5 Jan 1942	1164
6 Feb 1943	633
30 June 1943	1404

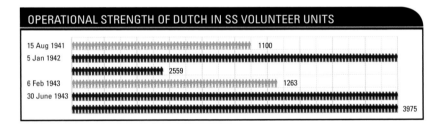

OPERATIONAL STRENGTH OF DUTCH IN SS VOLUNTEER UNITS

15 Aug 1941	1100
5 Jan 1942	2559
6 Feb 1943	1263
30 June 1943	3975

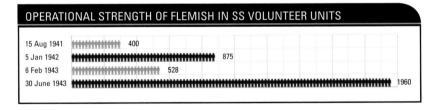

OPERATIONAL STRENGTH OF FLEMISH IN SS VOLUNTEER UNITS

15 Aug 1941	400
5 Jan 1942	875
6 Feb 1943	528
30 June 1943	1960

Greece was another nation that produced a minor contribution to the *Waffen-SS* – possibly some 1000 men may have served in Himmler's army following the German occupation of Greece in 1941. Greece was particularly hard hit by food shortages in the occupation period, pushing the population down to starvation levels on many occasions, so for some joining the German forces may well have been a quick route out of such hardship. Many of the men who went down this route ended the war deployed in Denmark, where they might escape the wrath of the Greek population back home.

The Indian Legion

The *Legion Freies Indien* (Free India Legion) was a curiosity in both the history of the *Wehrmacht* and of the *Waffen-SS*. It began forming in the spring of 1941, when Indian POWs, previously serving as Commonwealth troops in North Africa, were recruited

WAFFEN-SS RECRUITMENT FIGURES, LEGION PROGRAMME, SUMMER 1942

	1			2			3			4			5 = 3 + 4			
SS-Ersatz-kommando	Gesamtzahl der bis jetzt einberufenen Freiwilligen			Gesamtzahl der nach Ablauf einer Dienstzeit oder Verpflichtung Zurückgekehrten			Gesamtzahl der augenblicklich bei der Truppe Befindlichen (einschl. E-Einheit u. Lazarett)			Gesamtzahl der Toten (Gefallenen, Verstorbenen, Vermißten)			Insgesamt bei der Truppe einschl. Toten und Verwundeten. ?			
	SS	Leg.	zus.	SS	Leg.	zus.	SS	Leg.	zus.	SS	Leg.	zus.	SS	Leg.	zus.	
Flandern	1853	2636	4489	265	410	675	1525	1960	3485	63	266	329	1588	2226	3814	
Niederlande	7679	5873	13552	1666	1329	2995	5546	3975	9521	467	569	1036	6013	4544	10557	
Dänemark	2917	1896	4813	498	311	809	2142	1404	3546	277	181	458	2419	1585	4004	
Norwegen	2164	2296	4460	580	824	1404	1465	1314	2779	119	158	277	1584	1472	3056	
Insgesamt	14613	12701	27314	3009	2874	5883	10678	8653	19331	926	1174	2100	11604	9827	21431	

Stichtag: 30.6.1943

Th/Dr. 28.7.1943

This document from July 1942 details the total numbers recruited in the SS and the legions from Flanders, the Netherlands, Denmark and Norway.

The columns indicate:
1) Total enlisted figures to date;
2) Total whose service has expired;
3) Total currently in service;
4) Total of dead and missing; and
5) Totals for service, including dead and wounded.

ETHNICITIES PRESENT IN FOREIGN OR PART-FOREIGN *WAFFEN-SS* DIVISIONS

Division	Ethnicities
5th SS-Panzer Division *Wiking*	Dutch, Danes, Norwegians, Finns, Walloons, Flemish
6th SS-Mountain Division *Nord*	Finns
7th SS-Volunteer Mountain Division *Prinz Eugen*	Romanians, Hungarians, Yugoslavs
8th SS-Cavalry Division *Florian Geyer*	Romanians, other Eastern European
11th SS-Volunteer Panzergrenadier Division *Nordland*	Danes, Estonians, Finns, Latvians, Dutch, Norwegians, Swedes, Swiss, British
13th *Waffen* Mountain Division of the SS *Handschar* (Croatian No 1)	Croatians (Catholics, Serbs, Muslims)
14th *Waffen* Grenadier Division of the SS *Galizien* (Ukrainian No.1)	Ukrainians
15th *Waffen* Grenadier Division of the SS (Latvian No 1)	Latvians
18th SS-Volunteer Panzergrenadier Division *Horst Wessel*	Hungarians, Yugoslavs
19th *Waffen* Grenadier Division of the SS (Latvian No 2)	Latvians
20th *Waffen* Grenadier Division of the SS (Estonian No 1)	Estonians
21st *Waffen* Mountain Division of the SS *Skanderbeg* (Albanian No 1)	Albanians
22nd SS-Volunteer Cavalry Division of the SS *Maria Theresia*	Hungarians
23rd *Waffen* Mountain Division of the SS *Kama* (Croatian No 2)	Croatians, Bosnian Muslims
23rd SS-Volunteer Panzergrenadier Division *Nederland* (Netherlands No 1)	Dutch
24th *Waffen* Mountain Division of the SS *Karstjäger*	Italians, Slovenians, Croatians, Serbians, Ukrainians
25th *Waffen* Grenadier Division of the SS *Hunyadi* (Hungarian No 1)	Hungarians
26th *Waffen* Grenadier Division of the SS *Hungaria* (Hungarian No 2)	Hungarians
27th SS-Volunteer Grenadier Division *Langemarck* (Flemish No 1)	Flemish
28th SS-Volunteer Grenadier Division *Wallonien* (Walloon No 1)	Walloon Belgians
29th *Waffen* Grenadier Division of the SS *Italien* (Italian No 1)	Italians
29th *Waffen* Grenadier Division of the SS (Russian No 1)	Russians
30th *Waffen* Grenadier Division of the SS (Russian No 2)	Russians
30th *Waffen* Grenadier Division of the SS *Weißruthenische*	Russians
31st SS-Volunteer Grenadier Division *Böhmen-Mähren*	Czechs, Slovakians
33rd *Waffen* Cavalry Division (Hungarian No 3)	Hungarians
33rd *Waffen* Grenadier Division of the SS *Charlemagne* (French No 1)	French
34th SS-Volunteer Grenadier Division *Landstorm Nederland* (Netherlands No 2)	Dutch
36th *Waffen* Grenadier Division *Dirlewanger*	Soviets
37th SS-Volunteer Cavalry Division *Lützow*	Romanians, other Eastern European

by the Germans as resistance fighters to destabilize British India. After a protracted development and training period, the Free India Legion finally took the oath in August 1942.

The Free India Legion was around 2500 men strong, and was controlled initially by the *Wehrmacht*. It was organized along the lines of a standard German Army three-battalion regiment. In terms of its deployment, the Free India Legion was intended for operations in the Middle East and Asia, but few of these actually materialized, and instead it found itself shunted out of the way to reserve and coastal position duties in Western Europe, where it gained a reputation for poor discipline. In August 1944, along with many other volunteer legions, the Free India Legion was transferred to *Waffen-SS* control, becoming the *Indische Freiwilligen-Legion der* *Waffen-SS* (Indian Volunteer Legion of the *Waffen-SS*).

Following the Allied landings in Normandy on 6 June 1944, the Indian Legion saw some limited combat during the retreat back through France, often via contacts with the local French Resistance forces, although it did fight some engagements against British armoured formations. Later in the year the legion also saw service fighting in Italy, and it was there that it finally surrendered to the Allies in April 1945.

Muslim combatants

The Indian Legion is a distinct example of how the *Wehrmacht* and the *Waffen-SS* could cast a very wide net in the attempt to draw in manpower. The same was true of the inclusion of Muslim combatants into the German armed forces. The occupation of the Balkans and Eastern Europe, and the capture of thousands of Soviet troops from the Central Asian republics, brought the Germans into contact with vast swathes of Muslim soldiery, and it soon proved that they were not averse to using them as second-line infantry. Moreover, Himmler largely had a positive attitude towards Islam, seeing in it a robust and potentially militaristic faith that contrasted with what he saw as the weakness and passivity of Christianity. Indeed, in conversation with Joseph Goebbels, he was heard to state:

I have nothing against Islam, because it educates the men in this Division for me and promises them heaven if they fight and are killed in action. That's a highly practical and attractive religion for soldiers.
(Quoted in Trigg, 2008)

The largest Muslim *Waffen-SS* division was the 13th *Waffen* Mountain Division of the SS *Handschar* (Croatian No 1), which was composed of Bosnian Muslims. Formed from March 1943, the *Handschar* Division was deployed on home ground against Partisans and Chetniks (Serbian nationalist fighters), where the motivation of protecting hearth and home made its men committed fighters. In June 1944, it was joined by a sister division, the 23rd *Waffen* Mountain Division of the SS *Kama* (Croatian No 2). The 21st *Waffen* Mountain Division of the SS *Skanderbeg* (Albanian No 1) was primarily manned by Albanian Muslims. Other non-divisional Muslim forces included the *Osttürkischer Waffen-Verband der SS* (East Turkish *Waffen* Unit of the SS), which represented Muslim volunteers from Turkestan, Azerbaijan, Crimea and Idel-Ural (Volga Tatars), and the *1.Ostmuselmanische SS-Regiment* (1st East Mussulman SS Regiment). Apart from some rare moments of distinction, most of the Muslim units failed to perform competently in action. Indeed some, such as the 1st East Mussulman Regiment, went on to participate in notable war crimes, such as the hideous episode in bloodletting during the crushing of the Warsaw Uprising in August 1944 (see below).

The Cossacks were another Soviet ethnic group thoroughly alienated by Stalin, and so provided enough material to form a *Wehrmacht* division in the spring of 1943. While deployed to Yugoslavia for anti-Partisan duties, the division expanded into the XIV Cossack Corps. As with many of the *Wehrmacht* foreign formations, the Cossacks were eventually transferred to *Waffen-SS* command. Hence XIV Cossack Corps became XV SS-Cossack Cavalry Corps in early 1945, although the transfer was administrative in nature – the Cossacks retained *Wehrmacht* uniforms and insignia. The Cossacks, like the British, Greeks, French, Ukrainians and numerous others, proved the paucity of SS racial guidelines.

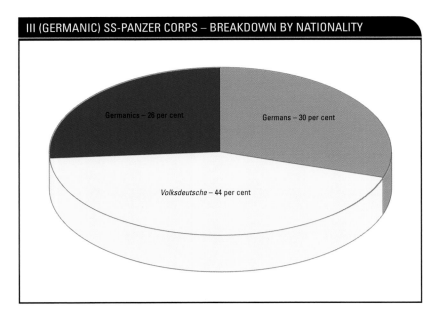

III (GERMANIC) SS-PANZER CORPS – BREAKDOWN BY NATIONALITY

Germanics – 26 per cent

Germans – 30 per cent

Volksdeutche – 44 per cent

Operational Record – the Best Divisions

A closer look at select foreign Waffen-SS *units and formations reveals similar patterns in their operational records. Although individual units were genuinely feared and competent, these tended to be islands in a sea of mediocrity, disloyalty and indiscipline.*

Regardless of their combat value, the German foreign legions were milked for every ounce of worth in terms of propaganda value. The following excerpt from *Signal* magazine, focusing on the foreign contribution from the Soviet Union, eulogizes the new material:

> *Russians, Ukrainians, Georgians... members of all races and tribes in the east have streamed in continually increasing numbers to the German armies for enrolment in a Volunteer Army which is fighting shoulder to shoulder with the Germans against the Soviets. This army has at its disposal infantry, cavalry, artillery and engineers, that is to say troops and weapons of all kinds. They have shown suprisingly quickly that the true soldierly spirit can soon be kindled in them when a great idea is at stake.*
>
> (Meyer, 1976)

The reality was largely different in many formations. 'Soldierly spirit' was often in short supply once the bullets began flying, particularly as relations between the foreigners and their German overlords could be mutually critical. Many foreign formations blamed instances of poor combat performance on a lack of material and tactical support from the German *Waffen-SS*, while in return

the German commanders accused the foreigners of unintelligent leadership, lack of fighting spirit and

ambiguous loyalties. As we shall see, problems with the late-war Eastern foreign units were particularly

NUMBER OF KNIGHT'S CROSSES AWARDED TO FOREIGN OR PART-FOREIGN *WAFFEN-SS* DIVISIONS	
Division	Number of Knight's Crosses
5th SS-Panzer Division *Wiking*	55
6th SS-Mountain Division *Nord*	4
7th SS-Volunteer Mountain Division *Prinz Eugen*	6
8th SS-Cavalry Division *Florian Geyer*	22
11th SS-Volunteer Panzergrenadier Division *Nordland*	25
13th *Waffen* Mountain Division of the SS *Handschar* (Croatian No 1)	4
14th *Waffen* Grenadier Division of the SS *Galizien* (Ukrainian No.1)	1
15th *Waffen* Grenadier Division of the SS (Latvian No 1)	3
18th SS-Volunteer Panzergrenadier Division *Horst Wessel*	2
19th *Waffen* Grenadier Division of the SS (Latvian No 2)	12
20th *Waffen* Grenadier Division of the SS (Estonian No 1)	5
21st *Waffen* Mountain Division of the SS *Skanderbeg* (Albanian No 1)	0
22nd SS-Volunteer Cavalry Division of the SS *Maria Theresia*	6
23rd *Waffen* Mountain Division of the SS *Kama* (Croatian No 2)	0
23rd SS-Volunteer Panzergrenadier Division *Nederland* (Netherlands No 1)	19
24th *Waffen* Mountain Division of the SS *Karstjäger*	0
25th *Waffen* Grenadier Division of the SS *Hunyadi* (Hungarian No 1)	0
26th *Waffen* Grenadier Division of the SS *Hungaria* (Hungarian No 2)	0
27th SS-Volunteer Grenadier Division *Langemarck* (Flemish No 1)	1
28th SS-Volunteer Grenadier Division *Wallonien* (Walloon No 1)	3
29th *Waffen* Grenadier Division of the SS *Italien* (Italian No 1)	0
29th *Waffen* Grenadier Division of the SS (Russian No 1)	0
30th *Waffen* Grenadier Division of the SS (Russian No 2)	0
30th *Waffen* Grenadier Division of the SS *Weißruthenische*	0
31st SS-Volunteer Grenadier Division *Böhmen-Mähren*	0
33rd *Waffen* Cavalry Division (Hungarian No 3)	0
33rd *Waffen* Grenadier Division of the SS *Charlemagne* (French No 1)	2
34th SS-Volunteer Grenadier Division *Landstorm Nederland* (Netherlands No 2)	3
36th *Waffen* Grenadier Division *Dirlewanger*	1
37th SS-Volunteer Cavalry Division *Lützow*	not known

severe, but there were part or wholly foreign formations that nonetheless managed to distinguish themselves.

Wiking Division

If we are to look for a success story in the foreign formations of the *Waffen-SS*, the 5th SS-Panzer Division *Wiking* is a good starting point. Created from three regiments – *Germania*, *Westland* and *Nordland* – the *Wiking* Division brought together foreigners from the newly conquered territories of Western Europe. However, we need to be cautious about treating this division as a foreign force, despite what the German newsreels showed. Here historian Chris Bishop outlines the reality of its ethnic membership:

The first truly international division of the Waffen-SS, Wiking *numbered Dutch, Danes, Norwegians, Finns, Walloons and Flemings among its personnel, together with a smattering of* Volksdeutsche *from the Balkans. However, in spite of the propaganda, which made much of its international nature, the bulk of the division's personnel (as much as 90 per cent) was German.*

(Bishop, 2005)

Such a bias towards native German personnel, and the use of diverse foreign elements, is ironic given the division's name – the *Wiking* (Viking) appellation was meant to describe a

---

DIVISIONAL STRENGTH OF FOREIGN OR PART-FOREIGN *WAFFEN-SS* DIVISIONS, 1945

Division	Strength
5th SS-Panzer Division *Wiking*	14,800
6th SS-Mountain Division *Nord*	15,000
7th SS-Volunteer Mountain Division *Prinz Eugen*	20,000
8th SS-Cavalry Division *Florian Geyer*	13,000
11th SS-Volunteer Panzergrenadier Division *Nordland*	9000
13th *Waffen* Mountain Division of the SS *Handschar* (Croatian No 1)	12,700
14th *Waffen* Grenadier Division of the SS *Galizien* (Ukrainian No 1)	22,000
15th Waffen Grenadier Division of the SS (Latvian No 1)	16,800
18th SS-Volunteer Panzergrenadier Division *Horst Wessel*	11,000
19th *Waffen* Grenadier Division of the SS (Latvian No 2)	9000
20th *Waffen* Grenadier Division of the SS (Estonian No 1)	15,500
21st Waffen-Mountain Division of the SS *Skanderberg* (Albanian No.1)	5000
22nd SS-Volunteer Cavalry Division *Maria Theresia*	8000
23rd *Waffen* Mountain Division of the SS *Kama* (Croatian No 2)	c.5000
23rd SS-Volunteer Panzergrenadier Division *Nederland* (Netherlands No 1)	6000
24th *Waffen* Mountain Division of the SS *Karstjäger*	3000
25th *Waffen* Grenadier Division of the SS *Hunyadi* (Hungarian No 1)	15,000
26th *Waffen* Grenadier Division of the SS *Hungaria* (Hungarian No 2)	13,000
27th SS-Volunteer Grenadier Division *Langemarck* (Flemish No 1)	7000
28th SS-Volunteer Grenadier Division *Wallonien* (Walloon No 1)	4000
29th *Waffen* Grenadier Division of the SS *Italien* (Italian No 1)	15,000
29th *Waffen* Grenadier Division of the SS (Russian No 1)	not known
30th *Waffen* Grenadier Division of the SS (Russian No 2)	4500
30th *Waffen* Grenadier Division of the SS *Weißruthenische*	not known
31st SS-Volunteer Grenadier Division *Böhmen-Mähren*	11,000
33rd *Waffen* Cavalry Division (Hungarian No 3)	not known
33rd *Waffen* Grenadier Division of the SS *Charlemagne* (French No 1)	7000
34th SS-Volunteer Grenadier Division *Landstorm Nederland* (N/lands No 2)	7000
36th *Waffen* Grenadier Division *Dirlewanger*	8000
37th SS-Volunteer Cavalry Division *Lützow*	not known

primarily Nordic formation. Yet the fact remained that a significant portion of the *Wiking* Division was foreign, and if that portion underperformed in combat it would soon reveal itself.

Wiking's first major combat deployment was the launch of Operation *Barbarossa* in June 1941. From the outset, the division proved its worth, being a lead unit in crossing the Dnieper River, after which it battled its way on as far as Rostov. *Wiking* soon gained a reputation for being dogged in both defence and attack, and hence it was used as a spearhead division for the Germans' summer 1942 offensive down into the Caucasus. It had also gone through several structural incarnations – first as a motorized division, then as a Panzergrenadier division, and finally, in October 1943, being upgraded to full Panzer division status.

From 1943 until the end of the war, the *Wiking* division fought an epic defensive retreat, and suffered huge losses in the process. Refitting in Poland in the summer of 1944 meant that it was spared facing Operation *Bagration*, the massive Soviet offensive that effectively wiped out the German Army Group Centre, but the division was then committed to helping shore up the German defence along the Vistula River. Its last great offensive action was an attempt to relieve German forces trapped under Soviet siege in Budapest in early 1945, but after this action failed it was transferred to Austria.

The survivors of *Wiking* finally surrendered in April 1945, having made an epic combat journey from the depths of southern Russia. The division had proved that foreign personnel, at least when buttressed by committed German troops, could fight as hard as any other formation.

8th SS-Cavalry Division
Another effective part-foreign *Waffen-SS* division was the 8th SS-Cavalry Division *Florian Geyer*. The origins of the division were purely German, with various SS cavalry units eventually forming into the SS-Cavalry Brigade under keen horseman and cavalry officer Hermann Fegelein. Yet the cavalry brigade was only able to make the leap to divisional status and strength with the addition of 9000 Hungarian *Volksdeutsche* volunteers in June 1942, and was designated the SS-Cavalry Division.

As a division, the formation was at first used as part of Army Group Centre's conventional forces, fighting in the Vyazma-Bryansk-Rzhev area. It then fought in regular operations for the next nine months, before being withdrawn to Bobruisk to recoup its losses and refit. Thereafter, the cavalry division was mainly charged with anti-Partisan operations in the German rear areas, a task that it performed adroitly owing to the exceptional manoeuvrability of its mounts in the forested areas favoured by the Partisans. Such was its talent in this form of warfare that in July 1943 it was redeployed away from the Eastern Front to Croatia, where it was used to combat Tito's Partisans.

The year 1944 brought a name change – in March it was titled the 8th SS-Cavalry Division *Florian Geyer*.

COMBAT PERFORMANCE CLASSIFICATIONS*
Good
SS *Wiking*
SS *Nordland*
Freikorps Danmark
SS *Wallonien* (1944)
SS *Langemarck* (1944)
SS *Legion Flandern*
Fair
SS *Nederland*
Spanish Volunteer Division
SS *Frankreich* (1944)
SS *Legion Niederlande*
French Legion (1944)
Walloon Legion
SS *Legion Norwegen*
SS *Landstorm Nederland*
Failure
French Legion (1941)
Spanish Legion
SS *Charlemagne*
Based on assessment by Kenneth W. Estes, A European Anabasis – Western European Volunteers in the German Army and SS, 1940–1945 – http://www.gutenberg-e.org/esk01/index.html

Under this name the largely Hungarian troops fought bitterly to defend their homeland, and it was during an attempted breakout from the siege of Budapest on 11 February 1945 that the division was destroyed. (Only 170 soldiers managed to reach the German lines.) Such unyielding commitment to battle proved that some foreign recruits could be amongst Hitler's most reliable soldiers. These examples are far from universal, however, and with the rapid expansion of the later war years the *Waffen-SS* took into its ranks far less reputable personnel.

FOREIGN WAFFEN SS DIVISION HONOUR TITLES

Divisional Number	Type/Title of Division	Meaning of Honour Title
5	SS-Panzer Division *Wiking*	'Viking' – reference to the medieval Norse warriors
6	SS-Mountain Division *Nord*	Simply means 'North'
7	SS-Volunteer Mountain Division *Prinz Eugen*	Named after Prince Eugene of Savoy (1663–1736), Austrian field marshal
8	SS-Cavalry Division *Florian Geyer*	Named after Florian Geyer (c.1490–1525), a Franconian knight
11	SS-Volunteer Panzergrenadier Division *Nordland*	Means 'Northern Land'
13	*Waffen* Mountain Division of the SS *Handschar* (Croatian No 1)	German for *Handlär*, Croat term meaning 'scimitar'
14	*Waffen* Grenadier Division of the SS *Galizien* (Ukrainian No 1)	German for 'Galicia'
18	SS-Volunteer Panzergrenadier Division *Horst Wessel*	Named after Horst Wessel (1907–30), martyred Berlin SA leader
21	*Waffen* Mountain Division of the SS *Skanderbeg* (Albanian No 1)	Named after Skanderbeg or Iskender-Beg (c.1405–68), more accurately Gjergi Kastriota, Albanian freedom fighter against the Turks
22	SS-Volunteer Cavalry Division *Maria Theresia*	Named after Empress Maria Theresia (1717–80), a Roman-German empress
23	*Waffen* Mountain Division of the SS *Kama* (Croatian No 2)	Named after Turkish sword
23	SS-Volunteer Panzergrenadier Division *Nederland* (Netherlands No 1)	Meaning 'Netherlands'
24	*Waffen* Mountain Division of the SS *Karstjäger*	Refers to Karst region of northwest Yugoslavia
25	*Waffen* Grenadier Division of the SS *Hunyadi* (Hungarian No 1)	Refers to Johann (or János) Hunyadi (c.1385–1456), a Hungarian military leader who fought against the Turks
26	*Waffen* Grenadier Division of the SS *Hungaria* (Hungarian No 2)	Meaning 'Hungary'
27	SS-Volunteer Grenadier Division *Langemarck* (Flemish No 1)	Named after Langemarck, a Belgian town in western Flanders, significant during World War I
28	SS-Volunteer Grenadier Division *Wallonien* (Walloon No 1)	Meaning 'Walloon'
29	*Waffen* Grenadier Division of the SS *Italien* (Italian No 1)	Meaning 'Italy'
31	SS-Volunteer Grenadier Division *Böhmen-Mähren*	Meaning 'Bohemia-Moravia'
32	SS-Volunteer Grenadier Division *30. Januar*	Named after date Hitler was made Reichschancellor
33	*Waffen* Grenadier Division of the SS *Charlemagne* (French No 1)	Named after Charlemagne, or Charles the Great (742–814), king of the Franks and Roman-German emperor
34	SS-Volunteer Grenadier Division *Landstorm Nederland* (Nertherlands No 2)	Meaning 'Land Storm Netherlands'
36	*Waffen* Grenadier Division *Dirlewanger*	Named after its commander, Dr Oskar Dirlewanger
37	SS-Volunteer Cavalry Division *Lützow*	Named after Adolf Freiherr von Lützow (1782–1834), a Prussian *Generalmajor*
38	SS-Panzergrenadier Division *Nibelungen*	Named after figures from Norse mythology

Operational Record – Late War Units

The energetic drive to expand the Waffen-SS *in 1943–45 resulted in major acquisitions of Eastern manpower combined with a sharp drop in recruitment standards. The result was a collection of divisions and brigades of questionable value to the* Waffen-SS.

The relaxation of *Waffen-SS* recruitment policies largely came from the military crisis faced by the German armed forces by early 1943. The defeat of German forces at Stalingrad and the subsequent Soviet offensives, the sheer length of the Eastern Front, the military commitments in Italy and the gathering storm of the Allied strategic air campaign back home all stretched the Reich's manpower to the limits. For Himmler, a solution came readily in the form of the opening of the *Waffen-SS* ranks to Slavs, something considered unthinkable only two years previously.

The first major manifestation of this policy came in the form of the SS-Volunteer Division *Galizien* (Galicia), authorized in April 1943 and built up from Ukrainian personnel. ('Galicia' was the term the Germans used for the western Ukraine.) The early combat history of the *Galizien* Division was illustrative of problems that would face the multitude of Eastern European and Soviet divisions and brigades created between 1943 and 1945. It was poorly trained and badly led, and was armed with a mix of what weapons the men had brought with them and what could be scrounged from the German forces. Committed to fighting at Brody in June 1944, the outcome was predictable – the division was

encircled and destroyed, with 12,000 of its 15,000 troops being either killed or captured by the Soviet forces.

The remnants of the division were used as the core of the new *14.Galizische SS-Freiwilligen-Division*, and in August 1944 it was deployed to Slovakia for anti-Partisan warfare. More name changes came

later, first to the 14th *Waffen* Grenadier Division of the SS *Galizien* (Ukrainian No 1) then, in April 1945, to the 1st Ukrainian Division of the Ukrainian National Army.

War crimes
Many of the late-war *Waffen-SS* foreign formations were deployed

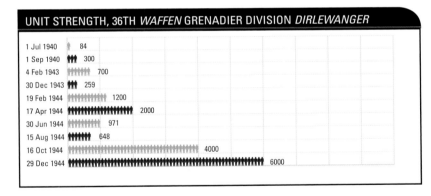

UNIT STRENGTH, 36TH *WAFFEN* GRENADIER DIVISION *DIRLEWANGER*

1 Jul 1940	84
1 Sep 1940	300
4 Feb 1943	700
30 Dec 1943	259
19 Feb 1944	1200
17 Apr 1944	2000
30 Jun 1944	971
15 Aug 1944	648
16 Oct 1944	4000
29 Dec 1944	6000

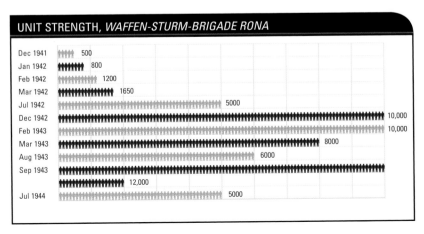

UNIT STRENGTH, *WAFFEN-STURM-BRIGADE RONA*

Dec 1941	500
Jan 1942	800
Feb 1942	1200
Mar 1942	1650
Jul 1942	5000
Dec 1942	10,000
Feb 1943	10,000
Mar 1943	8000
Aug 1943	6000
Sep 1943	12,000
Jul 1944	5000

as anti-Partisan troops. This usage had two benefits. First, it reduced the number of main German divisions that had to be diverted to rear-area security duties. Second, the character of many of the foreign soldiers seemed ideally suited to the reprisal mentality utilized in fighting Partisans.

The fact is that many of the late-war *Waffen-SS* divisions and brigades were of very low character indeed, and hence participated in some ghastly war crimes. Of the

many horrors perpetrated by the *Waffen-SS*, the crushing of the Warsaw Uprising in August–October 1944 stands out in sickening relief.

The task of handling the uprising, which began on 1 August 1944, was the responsibility of *Kampfgruppe Reinefarth*, named after its commander, Heinrich Reinefarth, the *SS- und Polizei Führer* in *Reichsgau* Wartheland. Amongst its ranks, the *Kampfgruppe Reinefarth* included two major formations: the *SS-Sturmbrigade Dirlewanger* (SS-Storm

Brigade *Dirlewanger*) led by *SS-Oberführer* Oskar Dirlewanger, and the *Waffen-Sturm-Brigade RONA*, headed by the former Soviet citizen Bronislav Kaminski.

Both units were perfect examples of how low *Waffen-SS* recruitment standards could fall. Dirlewanger himself was a World War I and Spanish Civil War veteran as well as a convicted child sex offender. A close friend of Berger, Dirlewanger was in 1940 allowed to take charge of a new SS unit made up of convicted

FOREIGN *WAFFEN-SS* BRIGADES

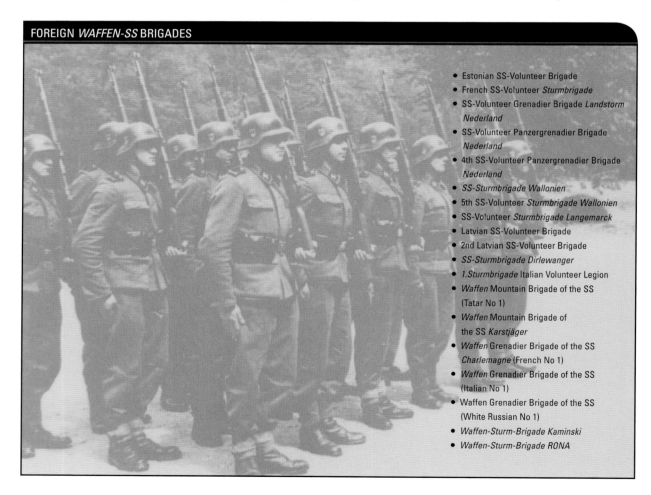

- Estonian SS-Volunteer Brigade
- French SS-Volunteer *Sturmbrigade*
- SS-Volunteer Grenadier Brigade *Landstorm Nederland*
- SS-Volunteer Panzergrenadier Brigade *Nederland*
- 4th SS-Volunteer Panzergrenadier Brigade *Nederland*
- *SS-Sturmbrigade Wallonien*
- 5th SS-Volunteer *Sturmbrigade Wallonien*
- SS-Volunteer *Sturmbrigade Langemarck*
- Latvian SS-Volunteer Brigade
- 2nd Latvian SS-Volunteer Brigade
- *SS-Sturmbrigade Dirlewanger*
- *1.Sturmbrigade* Italian Volunteer Legion
- *Waffen* Mountain Brigade of the SS (Tatar No 1)
- *Waffen* Mountain Brigade of the SS *Karstjäger*
- *Waffen* Grenadier Brigade of the SS *Charlemagne* (French No 1)
- *Waffen* Grenadier Brigade of the SS (Italian No 1)
- Waffen Grenadier Brigade of the SS (White Russian No 1)
- *Waffen-Sturm-Brigade Kaminski*
- *Waffen-Sturm-Brigade RONA*

TRANSCRIPT FROM NUREMBERG TRIAL PROCEEDINGS, 7 JANUARY 1946. CROSS EXAMINATION BY COLONEL POKROVSKY OF ERICH VON DEM BACH-ZELEWSKI

COL. POKROVSKY: *Do you know anything about the existence of a special brigade consisting of smugglers, poachers, and persons released from prison?*

VON DEM BACH-ZELEWSKI: *When all the troops really suitable for anti-Partisan warfare had been withdrawn, an anti-Partisan battalion under the command of Dirlewanger was formed and attached to Army Group Center at the end of 1941 or the beginning of 1942. This battalion was gradually strengthened by the addition of reserve units until it reached the proportions, first, of a regiment and, later, of a brigade. This 'Dirlewanger Brigade' consisted for the most part of previously convicted criminals; officially it consisted of so-called poachers, but it did include real criminals convicted of burglary, murder, et cetera.*

COL. POKROVSKY: *How do you explain the fact that the German Army Command so willingly strengthened and increased its forces by adding criminals to them and then using these criminals against the Partisans?*

VON DEM BACH-ZELEWSKI: *I am of the opinion that this step was closely connected with a speech made by Heinrich Himmler at Weselsburg at the beginning of 1941, prior to the campaign against Russia, when he spoke of the purpose of the Russian campaign, which was, he said, to decimate the Slav population by 30 million, and that it was in order to achieve this purpose that troops of such inferior caliber were introduced.*

COL. POKROVSKY: *Is it correct then to say that the character of the troops used by the commanders to fight the Partisans had been given careful consideration? Did they receive precise instructions how to treat the population and how to fight against the Partisans? I am now referring to the proposed and officially sanctioned extermination of the population.*

VON DEM BACH-ZELEWSKI: *Yes, I think this purpose was a decisive factor in the selection of certain commanders and formations.*

---

criminals, pulled out from the concentration camps and given the chance to prove themselves again through military service.

Sonderkommando Dirlewanger (Special Unit *Dirlewanger*), as it was known, became notorious for committing horrifying crimes against civilians and POWs in Poland and Belorussia; in the latter it is estimated that the unit killed some 120,000 civilians between 1942 and 1944. It also participated in front-line actions, and from January 1942 it was authorized to use Russian and Ukrainian personnel to fill out the gaps in its ranks. The number of foreigners in *Sonderkommando Dirlewanger* increased steadily, and

by February 1943, when it became *Sonderregiment Dirlewanger*, nearly 50 per cent of its troops were Soviet citizens. Furthermore, the recruits taken into the ranks eventually included individuals such as patients from psychiatric hospitals and sex offenders.

Kaminski Brigade

Even as Dirlewanger's troops were slaughtering Partisans and civilians alike in Belorussia, another anti-Partisan force had formed, this time from within the ranks of pro-German Soviets. Bronislav Kaminski, a Red Army veteran and engineer, had risen to command a local anti-Partisan militia around the town of Lokot,

south of Bryansk. The militia naturally started to cooperate with local *Wehrmacht* and *Waffen-SS* forces, acting in the roles of translators, guides and auxiliary combat troops. By the end of 1942, Kaminski's force was 10,000 men strong. Succumbing to delusions of grandeur, Kaminski renamed his formation the *Russkaya Osvoboditelnaya Narodnaya Armiya* (Russian National Army of Liberation; RONA).

Although the Kaminski Brigade, as it remained known by the German forces, was not composed of criminals per se, the calibre of its manpower was still dreadfully low. Desertions were frequent, and the anti-Partisan operations conducted by the unit often descended into exercises in killing – after one anti-Partisan sweep, the official report listed 12,531 civilians 'evacuated' (but most likely executed).

Warsaw Uprising

Dirlewanger and Kaminski's troops found a common destiny in the Warsaw Uprising of 1944. They were not the only German troops used in the two-month street battle to suppress the Polish resistance fighters. There was already a substantial Warsaw garrison, plus significant numbers of *Waffen-SS* and SS police. Yet on 4 August, *SS-Obergruppenführer* Erich von dem Bach-Zelewski was appointed overall commander for German forces in Warsaw. He organized his forces into two main battle groups, in which both *Sonderregiment Dirlewanger* and the Kaminski Brigade and were included.

History sometimes presents the crushing of the Warsaw Uprising as little but a German massacre, yet even Kaminski and Dirlewanger's soldiers experienced two months of exceptionally hard fighting, courtesy of a desperate enemy. The *Dirlewanger*'s casualty rate, for example, exceeded 300 per cent, the ranks refilled by an increasingly low grade of individual. Himmler himself commented that 'This is the fiercest of our battles since the start of the war. It compares to the street battles of Stalingrad.'

The SS units deployed in Warsaw were therefore short on mercy anyway, but under Himmler's orders they were essentially given free rein to unleash fury upon the belligerent Poles in whatever manner they

chose. The consequence was that the twisted elements of the units, many of them drunk, gave open expression to their basest desires in a terrible programme of slaughter, rape and torture. No one was spared – there were documented reports of babies being thrown onto bayonets. Women unfortunate enough to be captured were typically gang-raped

and then murdered. In the Wola and Ochota boroughs alone, it is estimated that some 40,000 civilians had been killed by 8 August. By the end of the action, when all resistance had been silenced and many of the survivors deported to concentration camps, civilian deaths may have numbered as high as 200,000.

30TH WAFFEN-GRENADIER DIVISION DER SS (RUSSISCHE NR.2)	
Commanders	
SS-Obersturmbannführer Hans Siegling	18 Aug 1944 (date appointed)
Divisional Strength	
Dec 1944	4400
Order of Battle	
Waffen-Grenadier-Regiment der SS 75	Waffen-Grenadier-Regiment der SS 76
Waffen-Grenadier-Regiment der SS 77	SS-Artillerie-Abteilung 30
SS-Aufklärungs-Abteilung 30	SS-Füsilier-Kompanie
SS-Pionier-Kompanie	SS-Nachrichten-Kompanie
SS-Sanitäts-Kompanie	SS-Panzerspäh-Kompanie
SS-Feldersatz-Bataillon	

33RD WAFFEN-GRENADIER DIVISION DER SS *CHARLEMAGNE*	
Commanders	
SS-Oberführer Edgard Puaud	Feb 1945 (date appointed)
SS-Brigadeführer Gustav Krukenberg	1 Mar 1945
SS-Standartenführer Walter Zimmermann	24 Apr 1945
Divisional Strength	
25 Feb 1945	7500
23 Apr 1945	1100
2 May 1945	30
Order of Battle	
SS-Waffen-Grenadier-Regiment 57	SS-Sturm-Bataillon 58
SS-Waffen-Grenadier-Regiment 58	SS-Artillerie-Abteilung 33
SS-Panzerjäger-Abteilung 33	SS-Pionier-Kompanie 33
SS-Nachrichten-Kompanie 33	SS-Feldersatz-Kompanie 33
SS-Nachschub-Bataillon 33	

OSKAR DIRLEWANGER – ESSENTIAL DATA

■ Oskar Dirlewanger's brutal style of leadership seems to have reflected a deep-seated sadism and a horrible tendency towards sexual violence.

Birth:	26 September 1895
Death:	1 June 1945 (tortured to death by Polish guards)
SS ID number:	357267
Place of birth:	Würzburg
Military service (pre-1939):	Infantry officer in World War I
	Joined Freikorps in 1919
	Condor Legion (1936–39)
Education:	PhD in Political Science (1922)
NSDAP membership:	From 1922
Criminal convictions:	Convicted of rape of 13-year-old girl and of molesting other children; sentenced to two years imprisonment
Decorations:	Iron Cross 2nd Class
	Iron Cross 1st Class
	German Cross in Gold
	Knight's Cross of the Iron Cross
WWII commands:	Commandant Dzików SS labour camp
	SS-Sturmbrigade Dirlewanger
Highest rank achieved:	SS-Oberführer der Reserve

Although Kaminski and Dirlewanger's troops had certainly sustained heavy casualties, their value as combat troops was negligible. Even Bach-Zelewski, under interrogation in a post-war trial, stated that the Kaminski Brigade in particular:

...had no military combat value whatsoever, with both officers and soldiers having not even a hint of tactical understanding. (...) I saw Kaminski's men removing entire cartloads of stolen jewelry, gold watches, and precious stones. The capture of a liquor supply was more important for the brigade than the seizure of a position commanding the same street. Each assault has been instantly stopped, because after taking the objective over, units dispersed into loose plundering hordes.

Unreliable comrades

In the end, the Kaminski Brigade was actually pulled out of the fighting because its sheer indiscipline was as much a problem for *Waffen-SS* local area commanders as it was for the Poles. Despite such a damning indictment, and the criticisms of many other local commanders, the two units were eventually given divisional status – the Kaminski Brigade became the 29th *Waffen* Grenadier Division of the SS (Russian No 1) while Dirlewanger's units were transformed into the 36th *Waffen* Grenadier Division of the SS *Dirlewanger*. And Dirlewanger himself was promoted.

War crimes became common amongst the *Waffen-SS* foreign divisions, particularly amongst men settling regional scores under German authority. (The Albanian 21st *Skanderbeg* Division, for example, killed thousands of Serb civilians during ethnic-cleansing operations in Kosovo.) In return, many of the foreign divisions had suffered dreadfully high casualties by the end of the war, as they were thrown into the maelstrom as expendable troops. Furthermore, those that did survive the war faced an equally perilous future back in the hands of the countrymen they had betrayed.

CHAPTER 5

Einsatzgruppen and Totenkopfverbände

Between 1939 and 1945, some six million Jews were murdered in an industrial style of slaughter such as the world had never seen. The SS was the engine of this mass murder, which was the brainchild of high-ranking SS officers such as Heinrich Himmler, Reinhard Heydrich, Adolf Eichmann and Theodor Eicke.

There were two principal forces behind the killings. The Einsatzgruppen *(Task Forces) were mobile murder squads. Operating in the villages, towns, cities, fields and woodlands of the Eastern occupied territories, they conducted executions on a staggering scale through bullet and mobile gas van. The* Totenkopfverbände, *by contrast, were the guards that oversaw the concentration and extermination camps, where millions of Jews and other 'undesirables' were sent to their deaths. The activities of these two elements, plus many other units of the SS, have ensured that the name 'SS' has been almost synonymous with evil ever since.*

◼ **Young** *Totenkopfverbände* **members photographed in Germany in 1938,**

Einsatzgruppen – Origins and Organization

The Einsatzgruppen *were the terrible culmination of six years of expanding anti-Semitic policy in Germany. They were Himmler's means of delivering the 'Final Solution' directly within the territories of occupied countries.*

The work of the *Einsatzgruppen* in Poland, the Baltic states and the occupied Soviet territories beggars belief. During the height of the *Einsatzgruppen* operations, SS killing squads, often aided by indigenous anti-Semitic police or locals, would at close quarters kill thousands of civilians – men, women and children – typically by shooting but also via mobile gas vans. Himmler himself witnessed an *Einsatzgruppen* operation in 1941 (see below 'Operations' section), and was so shaken by the experience that he commissioned the search for a more 'humane' method of execution – kinder, that is, on the executioners, not on the victims.

To comprehend the world of the *Einsatzgruppen*, we need to put them in the context of their times. For as we shall see, they were the result of policies implemented at the highest levels of power.

Turning on the Jews

Hitler rose to power in a society that, although deemed civilized and sophisticated, still retained ancestral undercurrents of anti-Semitism. Such prejudice had centuries-old roots in Europe, but in Germany it often coalesced around feelings that the small Jewish population enjoyed affluence by virtue of a 'parasitic' relationship with German society.

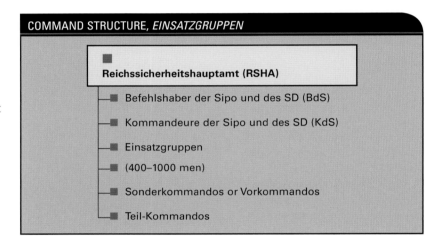

COMMAND STRUCTURE, *EINSATZGRUPPEN*

- **Reichssicherheitshauptamt (RSHA)**
  - Befehlshaber der Sipo und des SD (BdS)
  - Kommandeure der Sipo und des SD (KdS)
  - Einsatzgruppen
  - (400–1000 men)
  - Sonderkommandos or Vorkommandos
  - Teil-Kommandos

Historian Geoff Layton expands:

The Jews became easy scapegoats for the discontent and disorientation felt by many people as rapid industrialisation and urbanisation took place. The Jewish community was easily identifiable because of its different traditions, and became the focus of envy because it was viewed as privileged. In 1933, for example, although Jews comprised less than 1 per cent of the German population, they composed more than 16 per cent of lawyers, 10 per cent of doctors and 5 per cent of editors and writers.

(Layton, 2000)

The Jews were a visible and distinct community that attracted social envy and ideological hostility. Hitler turned those forces into outright persecution, steadily stripping Jews of their civic rights. From positions of influence, by 1937 they would become pariahs in their own country.

Legalizing persecution

Looking back at the 1930s, it is hard for us today to understand how the German people accepted the anti-Jewish legislation passed by the Nazi government. Yet acknowledging the widespread anti-Semitic context outlined above, we should also accept that the road to the Holocaust was gradualist – it occurred little by little over a period of around nine years (1933–42), so society adjusted to the policies one at a time. Add to this fact the apparent benefits Hitler brought to the German economy, plus the effects of Nazi propaganda, and the acceptance of persecution is a little more understandable. (There was also the fear of standing up to the authorities – it took a brave individual to speak out under the shadow of a *Gestapo* prison).

Yet although the overall process was gradualist, there was no doubt that Hitler was set on rigorously pursuing an anti-Jewish agenda. In 1933 alone, there was a raft of legislation attacking Jewish civil rights. The Law for the Restoration of the Professional Civil Service removed Jews from civil service employment; later that same month (April), the Law Against the Overcrowding of German Schools and Universities restricted Jews to 1.5 per cent of the educational population, and they were banned from admission to the Bar. In July, Jewish migrants from territories such as Russia and Poland were stripped of citizenship; from October Jews could no longer be journalists.

Similar legislation continued throughout 1934 and 1938, most of it designed to expel Jews from public positions or respected vocations. They were excluded from service in the German armed forces, and were dismissed from all public offices from November 1935. By the end of 1936, Jews could no longer practise as doctors, dentists, lawyers, notaries or teachers (of 'Aryan' pupils). More fundamental general legislation was the Reich Citizenship Law, which essentially stripped Jews of their German civil rights (forbiddingly putting them beyond the protection of the law), and the Law for the

Protection of German Blood and German Honour, which forbade intermarriage or sexual relations between Jews and non-Jews.

Losing their country

Steadily the Jews were being squeezed out of German society. Furthermore, in 1938 Hitler switched his focus to Jewish businesses and

assets. 'Aryanization' laws in March 1938 liquidated many Jewish firms, and in April all Jewish assets worth more than 5000 Reichsmarks had to be registered with the state, so that they could be used by Göring's Four-Year Plan office. In November 1939, a huge 'compensation fee' of 1000 million Reichsmarks was imposed on the German Jewish community, to be

VIPS TO BE ARRESTED BY *EINSATZGRUPPEN* OPERATIONS IN THE UNITED KINGDOM	
Person	*Position*
Aldous Huxley	Author
Anthony Eden	Secretary of State for War
Beatrice Webb	Pioneering socialist and economist
Bertrand Russell	Philosopher, historian and pacifist
C.P. Snow	Physicist and novelist
Chaim Weizmann	Zionist leader
David Low	Cartoonist
Duff Cooper	Cabinet Minister of Information
E.M. Forster	Author
Edvard Benes	President of the Czech government-in-exile
Ernst Hanfstaengl	German financier, refugee
Gilbert Murray	Classical scholar and League of Nations activist
H.G. Wells	Author and socialist
Harold Laski	Political theorist, economist and author
Hermann Rauschning	German refugee, former friend of Hitler
Ignacy Jan Paderewski	Former Prime Minister of Poland
J.B. Priestley	Anti-Nazi popular broadcaster and fiction writer
J.B.S. Haldane	Geneticist and evolutionary biologist
Jan Masaryk	Foreign Minister of the Czech government-in-exile
Neville Chamberlain	Former Prime Minister
Noël Coward	Actor
Paul Robeson	Singer and Communist
Rebecca West	British-Irish suffragist and writer
Robert Baden-Powell	Founder and leader of Scouting movement
Sigmund Freud	Jewish founder of psychoanalysis
Sir Norman Angell	Labour MP, Nobel Peace Prize winner
Sir Philip Gibbs	Journalist and novelist
Stephen Spender	Poet, novelist and essayist
Vera Brittain	Feminist writer and pacifist
Violet Bonham-Carter	Anti-fascist liberal politician
Virginia Woolf	Novelist and essayist
Winston Churchill	Prime Minister

EINSATZGRUPPEN ORGANIZATION, POLAND 1939

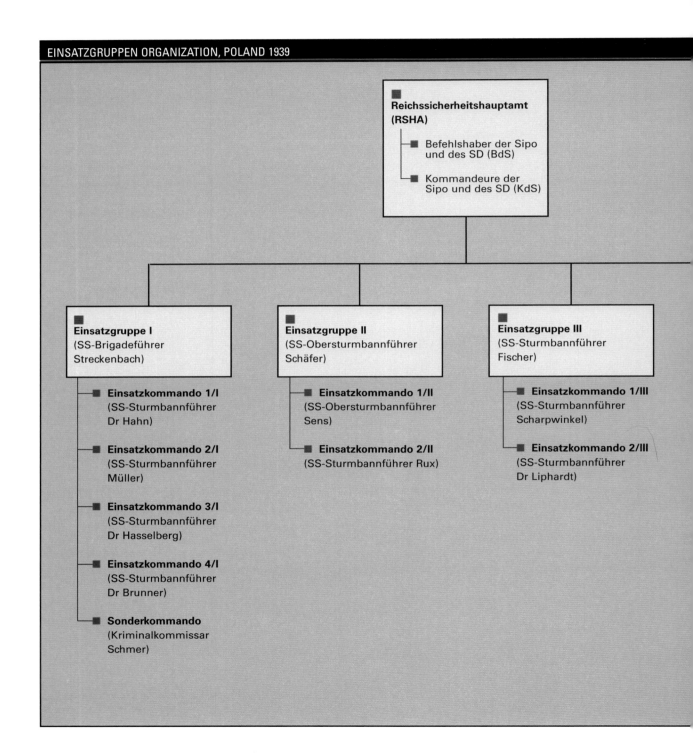

Reichssicherheitshauptamt (RSHA)

- Befehlshaber der Sipo und des SD (BdS)
- Kommandeure der Sipo und des SD (KdS)

Einsatzgruppe I (SS-Brigadeführer Streckenbach)

- **Einsatzkommando 1/I** (SS-Sturmbannführer Dr Hahn)
- **Einsatzkommando 2/I** (SS-Sturmbannführer Müller)
- **Einsatzkommando 3/I** (SS-Sturmbannführer Dr Hasselberg)
- **Einsatzkommando 4/I** (SS-Sturmbannführer Dr Brunner)
- **Sonderkommando** (Kriminalkommissar Schmer)

Einsatzgruppe II (SS-Obersturmbannführer Schäfer)

- **Einsatzkommando 1/II** (SS-Obersturmbannführer Sens)
- **Einsatzkommando 2/II** (SS-Sturmbannführer Rux)

Einsatzgruppe III (SS-Sturmbannführer Fischer)

- **Einsatzkommando 1/III** (SS-Sturmbannführer Scharpwinkel)
- **Einsatzkommando 2/III** (SS-Sturmbannführer Dr Liphardt)

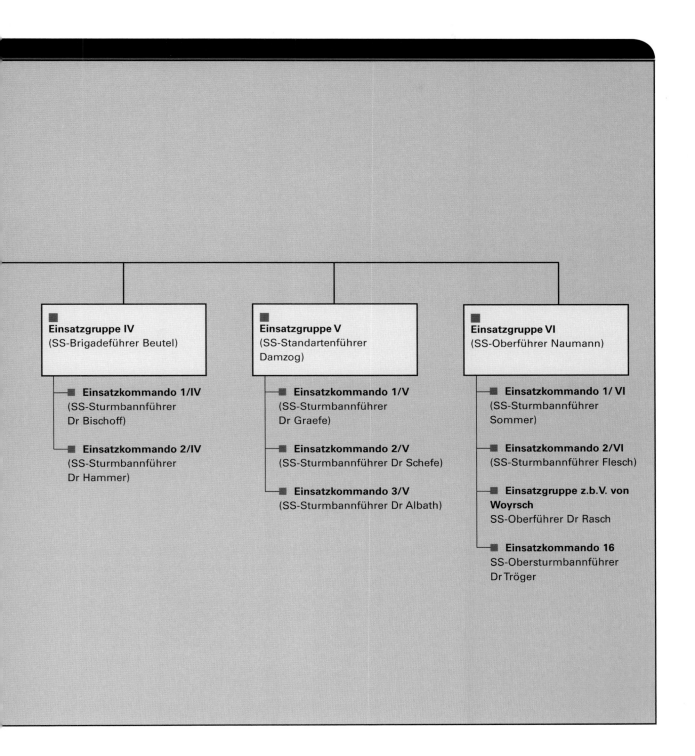

Einsatzgruppe IV
(SS-Brigadeführer Beutel)

- **Einsatzkommando 1/IV**
(SS-Sturmbannführer
Dr Bischoff)

- **Einsatzkommando 2/IV**
(SS-Sturmbannführer
Dr Hammer)

Einsatzgruppe V
(SS-Standartenführer
Damzog)

- **Einsatzkommando 1/V**
(SS-Sturmbannführer
Dr Graefe)

- **Einsatzkommando 2/V**
(SS-Sturmbannführer Dr Schefe)

- **Einsatzkommando 3/V**
(SS-Sturmbannführer Dr Albath)

Einsatzgruppe VI
(SS-Oberführer Naumann)

- **Einsatzkommando 1/ VI**
(SS-Sturmbannführer
Sommer)

- **Einsatzkommando 2/VI**
(SS-Sturmbannführer Flesch)

- **Einsatzgruppe z.b.V. von
Woyrsch**
SS-Oberführer Dr Rasch

- **Einsatzkommando 16**
SS-Obersturmbannführer
Dr Tröger

collected through liquidated assets, and in February 1939 Jews were even required to surrender their precious metals and jewellery.

Under such malign legislation, it is little wonder that thousands of Jews chose to pack their bags and run for seemingly safer territories abroad. The fortunate ones put sea between them and Germany, going to Britain and the United States, for example. Less fortunate were those who went to other mainland European countries, ones that Hitler's forces would later occupy in 1940.

Note also that Jews were not the only people being singled out by Hitler's racial excesses. Gypsies and blacks were also victims of persecutory legislation.

Open violence

The anti-Jewish laws of the 1930s were still a long way from the gas chambers of Auschwitz, but there were signs of a violent destiny for the Jews. Attacks by members of the Nazi Party, *Sturmabteilung* (SA) and SS against Jews and Jewish shops escalated steadily, the perpetrators having the reassurance that there would be little or no legal comeback from such actions.

The violence reached its pre-war apogee on 9 November 1938, following the murder of German diplomat Ernst vom Rath by a Polish Jew in Paris. In a state-sanctioned night of mayhem, 91 Jews were murdered, more than 200 synagogues were burned and 7500 Jewish businesses were ransacked. *Kristallnacht* ('Night of the Broken Glass') was followed by mass arrests of Jewish men, who were sent off to

Germany's burgeoning concentration camp system, where they faced a bleak future.

Kristallnacht was fundamentally led by the SS in the person of Reinhard Heydrich, head of the *Sicherheitspolizei* (*Sipo*) and *Sicherheitsdienst* (SD) security services. Heydrich would be integral to the later *Einsatzgruppen* operations (see the document on the opposite page), but on this particular night he gained some early experience in organizing mass terror. His instructions to SS and state police leaders, reproduced on page 28, show a curious mindset. For example, while it was permitted to 'destroy' Jewish businesses, it was not permitted to loot them. Any Jews arrested were not to be 'ill-treated', a bizarre request considering what else they were being put through. On Heydrich's part there seems to have been the belief that violence could be given an ordered and almost respectable veneer, and a similar concern runs throughout the SS in implementing the Holocaust.

Building the *Einsatzgruppen*

The foundations of the *Einsatzgruppen* actually pre-date the war. The precursors were the *Einsatzkommandos* (Task Commands), special units formed from collections of police, *Gestapo*, SD and *Sipo* members, which were used to apprehend anti-Nazi politicians and intellectuals in the aftermath of the annexation of Austria in 1938. Having proved their worth, the new *Einsatzgruppen* were formed in the run-up to the German occupation of Czechoslovakia in

March 1939. (The *Einsatzgruppen* were already established in government offices in the Sudetenland, which had been occupied by the Germans in 1938.) With the possibility that the invasion might be a full-blown military operation, the *Einsatzgruppen* were given authorization to use lethal force where necessary. Only the fact that the occupation of Czechoslovakia was essentially bloodless prevented an early test of the *Einsatzgruppen*'s new range of authority.

Formal killing squads

The status of the *Einsatzgruppen* changed dramatically with the invasion of Poland in September 1939. This was the true beginning of Hitler's racial war against the *Untermenschen*, and accordingly the *Einsatzgruppen* received a clarified purpose. In the post-war trials of SS personnel, Adolf Eichmann, the man ultimately charged with the Holocaust deportation programme, told the court that 'The purpose of the *Einsatzgruppen* was to murder Jews and deprive them of their property.' This clipped, brutally framed objective was confirmed by Erich Bach-Zelewski, who viewed the main aims of the *Einsatzgruppen* as 'the annihilation of the Jews, gypsies, and political commissars'.

The violence brought by the *Einsatzgruppen* was not detached impromptu field killings, but was approved and ordered from the highest levels of the SS command. Both Himmler and Heydrich are known to have met with *Einsatzgruppen* commanders and issue orders, and the death toll

LETTER FROM HEYDRICH TO THE CHIEFS OF ALL *EINSATZGRUPPEN* CONCERNING 'THE JEWISH QUESTION IN THE OCCUPIED TERRITORY', 21 SEPTEMBER 1939

The following document was presented at the Nuremberg Trials, and provides a clear insight into Einsatzgruppen policy in Poland and for further actions in the Soviet Union.

The Chief of the Security Police
PP (II) -288/39 Secret.
Berlin, 21 September 1939.

Express Letter

To the Chiefs of all Einsatzgruppen of the Security Police
Re: The Jewish question in the occupied territory.

With reference to the conference which took place today in Berlin, I would like to point out once more that the total measures *planned* (i.e., the final aim) are to be kept *strictly secret*.

A distinction is to be made between,
1. The final aim (which will take some time), and
2. Sections of the carrying out of this aim (which can be carried out within a short space of time).

The measures planned require the most thorough preparation both from the technical and the economic point of view. It goes without saying that the tasks in this connection cannot be laid down in detail. The following instructions and directives simultaneously serve the purpose of urging the chiefs of the Einsatzgruppen to practical consideration.

I

The first necessity for the attaining of the final aim is the concentrating of the country Jews in the big towns. This is to be carried out immediately.

A distinction is to be made between (1) the territories of Danzig and West Prussia, Posen, Eastern Upper Silesia, and (2) the remaining occupied territories. As far as possible the territories enumerated under (1) are to be cleared of Jews, but the very least to be aimed at is the formation of very few 'concentration' towns.

In the territories mentioned under (2) as few 'concentration' points as possible are to be established in order to facilitate later measures. Care must be taken that only such towns be chosen as concentration points as are either railroad junctions or at least lie on a railway.

It is laid down on principle that Jewish communities of less than 500 persons are to be dissolved and to be sent to the nearest 'concentration' town.

This decree does not concern the territory of Einsatzgruppe I which, lying east of Krakow, is bordered by Polanico, Jaroslav, the new demarcation line and the former Slovak-Polish frontier. Within this territory only a temporary census of Jews need be taken. The rest is to be done by the Jewish Council of Elders dealt with below.

II

Jewish Council of Elders

1. In every Jewish community a Jewish Council of Elders is to be set up which, as far as possible, is to be formed from persons in authority and rabbis who have remained behind. Up to 24 male Jews (according to the size of the Jewish community) are to form the Council of Elders. It is to be made fully responsible, within the meaning of the word, for the exact and punctual carrying out of all instructions issued or to be issued.

2. In the event of the sabotaging of such instructions, the strictest measures are to be announced to the council.

3. The Jewish councils are to undertake a temporary census of the Jews, if possible arranged according to sex, ages

(CONTINUED NEXT PAGE)

LETTER FROM HEYDRICH TO THE CHIEFS OF ALL *EINSATZGRUPPEN* CONCERNING 'THE JEWISH QUESTION IN THE OCCUPIED TERRITORY', 21 SEPTEMBER 1939

(a) up to 16 years, (b) from 16 to 20 years, and (c) over and according to the principal professions-in their localities, and to report thereon within the shortest possible period.

4. The Councils of Elders are to be advised of the days fixed and the appointed times of the evacuation, the possibilities of evacuation, and finally the evacuation routes. They are then to be made personally responsible for evacuation of the Jews from the country. The reason for the concentrating of Jews in the towns is to be that Jews have to a very great extent participated in franc-tireur attacks and pillage.

5. The Councils of Elders in the 'concentration' towns are to be made responsible for the suitable accommodation of the Jews from the country. The concentration of the Jews in the towns will probably, in the interests of general security, call for certain regulations in these towns, e. g., that certain quarters of the town be altogether forbidden to the Jews; that in the interests of economic necessity, they be forbidden to leave the Ghetto, forbidden to go out after a certain hour in the evening, etc.

6. The Council of Elders is to be made responsible for the suitable feeding of the Jews during their transportation to the towns. No objections are to be made if the departing Jews take their movable possessions with them, as far as this is technically possible.

7. Jews who do not comply with the order to move to the towns are, in certain cases, to be given a short respite. They are to be advised of the most strict punishment if they do not comply with this time limit.

III

All necessary measures are, on principle, always to be taken in the closest agreement and cooperation with the German civil administration and the competent local military authorities.

When carrying out this action care is to be taken that the economic security of the occupied territories suffers no damage.

1. The needs of the army are to be the first consideration, e. g., it will hardly be possible, to begin with, to avoid leaving behind Jewish traders here and there who, for lack of other possibilities, must definitely remain behind for the provisioning of the troops. In such cases, however, the speedy Aryanization of these industries is to be aimed at, in agreement with the competent local German administrative authorities, and the migration of the Jews completed.

2. It goes without saying that Jewish branches of industry and trade which are vital to the life of the community, the war effort, or the Four Year Plan must be maintained in order to safeguard economic interest in the occupied territories. In such cases, also, the quickest possible Aryanization is to be aimed at and the migration of the Jews completed.

3. Finally, the food question in the occupied territories is to be taken into consideration. For example, if possible, land belonging to Jewish settlers is to be farmed with their own by the neighboring German or Polish peasants, in an official capacity, so that the gathering in of the harvest still in the fields or the continued cultivation can be safeguarded. With regard to this important question, contact is to be made with agricultural expert consultants of the chief of civil administration.

4. In all cases where the interests of the security police on one hand and the German civil administration on the other are not in agreement, the individual measures in question are to be reported to me as quickly as possible before their execution and my decision awaited.

IV

The chiefs of the Einsatzgruppen will report to me continually regarding the following circumstances:

1. Census of Jews in their districts (if possible in the above-mentioned groups). The numbers are to be divided into Jews who will be migrating from the country and those who are already in the towns.

2. Names of towns selected as 'concentration' points.

3. The time limits set for the migration of the Jews to the towns.

4. Summary of all Jewish branches of industry and trade which are vital to the life of the community, the war effort, or the Four Year Plan. If possible the following facts are to be established:

a. The type of undertaking (together with estimate of the possibility of the adaptation of the undertaking to one vital to the life of the community, the war effort, or the Four Year Plan.

b. Which of these undertakings it is most urgent to Aryanize (to avoid damage of any kind)? How is it proposed to effect the Aryanization? Germans or Poles (this decision is dependent on the importance of the industry).

c. What is the number of the Jews employed in these industries (among those in the influential positions)? Can the industry be maintained without any more ado after the evacuation of the Jews, or does this require the allocation of German or Polish workers? To what extent? Insofar as it is necessary to bring in Polish workers, care must be taken to obtain them principally from the former German Provinces, so that the Polish element there is consequently broken up. This question can only be dealt with through the intervention and cooperation of the organized German labor offices.

V

In order to attain the aims which have been set, I expect the fullest cooperation from all forces of the security police and the security service.

The neighbouring chiefs of the Einsatzgruppen must immediately get into touch with one another, in order that the territories in question may be dealt with in their entirety.

VI

The OKH, the Plenipotentiary for the Four Year Plan (for the attention of State Secretary Neumann), the Reich Ministries of the Interior (for the attention of State Secretary Stuckart), for Food and Economy (for the attention of State Secretary Landfried), as well as the chiefs of the civil administration of the occupied territories have received a draft copy of this decree.

[Signed] HEYDRICH
Certified :
[Signed] Schmidt
Chancellery Employee

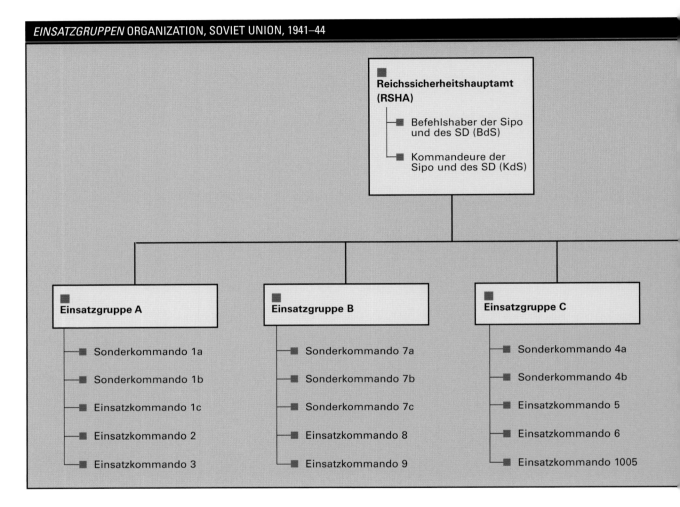

EINSATZGRUPPEN ORGANIZATION, SOVIET UNION, 1941–44

Reichssicherheitshauptamt (RSHA)
- Befehlshaber der Sipo und des SD (BdS)
- Kommandeure der Sipo und des SD (KdS)

Einsatzgruppe A
- Sonderkommando 1a
- Sonderkommando 1b
- Einsatzkommando 1c
- Einsatzkommando 2
- Einsatzkommando 3

Einsatzgruppe B
- Sonderkommando 7a
- Sonderkommando 7b
- Sonderkommando 7c
- Einsatzkommando 8
- Einsatzkommando 9

Einsatzgruppe C
- Sonderkommando 4a
- Sonderkommando 4b
- Einsatzkommando 5
- Einsatzkommando 6
- Einsatzkommando 1005

reports of *Einsatzgruppen* and *Einsatzkommando* leaders were read centrally by the SS leadership.

Organization

For the Poland operation, five *Einsatzgruppen* were formed, each of them attached to a specific *Wehrmacht* army. Note, however, that in Poland and later in the Soviet Union the *Wehrmacht* had no authority to interfere in *Einsatzgruppen* operations, no matter how ghastly. On several occasions high-ranking Army officers were witnesses to death squad actions, but their official complaints fell on deaf ears. When General Gerd von Rundstedt, for example, complained about the actions of one *Einsatzgruppe* in Upper Silesia, Hitler's response was to remove military-controlled regions and place Poland under a system of *Gauleiter*, therefore giving the Party jurisdiction over all activities. Rundstedt was eventually replaced by General Johannes Blaskowitz, but he too felt compelled to report *Einsatzgruppen* actions to Berlin. The result was that Blaskowitz and all his staff were eventually removed on the personal request of Hans Frank, the head of the General Government, and relations between the Army and the SS dropped to an all-time low.

Having said this, there is photographic and documentary evidence of *Wehrmacht* personnel

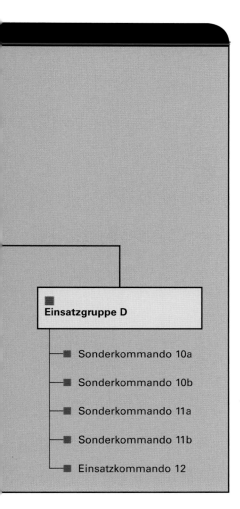

Einsatzgruppe D

- Sonderkommando 10a
- Sonderkommando 10b
- Sonderkommando 11a
- Sonderkommando 11b
- Einsatzkommando 12

now on killing rather than police-type work, *Waffen-SS* personnel now made up the bulk of the units. The rest came from the full range of police and security services, implicating a broad cross-section of German society in the murders. (Note, however, that *Einsatzgruppen* personnel all wore SD field-grey service uniforms.) As we shall see later, local manpower was also important to enable the *Einsatzgruppen* to perform their largest killing actions.

The *Einsatzgruppen* operated in the German rear areas, systematically targeting Jewish communities for extermination actions. In occupied Poland, the murder squads were governed by *Gestapo Leiststellen* (Regional HQs) and SD *Abschnitte*, acting under the *Sipo und SD* commander in each district. (The actual full title of the *Einsatzgruppen* was the *Einsatzgruppen der Sicherheitspolizei und des SD*, a clear indication of their positioning within

the SS.) The command chain then ran all the way up to the RSHA and beyond to the RFSS – Heinrich Himmler himself.

Soviet operations
For the invasion of the Soviet Union and Baltic states in June 1941, the *Einsatzgruppen* underwent some reordering. They were arranged into four *Gruppen*, using the letters A–D. *Einsatzgruppe* A was attached to Army Group North, *Einsatzgruppe* B to Army Group Centre, *Einsatzgruppe* C to Army Group South, and *Einsatzgruppe* D to the Eleventh Army, which was part of Army Group South. In this way, the *Einsatzgruppen* were able to operate along the entire length of the Eastern Front. It was not only Jews on the list of targets for the *Einsatzgruppen.* The killing squads also targeted 'political enemies' such as NKVD (Soviet secret police) agents and Soviet commissars, plus anyone who fitted into a variety of 'undesirable' categories.

being present at and possibly assisting in *Einsatzgruppen* operations, so we must be cautious in claiming that the *Wehrmacht* always occupied the moral high ground.

There were eventually six *Einsatzgruppen* in total in Poland, numbered I–VI, and each *Einsatzgruppe* was divided into *Einsatzkommandos* that numbered about 100 men each. The composition of the *Einsatzgruppen* was interesting. Given that the focus was

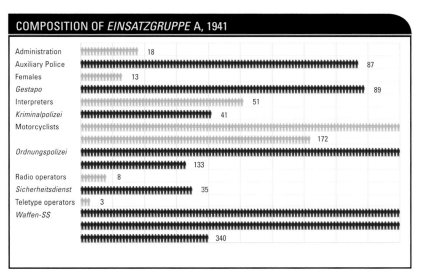

COMPOSITION OF *EINSATZGRUPPE* A, 1941

Administration	18
Auxiliary Police	87
Females	13
Gestapo	89
Interpreters	51
Kriminalpolizei	41
Motorcyclists	172
Ordnungspolizei	133
Radio operators	8
Sicherheitsdienst	35
Teletype operators	3
Waffen-SS	340

Operations

Einsatzgruppen 'operations' were little more than exercises in systematic murder. They killed young and old, men and women, scooping up entire communities for dreadful ends in woods, fields, ravines and town squares.

A revealing insight into both the chilling work of the *Einsatzgruppen*, and the curious relationship between Himmler and the Holocaust, can be seen in the post-war testimony of Erich Bach-Zelewski at the Nuremberg trials:

In August 1941, Himmler ordered Artur Nebe, leader of an Einsatzgruppe in Minsk, to murder one hundred people in his presence, among them numerous women. I stood at the side of Himmler and observed him. When the first shots were heard and the victims collapsed, Himmler began to feel ill. He reeled, almost fell to the ground, and then pulled himself together. He then hurled abuse at the firing squad because of their

poor marksmanship. Some of the women were still alive, for the bullets had simply wounded them.

It is indeed ironic that the man who oversaw the murder of more than six million Jews was unable to stomach viewing the process of killing itself. (He had similar physical responses when visiting extermination camps.) Yet what is equally aberrant is the fact that Bach-Zelewski seems sufficiently inured to the killing of 100 people to be more interested in Himmler's reaction than the sight before him.

The levels of inhumanity reached by the *Einsatzgruppen* are not easily grasped. Entire territories were combed of Jews – men, women, children, babes in arms – who were herded into remote locations and

shot, beaten, buried or tortured to death, often with the help of local police and collaborators.

Psychologically, it is extremely hard to unpack what occurred, and can be ascribed to a mix of racial enmity, brutal training, the abdication of moral responsibility under orders, and simple brutal personalities. What was beyond doubt, however, was that they did a very effective job. Gordon Williamson points out that:

By the first winter of the war in the Soviet Union, almost half a million Jews had been murdered by the Einsatzgruppen. Einsatzgruppe A alone had murdered almost a quarter of a million, B some 45,000, C 95,000 and D 92,000. Behind the

▶ **OPERATIONAL AREAS**
The operational areas of the *Einsatzgruppen* from June 1941 extended from the Baltic states in the north down to the southern Ukraine. At first the *Einsatzgruppen* simply moved behind the German forces advancing in Operation *Barbarossa*, but then established fixed command regions, organized under a police and security service command structure. The *Einsatzgruppen* operated in these regions with impunity until the Soviet advances of 1943 and 1944 pushed them back.

DATES ON WHICH *EINSATZGRUPPEN* AND SUB-UNITS WERE DISBANDED			
Formation/Unit	Date disbanded	Formation/Unit	Date disbanded
Einsatzgruppe A	17 Oct 1944	Einsatzgruppe C	28 Aug 1943
Sonderkommando 1a	15 Oct 1944	Sonderkommando 4a	28 Aug 1943
Sonderkommando 1b	1 Oct 1943	Sonderkommando 4b	7 Jan 1944
Einsatzkommando 1c	28 Nov 1942	Einsatzkommando 5	6 Jan 1942
Einsatzkommando 2	Mar 1944	Einsatzkommando 6	5 Aug 1943
Einsatzkommando 3	Jan 1945	Einsatzkommando 1005	16 Oct 1944
Einsatzgruppe B	29 Aug 1944	Einsatzgruppe D	15 July 1943
Sonderkommando 7a	28 Nov 1944	Sonderkommando 10a	11 July 1943
Sonderkommando 7b	14 Oct 1944	Sonderkommando 10b	7 May 1943
Sonderkommando 7c	Dec 1943?	Sonderkommando 11a	12 May 1943
Einsatzkommando 8	26 Apr 1944	Sonderkommando 11b	23 Feb 1943
Einsatzkommando 9	16 Mar 1944	Einsatzkommando 12	1 Mar 1943

Einsatzkommandos came police and auxiliary volunteers from the occupied territories to deal with any stragglers the Einsatzkommandos had missed, and a grisly race ensued to see who could report the highest 'score' of executions.

(Williamson, 2002)

Williamson goes on to note that the *Einsatzgruppen* were also utilized for 'anti-Partisan' operations, this title providing a useful cover for killing operations in which almost every civilian encountered fell under the category of 'Partisan'.

In total, it is estimated that the *Einsatzgruppen* murdered somewhere in the region of 1.5 million people between 1939 and 1944. Here we will look deeper into their modus operandi, and explore the tensions that came with personally delivering mass murder.

Operating methods

The *Einsatzgruppen* advancing into Poland in 1939 were under direct orders from Heydrich to liquidate without mercy any Jews or members of the Polish intelligentsia they ran across during their sweep operations. It is often overlooked that

MAP OF OPERATIONAL AREAS OF EASTERN *EINSATZGRUPPEN,* 1941–44*

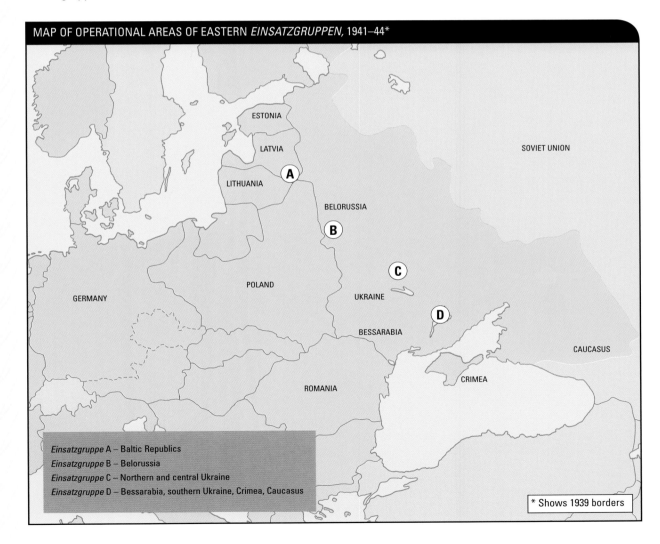

Einsatzgruppe A – Baltic Republics
Einsatzgruppe B – Belorussia
Einsatzgruppe C – Northern and central Ukraine
Einsatzgruppe D – Bessarabia, southern Ukraine, Crimea, Caucasus

* Shows 1939 borders

EINSATZGRUPPEN AND TOTENKOPFVERBÄNDE

JEWISH EXECUTIONS CARRIED OUT BY *EINSATZGRUPPEN*, BALTIC STATES AND BELORUSSIA, JUNE–DECEMBER 1941

◄ **EXECUTIONS, BALTIC STATES/BELORUSSIA, 1941**
The map shows the numbers of Jews killed by the *Einsatzgruppen* in the Baltic states and Belorussia during the second half of 1941. These territories were the province of *Einsatzgruppen* A and B, the former having one of the worst records for atrocities of any *Einsatzgruppe*. The Baltic states sat well behind the front line, and contained highly anti-Semitic elements amongst their own citizenry, so containing and then murdering local Jews was relatively easy.

the *Einsatzgruppen* were also employed during the campaign in Western Europe in 1940. The different racial perspective of that campaign, however, meant that what were murder squads in the East essentially became police and intelligence squads in the West, securing important government offices and papers. When they turned east again in mid-1941, the gloves came off and they were once again instructed to act as a purge of the Jewish people.

The basic operating procedure of the *Einsatzgruppen* ran as follows. The units would enter a village, town or city, targeting those areas in which large numbers of Jews were known to live. The inhabitants were then ordered to assemble, typically in the town or village square. Some individuals would liaise with local police or any anti-Semitic elements to help identify Jews or flush out those that had gone into hiding. Once assembled, the Jews were destined for deportation to a camp, transfer to a ghetto, or immediate killing.

When the last-mentioned option was chosen, the organization of murder would vary according to the surroundings and the numbers of victims involved. In out-of-the-way rural areas, and with smaller numbers of people, victims might simply be shot in the village square or taken into nearby woods and fields and executed. An alternative method of mass execution was to herd large numbers of citizens into a church or similar public building, then set the building alight, with SS soldiers waiting outside with small arms to gun down any who managed to break free from the flames.

In larger urban areas, the citizens might be transported en masse to more remote locations such as forests or large ravines, where they would be killed in several days of very intensive murder. Former *Einsatzgruppe* D commander Otto Ohlendorf, at the trial of *Einsatzgruppen* members in Nuremberg between 1947 and 1948, testified to prosecuting attorney John Arlan Amen as to what typically happened at the killing sites:

Amen: *Did you personally supervise any mass murders?*
Ohlendorf: *I attended two mass murders as an inspector.*
Amen: *Will you explain to the Court the procedures used.*
Ohlendorf: *The site generally chosen was at a deep trench or extensive dugout.*

SOVIET/BALTIC-BASED *EINSATZGRUPPEN* COMMANDERS

Einsatzgruppe A

SS-Brigadeführer Dr Walter Stahlecker	(June 1941–Mar 1942)
SS-Brigadeführer Heinz Jost	(Mar–June 1942)
SS-Oberführer Dr Hubert Achamer-Pifrader	(June 1942–Sep 1943)
SS-Gruppenführer Friedrich Panzinger	(Sep 1943–May 1944)
SS-Brigadeführer Dr Wilhelm Fuchs	(May–Oct 1944)

Einsatzgruppe B

SS-Brigadeführer Artur Nebe	(June–Nov 1941)
SS-Brigadeführer Erich Naumann	(Nov 1941–Mar 1943)
SS-Obersturmbannführer Horst Böhme	(Mar–Aug 1943)
SS-Oberführer Dr Erich Ehrlinger	(Aug 1943–Apr 1944)
SS-Standartenführer Heinz Seetzen	(Apr–Aug 1944)
SS-Obersturmbannführer Horst Böhme	(Aug 1944)

Einsatzgruppe C

SS-Brigadeführer Dr Otto Rasch	(June–Oct 1941)
SS-Gruppenführer Dr Max Thomas	(Oct 1941–Augt 1943)

Einsatzgruppe D

SS-Brigadeführer Otto Ohlendorf	(June 1941–July 1942)
SS-Brigadeführer Walther Bierkamp	(July 1942–July 1943)

EXTRACT FROM OPERATIONAL SITUATION REPORT USSR NO. 106, 7 OCTOBER 1941, FROM THE CHIEF OF THE SECURITY POLICE AND THE SD, 7 OCTOBER 1941 (DOCUMENT TRANSLATED FOR NUREMBERG TRIALS).

Executions and Other Measures

Partly because of the better economic situation of the Jews under the Bolshevist regime and their activities as informers and agents of the NKVD, partly because of the explosions and the resulting fires, the public feeling against the Jews was very strong. As an added factor it was proved that the Jews participated in the arson. The population expected adequate retaliatory measures by the German authorities. Consequently all Jews of Kiev were requested, in agreement with the city commander, to appear on Monday, 29 September by 8 o'clock at a designated place. These announcements were posted by members of the Ukrainian militia in the entire city. Simultaneously it was announced orally that all Jews were to be moved. In collaboration with the group [Gruppe] staff and 2 Kommandos of the police regiment South, the Sonderkommando 4a executed on 29 and 30 September, 33,771 Jews. Money, valuables, underwear and clothing were secured and placed partly at the disposal of the NSV Nazi Party Public Welfare Organization for use of the racial Germans, partly given to the city administration authorities for use of the needy population. The transaction was carried out without friction. No incidents occurred. The 'Resettlement measure' against the Jews was approved throughout by the population. The fact that in reality the Jews were liquidated was hardly known until now, according to up-to-date experiences it would, however, hardly have been objected to. The measures were also approved by the Wehrmacht. The Jews who were not yet apprehended as well as those who gradually returned from their flight to the city were in each case treated accordingly.

Simultaneously a number of NKVD officials, political commissars, and Partisan leaders was arrested and liquidated.

The Bandera [Ukrainian independence movement] men had lost their impact through the arrests before Kiev effected by the Kommandos and their activity was reduced to the mere distribution of leaflets and the posting of placards. Three arrests were effected, further arrests are planned.

Communications with the local authorities were immediately established by the group staff as well as the Sonderkommando 4a and the Einsatzkommando 5 also stationed in Kiev. A constant cooperation with these authorities was accomplished and the actual problems were discussed in daily consultations.

On the activity of the Einsatzkommando, it must be reported in detail in separate action reports, because of the great extent of the material.

Amen: *In what position were the victims shot?*

Ohlendorf: *Either standing or on their knees.*

Amen: *What happened to the corpses once they had been shot?*

Ohlendorf: *They were buried.*

Amen: *What measures were taken to ensure that the victims were actually dead?*

Ohlendorf: *The unit commanders were ordered to attend to this and if necessary to finish off those who were still alive.*

Amen: *Were all the victims, women, men and children, murdered in the same manner?*

Ohlendorf: *Until the spring of 1942, yes. Then we received an order from Himmler that in the future women and children should be killed in the gas wagons.*

The trenches to which Ohlendorf refers were either dug prior to the executions by teams of specially conscripted locals, or on many occasions were actually dug by the victims themselves.

Willing accomplices

We have already noted how the *Einsatzgruppen* were assisted in their killings by local people. Indeed, the final results of the murder campaigns were unlikely to have been so impressive had it not been for the willing assistance of local people. Historian Lawrence Rees, for example, has explored the activities of Lithuanian police and civilians in assisting the operations of *Einsatzgruppe* A in the Baltic. His findings present horrifying reading, and show that in many cases the SS soldiers simply stood by and let Lithuanians do all the killing for them. In one case in Kaunas, Lithuania's second city, local crowds gathered to watch Jews be killed by a man known to posterity as the 'Death-dealer of Kaunas'. A *Wehrmacht* officer recounted:

There was a large number of women in the crowd and they had lifted up their children or stood them on chairs or boxes so that they could see better. At first I thought this must be a victory celebration or some type of sporting event because of the cheering, clapping and laughter that kept breaking out. However, when I enquired what was happening, I was told that the 'Death-dealer of Kovno [Kaunas]' was at work... In response to a cursory wave, the next man then stepped forward and was beaten to death with the wooden club in the most bestial manner.

(Rees, 2002)

During more organized killing operations, Lithuanian soldiers, police and civilians seemed perfectly willing, when plied with drink, to shoot dead hundreds of women and children. An *Einsatzgruppe* A situation report dated 6 July 1941 noted that 'Public feelings among the Lithuanians in Kaunas are good and are pro-German.' Another report five days later explained in more detail the extent of local support:

The attitude of the Lithuanian population is friendly towards the Germans so far. They help the German soldiers, the police officials, and the other organizations already functioning in this area as much as possible. Their cooperation consists chiefly in looking for and turning over Lithuanian Communists, dispersed Red Army soldiers, and Jews. After the retreat of the Red Army, the population of Kaunas killed about 2,500 Jews during a spontaneous uprising. In addition, a rather large number of Jews was shot by the Auxiliary Police Service.

The events in Lithuania were far from exceptional. *Einsatzgruppe* D noted that there was 'good cooperation' with the Romanian Army and Gendarmerie in its actions. A

EINSATZGRUPPEN COMMANDERS

Einsatzgruppen	Commander	Rank	Date of birth/death	Fate
Einsatzgruppe A	Dr. Franz Walter Stahlecker	SS-Brigadeführer	1900–42	Killed in action
Einsatzgruppe B	Artur Nebe	SS-Brigadeführer	1894–1945	Executed by Nazis for treason
Einsatzgruppe C	Otto Rasch	SS-Gruppenführer	1891–1948	Indicted for war crimes, but died 1948
Einsatgruppe D	Otto Ohlendorf	SS-Gruppenführer	1907–51	Executed for war crimes

EXTRACT FROM THE JÄGER REPORT

The following are just two pages from a six-sheet document listing the killings of Jews in Lithuania by *Einsatzkommando* 3, written by the commander of the liquidation squad. The final total of executions listed on sheet six was 137,346.

2.10.41	Zagare	633 Jews, 1,107 Jewesses, 496 Jewish children (as these Jews were being led away a mutiny rose, which was however immediately put down; 150 Jews were shot immediately; 7 partisans wounded)	2,236
4.10.41	Kauen-F.IX	315 Jews, 712 Jewesses, 818 Jewish children (reprisal after German police officer shot in ghetto)	1,845
29.10.41	Kauen-F.IX	2,007 Jews, 2,920 Jewesses, 4,273 Jewish children (mopping up ghetto of superfluous Jews)	9,200
3.11.41	Lazdijai	485 Jews, 511 Jewesses, 539 Jewish children	1,535
15.11.41	Wilkowiski	36 Jews, 48 Jewesses, 31 Jewish children	115
25.11.41	Kauen-F.IX	1,159 Jews, 1,600 Jewesses, 175 Jewish children (resettlers from Berlin, Munich and Frankfurt am main)	2,934
29.11.41	Kauen-F.IX	693 Jews, 1,155 Jewesses, 152 Jewish children (resettlers from from Vienna and Breslau)	2,000
29.11.41	Kauen-F.IX	17 Jews, 1 Jewess, for contravention of ghetto law, 1 Reichs German who converted to the Jewish faith and attended rabbinical school, then 15 terrorists from the Kalinin group	34
EK 3 detachment in Dunanberg in the period 13.7-21.8.41:		9,012 Jews, Jewesses and Jewish children, 573 active Comm.	9,585
EK 3 detachment in Wilna: 12.8-1.9.41 City of Wilna		425 Jews, 19 Jewesses, 8 Comm. (m.), 9 Comm. (f.)	461
2.9.41 City of Wilna		864 Jews, 2,019 Jewesses, 817 Jewish children (sonderaktion because German soldiers shot at by Jews)	3,700
		Total carried forward	99,084

12.9.41	City of Wilna	993 Jews, 1,670 Jewesses, 771 Jewish children	3,334
17.9.41	City of Wilna	337 Jews, 687 Jewesses, 247 Jewish children and 4 Lith. Comm.	1,271
20.9.41	Nemencing	128 Jews, 176 Jewesses, 99 Jewish children	403
22.9.41	Novo-Wilejka	468 Jews, 495 Jewesses, 196 Jewish children	1,159
24.9.41	Riesa	512 Jews, 744 Jewesses, 511 Jewish children	1,767
25.9.41	Jahiunai	215 Jews, 229 Jewesses, 131 Jewish children	575
27.9.41	Eysisky	989 Jews, 1,636 Jewesses, 821 Jewish children	3,446
30.9.41	Trakai	366 Jews, 483 Jewesses, 597 Jewish children	1,446
4.10.41	City of Wilna	432 Jews, 1,115 Jewesses, 436 Jewish children	1,983
6.10.41	Semiliski	213 Jews, 359 Jewesses, 390 Jewish children	962
9.10.41	Svenciany	1,169 Jews, 1,840 Jewesses, 717 Jewish children	3,726
16.10.41	City of Wilna	382 Jews, 507 Jewesses, 257 Jewish children	1,146
21.10.41	City of Wilna	718 Jews, 1,063 Jewesses, 586 Jewish children	2,367
25.10.41	City of Wilna	1,776 Jewesses, 812 Jewish children	2,578
27.10.41	City of Wilna	946 Jews, 184 Jewesses, 73 Jewish children	1,203
30.10.41	City of Wilna	382 Jews, 789 Jewesses, 362 Jewish children	1,553
6.11.41	City of Wilna	340 Jews, 749 Jewesses, 252 Jewish children	1,341
19.11.41	City of Wilna	76 Jews, 77 Jewesses, 18 Jewish children	171
19.11.41	City of Wilna	6 POW's, 8 Poles	14
20.11.41	City of Wilna	3 POW's	3
25.11.41	City of Wilna	9 Jews, 46 Jewesses, 8 Jewish children, 1 Pole for possesion of arms and other military equipment	64

situation report later in September 1941 observed that:

...the ever increasing security tasks cannot be solved by the Einsatzkommandos alone, since they are too weak for this purpose, mounting importance is being attached to the creation and organization of a regular police service. Well screened, particularly reliable Ukrainians are employed for this purpose; moreover, a network of confidential agents, predominantly composed of ethnic Germans, has been created with great success.

This report is particularly revealing, as it clearly states that the German forces alone were insufficient to cope with the demands of their extermination, deportation and ghettoization activities. It is an unpalatable fact that it was not only German Nazis who were responsible for the Holocaust. Yet disloyalty cuts both ways, and later in the war the Germans often found that previously allied locals jumped ship to assist the Partisans.

Case study – Babi Yar

The actions of *Einsatzgruppe* C at Babi Yar from 29 September 1941 are a typically horrifying example of how *Einsatzgruppen* operations were conducted, and how they generated such dizzying death tolls.

On 19 September 1941, Kiev, the capital of the Ukraine, fell to the Germans as part of Operation *Barbarossa*, and *Einsatzgruppe* C quickly moved into the streets to vent its wrath on the city's large Jewish community. The Jewish population of Kiev was huge, but any vestige of mercy was lost through the German casualties taken by booby traps left by the retreating Soviet forces.

Einsatzgruppe C's commander, *SS-Brigadeführer* Otto Rasch, consulted with the local HSSPF, *SS-Obergruppenführer* Friedrich Jeckeln, to decide on a course of action. The selected option was the liquidation of

all Kiev's Jews, the chosen execution site being the large ravine of Babi Yar just outside the city. The operation would be assisted by various security service and *Waffen-SS* personnel, plus units of local auxiliary police, formed into two special *Kommandos*, who appeared more than willing to help out with the operations.

First the Germans had to assemble the Jews. Leaflets were distributed that read out the following message:

All Jews of the city of Kiev and its environs must appear on Monday, September 29, 1941, by 8:00 AM on the corner of Melnikov and Dokterivsky streets (near the cemetery). You are to take your documents, money, valuables, warm clothes, linen etc. Whoever of the Jews does not fulfill

this order and is found in another place, shall be shot. Any citizen who enters the apartments that have been left and takes ownership of items will be shot.

On 29 September 1941, the first, huge columns of Jews were led out to the ravine at Babi Yar. As they approached the ravine, they were stopped and ordered to remove all their clothes and hand over their valuables. They were then channelled between tight ranks of SS soldiers to the edge of the ravine, where they were formed up into large groups and machine-gunned or shot individually and cast into the ravine. Some 33,771 people were killed in this way in a period of only two days, according to the official SS reports.

The Babi Yar ravine was the site of *Einsatzgruppen* murder operations for a long period after the initial actions against Kiev's Jews. Gypsies, Soviet POWs and psychiatric patients also joined the ranks of the dead in the bottom of the ravine, which ultimately may have held up to 100,000 corpses.

By mid-1943, the war was turning against the Germans, and it was desperately realized that Babi Yar constituted profound evidence against the SS. At that point the SS decided to remove that evidence, and during a grim six-week operation local concentration camp inmates were forced to exhume and burn the rotting bodies.

Paul Blobel, the commander of *Sonderkommando* 4a, a sub-unit of *Einsatzgruppe* C, later testified to the Nuremberg trial judges about the body removal operations, which he witnessed in August 1943:

SELECTED POLISH VILLAGES SUBJECTED TO NAZI 'PACIFICATION' OPERATIONS

Village name	Killed	Village name	Killed
Borów	232 (103 children)	Szczecyn	368 (71 children)
Cyców	111	Wanaty	109
Jamy	147	Zamosc	470
Kaszyce	117	Szczebrzeszyn	208
Kitów	174	Labunie	210
Krasowo-Czestki	257 (83 children)	Krasnogród	285
Krusze	148	Mokre	304
Kulno	100	Nielisz	301
Lipniak-Majorat	more than 370	Nowa Osada	195
Lazek	187	Radecznica	212
Michniów	203 (48 children)	Skierbieszow	335
Milejów	150	Stary Zamosc	287
Mrozy	more than 100	Suchowola	324
Olszanka	103	Sulów	252
Rajsk	more than 143	Tereszpol	344
Rózaniec	c.200	Wysokie	203
Skloby	265	Zwierzyniec	412
Smoligów	c.200	Kitowa	165
Sochy	183	Królewiec/Szalas	more than 100 each
Sumin	118		

During my visit in August I myself observed the burning of bodies in a mass grave near Kiev. This grave was about 55m [180ft] long, 3m [10ft] wide and 2.5m [8ft] deep. After the top had been removed the bodies were covered with inflammable material and ignited. It took about two days until the grave burned down to the bottom. I myself observed that the fire had glowed down to the bottom. After that the grave was filled in and the traces were now practically obliterated.

In this way the SS managed to remove many of the traces of its hideous work. Enough survivors and scraps of evidence remained, however, to bring the crime to light. Furthermore, although massacres such as that perpetrated at Babi Yar resulted in an enormous death toll, Himmler came to regard such killings as grossly inefficient, and looked for other methods of execution.

'Humane' killings

Himmler's witnessing of *Einsatzgruppen* operations seems to have had a curious effect on his outlook. Several speeches and testimonies indicate a growing concern not for the victims of the killings, but for the moral and mental health of the killers. His solution to this problem was to implement methods of execution that distanced the soldiers from their victims.

At this point in time, gassing was being developed both as a method of euthanizing mentally and physically disabled children and of delivering the emerging 'Final Solution'. In

September 1941, *SS-Obersturmbann- führer* Walter Rauff, an official in the RSHA, commissioned transportation service chief Friedrich Pradel to develop a special gassing truck that could be used as a means of mass execution in the Soviet territories. After the war, Rauff explained the logic of the gas vans in action:

So far as the extermination of Jews in Russia is concerned, I know that gas vans were used... I don't believe that Pradel took the initiative in the development of the gas vans. He must have been under orders, either from me or my superiors. Did I think twice about employing the gas vans? I couldn't say. At the time the most important consideration for me was the psychological stress felt by the men involved in the shootings. This problem was overcome by the use of gas vans.

(Kogon, 1993)

The gas vans used in the East were essentially regular box lorries, but with the box hermetically sealed and with the exhaust fumes diverted into the interior. The victims were herded inside the vehicle and the doors closed, whereupon they were killed by carbon monoxide poisoning.

After the war, an *Einsatzkommando* 5 driver named Wilhelm Findeisen testified to how the gas van procedure worked:

The gas van was deployed for the first time in Kiev. My job was to just drive the vehicle. The van was loaded by the local staff. About forty people were loaded inside. There were men, women, and children. I

was supposed to tell the people they were going to be put to work. The people were pushed up a short ladder and into the van. The van door was then bolted shut, and the hose was attached. It was already in place – I did that too, it was cold at the time. I drove through the town to the antitank ditches. There the doors of the vehicle were opened. Prisoners had to do this. The bodies were thrown into the antitank ditches.

(Kogon, 1993)

The gas vans did their work between late 1941 and 1944. Hundreds of

ESTIMATES OF HOLOCAUST DEATH TOLL, BY NATIONALITY		
Country	Initial Jewish Population	Estimated Killed
Austria	185,000	65,000
Belgium	65,700	28,900
Bohemia- Moravia	118,310	71,150
Denmark	7800	60
Estonia	4500	2000
Finland	2000	7
France	350,000	77,320
Germany	214,000	200,000
Greece	77,380	67,000
Hungary	800,000	596,000
Italy	44,500	7680
Latvia	95,000	80,000
Lithuania	168,000	143,000
Luxembourg	3000	1950
Netherlands	140,000	100,000
Norway	1700	762
Poland	3,300,000	3,000,000
Romania	342,000	287,000
Slovakia	88,950	71,000
USSR	3,020,000	1,100,000
Yugoslavia	78,000	63,300

thousands of Jews were murdered in this way, typically taking about 15 minutes to succumb to the fumes, usually while being driven to their graves. Such was Himmler's more humane method of execution.

Yet still the gas vans were an imperfect solution for Himmler, principally on account of the limited number of people that could be killed at any one time. The mechanism of murder needed to be upgraded in terms of scale if it was to achieve Himmler and Hitler's overall purpose of ridding Europe of its Jewish population.

▼ GHETTOS IN OCCUPIED EUROPE

The ghetto system was integral to the Final Solution. When _Einsatzgruppen_ moved into an urban area with a high concentration of Jews, a certain area of the city was sealed off by German forces and the Jews were relocated into the ghetto thus created. Once in the ghetto, the Jews could be controlled more easily in terms of deporting them to the concentration and extermination camps, or liquidating them in batches in _Einsatzgruppen_ operations. The horrible conditions inside the ghettos also added daily natural attrition to the Germans' advantage.

GHETTOS IN OCCUPIED EUROPE, 1939–45*

KEY
- ■ Ghetto established 1939–May 1941
- ■ Ghetto established June 1941–1943
- ■ Ghetto established 1944

* Shows 1939 borders

Totenkopfverbände and the Final Solution

Regardless of the undoubted bravery of the Waffen-SS *in combat, the SS is popularly remembered as being the human engine that drove the Holocaust. The SS was central to the conception, planning and execution of the Final Solution at every stage.*

The Holocaust was, in many ways, Himmler's personal project. There is no doubt that Hitler planted the seeds of *Die Endlösung* (The Final Solution), and protected the interests of the programme. An entry in Joseph Goebbels' diary for 12 December 1941 clarified the issue of responsibility:

With respect of the Jewish Question, the Führer *has decided to make a clean sweep. He prophesied to the Jews that if they again brought about a world war, they would live to see their annihilation in it. That wasn't just a catch-word.*

The world war is here, and the annihilation of the Jews must be the necessary consequence.

(McFee, http://www.holocaust-history.org/hitler-final-solution)

Combined with Hitler's obvious suport for the *Einsatzgruppen* operations in the East, and his close working relationship with Himmler, there is little doubt that Hitler's aspirations ignited the Holocaust.

Yet the detailed implementation of the mass murder programme was largely delivered through Himmler's SS. Such is not to say that the SS

was the only body that made the Holocaust a reality. As was seen in the case of the *Einsatzgruppen* in the previous section, the killing of millions was a project that required the assistance of a multitude of different people, and they included local and state officials, industrial concerns, police forces, civil servants and the general citizenry. Indeed, historian Michael Berenbaum has argued that in effect Germany became a 'genocidal state', with every portion of society sharing in the blame through either complicity or knowledge.

The SS, however, was the true centre of the Holocaust. Its top leadership commissioned both the *Einsatzgruppen* operations in the East and oversaw the establishment and running of the extermination camp system. *SS-Totenkopfverbände* guards manned the camps with appalling brutality. The ghetto and deportation systems were managed by SS officials. SS security agents were responsible for hunting down Jews within the occupied territories. At every stage, therefore, the SS was the shadow that hung over the Jews.

Euthanasia
Nazi ideology was obsessed with the idea of physical and hereditary 'health', and of keeping the Aryan people 'pure'. From that perspective, mental and physical disabilities were

WANNSEE CONFERENCE, 20 JANUARY 1942 – PARTICIPANTS LISTED IN OFFICIAL MINUTES OF MEETING	
Participant	*Position/Department*
SS-Obergruppenführer Reinhard Heydrich	Chief of the RSHA and *Reichsprotektor* of Bohemia-Moravia
Dr Josef Bühler	Government of the General Government
Dr Roland Freisler	Reich Ministry of Justice
SS-Gruppenführer Otto Hofmann	Race and Resettlement Main Office
SA-Oberführer Dr Gerhard Klopfer	NSDAP Chancellery
Ministerialdirektor Friedrich Wilhelm Kritzinger	Reich Chancellery
SS-Sturmbannführer Dr Rudolf Lange	Deputy Commander of the SS in Latvia
Reichsamtleiter Dr Georg Leibbrandt	Reich Ministry for the Occupied Eastern Territories
Dr Martin Luther	Foreign Office
Gauleiter Dr Alfred Meyer	Reich Ministry for the Occupied Eastern Territories
SS-Gruppenführer Heinrich Müller	Chief of *Amt* IV (*Gestapo*), Reich Main Security Office (RSHA)
Erich Neumann	Director, Office of the Four-Year Plan
SS-Oberführer Dr Karl Eberhard Schöngarth	SD, assigned to the General Government
Dr Wilhelm Stuckart	Reich Ministry for the Interior
SS-Obersturmbannführer Adolf Eichmann	Head of *Referat* IV B4 of the *Gestapo*, recording secretary

selected as obvious problems, and were denoted as a burden on both state and posterity. Nazi magazines included articles that emphasized the financial weight placed on the state and on families through having to deliver a lifetime's care to disabled individuals. Such propaganda was actually laying the groundwork for something far more insidious. In August 1939, a Nazi directive from the Minister of the Interior ordered physicians and maternity staff to report cases of disabilities in babies and children under three years old. From the following October, parents were encouraged to present such children at what were to surface appearances specialist pediatric centres – in fact the children were killed there by lethal injection or even by simply leaving them to starve.

This was just the beginning of the Nazi 'euthanasia' programme. Over time, the age group for selection was extended up to 17 years old, resulting in the murder of some 7000 mentally and physically disabled children. The programme, labelled *Aktion* T4 (Action T4), eventually adopted a broader and more comprehensive classification system – which included patients with conditions such as epilepsy and dementia – and therefore required more efficient killing methods. Six gassing centres were developed at secret locations, and between January 1940 and August 1941 some 70,273 people were executed there in fake shower blocks filled with carbon monoxide gas. These killings were a haunting indicator of what was to come, and the SS was centrally involved at every stage.

Heading *Aktion* T4 was SS officer Christian Wirth, a former *Kripo* agent. Wirth conducted the very first *Aktion* T4 gassing at the prison at Brandenburg an der Havel. (Note that Reich Chancellery officials Philipp Bouhler and Viktor Brack were also present at the gassing and it was Bouhler who suggested disguising the gas chambers as shower rooms.) Wirth would go on to run several more euthanasia centres before finally being appointed commandant of Belzec extermination camp in the winter of 1941. He would also assist in 'rationalizing' the processes of Treblinka camp. One SS man who served under Wirth recounted:

Wirth was more than brutal. In my opinion, his brutality was grounded more in his human nature, than as an emanation of his political mentality. He bellowed, screamed and threatened us, and hit members of the German camp garrison in the face. Other than Oberhauser, there was no-one in Belzec who was not afraid of Wirth.

Wirth was only one of the hardened SS individuals who participated in the *Aktion* T4 programme. SS men, for example, often dressed in white coats to appear as doctors while they transferred disabled patients out to the gassing centres. At the other extreme of the hierarchy, in December 1939 Himmler himself witnessed one of the gassings. It was evident that the euthanasia programme was a learning experience for all levels of the SS.

Public knowledge of the programme led to its cessation in theory in the summer of 1941, but by that time more than 70,000 people had been killed. Yet killing still continued in various covert ways throughout the rest of the war, and the *Aktion* T4 efforts blended into those of the *Einsatzgruppen* operations in the East – execution squads would target the patients in major municipal hospitals and asylums.

Between 1939 and 1941 it was evident that the SS was developing an industrial and scientific process of mass execution. Yet in terms of the Jews, there was no overall mechanism in place to coordinate the destruction of the entire ethnic group prior to 1941. That situation would

MASS EXTERMINATIONS IN THE DEATH CAMPS			
Camp	Commencement Date for Mass Killings	Main Method of Extermination	Estimated Death Toll
Chelmno	7 December 1941	Gas vans	320,000
Auschwitz-Birkenau	September 1941	Zyklon-B	1,200,000
Belzec	17 March 1942	Carbon monoxide gas	600,000
Sobibór	March 1942	Carbon monoxide gas	250,000
Treblinka	23 July 1942	Carbon monoxide gas	700,000
Majdanek	October 1942	Carbon monoxide and Zyklon B gas	1,380,000
Stutthof	June 1944	Zyklon-B gas	65,000

TOTENKOPF-STANDARTEN, WITH MANPOWER STRENGTHS

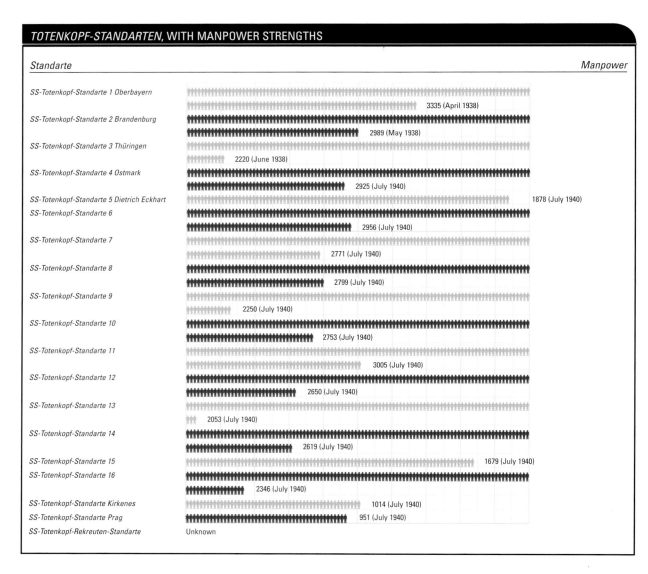

Standarte	Manpower
SS-Totenkopf-Standarte 1 Oberbayern	3335 (April 1938)
SS-Totenkopf-Standarte 2 Brandenburg	2989 (May 1938)
SS-Totenkopf-Standarte 3 Thüringen	2220 (June 1938)
SS-Totenkopf-Standarte 4 Ostmark	2925 (July 1940)
SS-Totenkopf-Standarte 5 Dietrich Eckhart	1878 (July 1940)
SS-Totenkopf-Standarte 6	2956 (July 1940)
SS-Totenkopf-Standarte 7	2771 (July 1940)
SS-Totenkopf-Standarte 8	2799 (July 1940)
SS-Totenkopf-Standarte 9	2250 (July 1940)
SS-Totenkopf-Standarte 10	2753 (July 1940)
SS-Totenkopf-Standarte 11	3005 (July 1940)
SS-Totenkopf-Standarte 12	2650 (July 1940)
SS-Totenkopf-Standarte 13	2053 (July 1940)
SS-Totenkopf-Standarte 14	2619 (July 1940)
SS-Totenkopf-Standarte 15	1679 (July 1940)
SS-Totenkopf-Standarte 16	2346 (July 1940)
SS-Totenkopf-Standarte Kirkenes	1014 (July 1940)
SS-Totenkopf-Standarte Prag	951 (July 1940)
SS-Totenkopf-Rekreuten-Standarte	Unknown

change in the early summer of 1941, when the concentration camp system was applied to new ends.

Concentration camps

Immediately upon taking power in 1933, Hitler needed a system in place for incarcerating enemies of the Nazi Party and state. What emerged at first was a mixed bag of prisons and minor detention camps dotted around the country, some run by the SA while others, such as the new camp at Dachau established in March 1933, were run by the SS.

Hitler's alienation from the SA in 1934 changed the landscape of the fledgling concentration camp system. From May of that year the SS took over control of the concentration camps, either adopting existing SA facilities or simply closing them down. By 1935 there were five main camps – Esterwegen, Lichtenburg, Moringen, Dachau and Sachsenburg – between them housing less than 4000 prisoners.

In charge of the concentration camp system was a man whose name would become synonymous with SS brutality – Theodor Eicke. Eicke was a fanatical Nazi loyalist who had joined the Party back in 1928. There were some serious questions about his mental health, his openly aggressive character prompting the *Gauleiter* of the Rhine- Palatinate, Josef Burckel, to attempt to detain him under psychiatric care on 21 March 1933. Yet Eicke's ideological loyalty (it was he who personally executed Ernst Röhm during the SA purge of 1934) and position as an *SS-Standartenführer* meant that he was destined for higher office under Himmler. In early July 1934 Eicke was promoted from his position at Dachau to *Inspekteur der Konzentrationslager und SS-Wachverbände* (Inspector of Concentration Camps and SS Guard Formations).

Eicke would be in charge of the concentration camps during their formative period between 1934 and 1939. Eventually he would go on to command the *Totenkopf* Division on active service, and his position passed to *SS-Gruppenführer* Richard Glücks. While in office, however, Eicke established a camp regime based upon terror, cruel (often fatal) discipline and a complete disregard for the well-being of the inmates, who to Eicke constituted the lowest form of life. He also oversaw the development of the *SS-Totenkopfverbände* (SS Death's Head Formations), the concentration camp guards put in place to run the camps at ground level. In the early days the guards underwent training at a special school in Dachau, and

thereafter went to serve the camp system with general cruelty. Historian Chris Ailsby here comments on the ethos that Eicke aimed to impart to the *SS-Totenkopfverbände*:

Eicke viewed the SS-Totenkopfverbände *(Death's Head unit) as an elite within the elite structure of the SS. This concept grew from the fact that the most dangerous political enemies of the state were incarcerated in the concentration camps and Hitler had given sole responsibility for guarding and running the camps to the* SS-Totenkopfverbände. *Eicke repeatedly pressed home his principles in orders, circulars and memoranda. The whole of the* SS-Totenkopfverbände *training was based on elitism, toughness and comradeship, together with a regime of ruthless discipline.*
(Ailsby, 1998)

An important point to note about the *SS-Totenkopfverbände* was that they were directly under the control of the camp commandant, rather than governed by a specific department within the camp. Therefore the actions of the camp guards typically had a straight link with the orders of the commander. Furthermore, the *SS-Totenkopfverbände* were, in the later extermination and concentration camps, heavily supported by auxiliaries from the occupied territories, typically fearsome Baltic, Russian or Ukrainian guards who could be some of the cruellest members of the camp force.

Between 1935 and 1939, the *SS-Totenkopfverbände* and the concentration camps expanded in both number and volume of inmates. New camps, including those established in Austria following the *Anschluss,* included Buchenwald, Mauthausen, Flossenbürg and Ravensbrück, the larger camps soon

RANKS OF THE *SS-TOTENKOPFVERBÄNDE*, FROM JULY 1940

- Reichsführer-SS
- SS-Obergruppenführer
- SS-Gruppenführer
- SS-Brigadeführer
- SS-Oberführer
- SS-Standartenführer
- SS-Obersturmbannführer
- SS-Sturmbannführer
- SS-Hauptsturmführer
- SS-Obersturmführer
- SS-Untersturmführer
- SS-Sturmscharführer
- SS-Hauptscharführer
- SS-Oberscharführer
- SS-Scharführer
- SS-Unterscharführer
- SS-Rottenführer
- SS-Sturmmann
- SS-Oberschütze
- SS-Schütze
- SS-Staffelbewerber

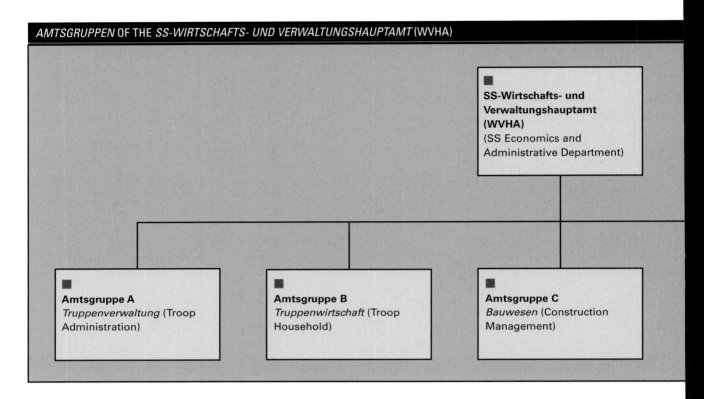

AMTSGRUPPEN OF THE *SS-WIRTSCHAFTS- UND VERWALTUNGSHAUPTAMT* (WVHA)

SS-Wirtschafts- und Verwaltungshauptamt (WVHA)
(SS Economics and Administrative Department)

Amtsgruppe A
Truppenverwaltung (Troop Administration)

Amtsgruppe B
Truppenwirtschaft (Troop Household)

Amtsgruppe C
Bauwesen (Construction Management)

exceeding 10,000 inmates each. Once the war began in September 1939, the growth of the camp system was explosive, both within Greater Germany and the occupied territories. Poland in particular became the recipient of major new camps. Unlike the German concentration camps of the 1930s, however, many of these establishments were designed around much different purposes.

The Final Solution

Die Endlösung was the ultimate programme for the extermination of European Jewry. Defining the exact moment when it was decided to murder all the Jews in occupied Europe is difficult. Certainly practical

arrangements began back in the early summer of 1941, when Hermann Göring ordered the head of the RSHA, Reinhard Heydrich, overseen by Himmler, to prepare a detailed proposal for achieving the Final Solution. A special commission was established to implement Operation *Reinhard*, the murder of Polish Jewry, and from September 1941 the first pure extermination camps began emerging in Poland. Previously, concentration camps had been primarily used as forced labour centres and places for the incarceration of political prisoners. The new camps – such as Treblinka, Chelmno, Sobibór, Majdanek and Belzec – were dedicated extermination centres, designed for

the industrial-scale killing of thousands of Jews by using specially designed gas chambers. The notorious Auschwitz-Birkenau complex also contained an extermination camp, although it should be noted that Auschwitz comprised three major camps, only one of which, Auschwitz II (Birkenau), was a death camp, albeit the most voracious of the killing centres.

The first experimental gassing of inmates at Auschwitz, using Zyklon-B cyanide gas, occurred on 3 September 1941, after which there were regular trials (usually on Soviet POWs) to refine the process. Many of the other camp commandants preferred to use carbon monoxide for

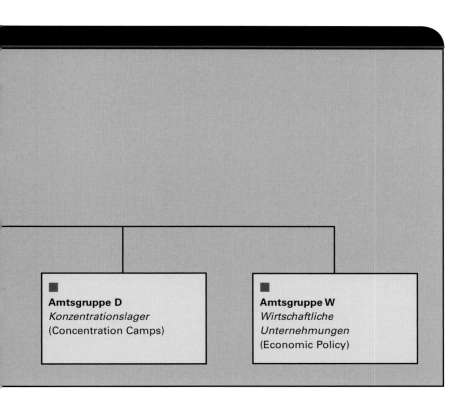

Amtsgruppe D
Konzentrationslager
(Concentration Camps)

Amtsgruppe W
*Wirtschaftliche
Unternehmungen*
(Economic Policy)

ghettoized, then deported to labour and/or extermination camps, where they would meet their end by gas, exhaustion or starvation. One key section of the chilling protocol ran as follows:

Under proper guidance, in the course of the final solution the Jews are to be allocated for appropriate labour in the East. Able-bodied Jews, separated according to sex, will be taken in large work columns to these areas for work on roads, in the course of which action doubtless a large portion will be eliminated by natural causes.

The possible final remnant will, since it will undoubtedly consist of the most resistant portion, have to be treated accordingly, because it is the product of natural selection and would, if released, act as the seed of a new Jewish revival (see the experience of history). In the course of the practical execution of the final solution, Europe will be combed through from west to east.

In the Wannsee Protocol, 'emigration' or 'evacuation' act as euphemisms for deportation and murder. Heydrich here proposes that the Jews are either killed through the 'natural causes' of forced labour, or from other means not defined, but already understood by those present.

Some Holocaust deniers have gone on to claim that the Wannsee Protocol certainly outlines a forced labour programme but not a plan for mass extermination. Yet there seems no doubt that in the minds of the Nazi hierarchy this was exactly what was intended. Robert Ley, who was

the gassing operations, provided either from bottled sources or, more typically, by simply venting engine exhaust fumes directly into the sealed gas chamber. Individuals such as Christian Wirth felt that carbon monoxide would generate less suspicion in the outside world than would ordering large quantities of Zyklon-B.

The Wannsee Conference

While the techniques of mass murder were being modelled, Heydrich was nearing the end of his planning process for the destruction of Europe's Jews. It culminated in the so-called Wannsee Conference, a meeting headed by Heydrich at Wannsee in the Berlin suburbs. The people attending the conference were admittedly not all SS members, but included figures from key Nazi state and Party offices. Yet the SS was represented not only by Heydrich as chair of the meeting, and mastermind of the proposal, but also by SS leaders from the *Gestapo* and SS field commanders who had experience of mass killings.

The purpose of the conference was nothing less than the discussion of the Final Solution, and the minutes of the meeting have survived. The Wannsee Protocol, as the final document was called, used veiled language to propose the total eradication of Jews in Europe. Essentially, Jews from all parts of the Greater German Reich were to be present at Wannsee, later told a conference in May 1942 that 'It is not enough to isolate the Jewish enemy of mankind, the Jews have to be exterminated.' It would be the responsibility of the SS to implement this objective.

Running the camps

For the Nazis to achieve their goals of stripping Germany and occupied Europe of its Jews, the process of collection and killing had to be conducted with industrial rigour. The darkest expression of this objective in action can be seen in a typical gassing operation, such as was used in all the major extermination camps, and in how the SS personnel fitted

into this process. It should be remembered that the following description is a generalization only, and the priorities might change according to the proportions of arrivals drawn off for execution and those destined first for labour duties.

Deported Jews would arrive by rail in cattle cars, having spent days on the train with no food and water – transit alone killed thousands of individuals. On arrival, they were met by the *SS-Totenkopfverbände*, who would immediately begin the process of separating the women and children from the men. (In some instances, however, the entire trainload of people would be consigned immediately to gassing.)

Herded off the train, the arrivals passed through a selection process in which SS medical staff distinguished between those could work, and those who would go to the gas chambers (women with dependent children, the children themselves, and the elderly were almost always in the latter category). Those selected for gassing were then moved straight to the execution block, where they were told to strip naked and prepare themselves for a shower or delousing. Great care was taken to maintain the illusion that nothing insidious awaited them. They were then funnelled into the gas chamber, where they would be executed either by Zyklon-B gas

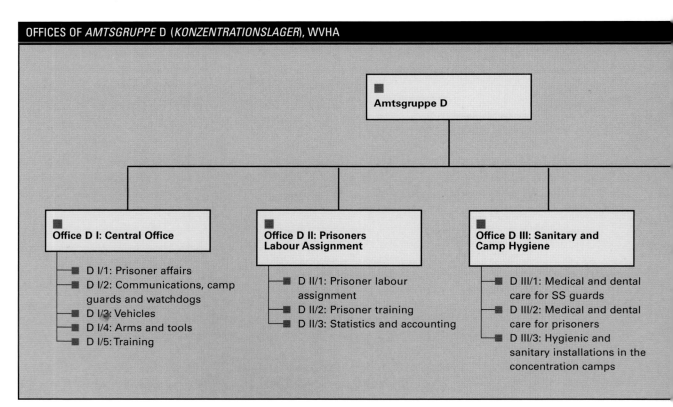

OFFICES OF *AMTSGRUPPE* D (*KONZENTRATIONSLAGER*), WVHA

Amtsgruppe D

Office D I: Central Office
- D I/1: Prisoner affairs
- D I/2: Communications, camp guards and watchdogs
- D I/3: Vehicles
- D I/4: Arms and tools
- D I/5: Training

Office D II: Prisoners Labour Assignment
- D II/1: Prisoner labour assignment
- D II/2: Prisoner training
- D II/3: Statistics and accounting

Office D III: Sanitary and Camp Hygiene
- D III/1: Medical and dental care for SS guards
- D III/2: Medical and dental care for prisoners
- D III/3: Hygienic and sanitary installations in the concentration camps

(delivered in the form of pellets dropped through holes in the roof) or by carbon monoxide gas. The deaths of several hundred people could be watched through an observation glass in the chamber door, and the whole killing process took some 15 to 20 minutes.

Once silence prevailed, the doors were opened and the gas allowed to disperse. Then the *Sonderkommando* (Special Unit) – Jewish prisoners forced to assist in the killing process – faced the hideous task of removing all the bodies for cremation. They were also responsible for removing any gold teeth from the corpses, this gold eventually being melted down and turned into an additional source of Reich revenue. All the Jews' belongings were also processed in separate facilities, many SS men building considerable wealth through robbing the valued possessions of the deceased.

Although killing hundreds of thousands of people was a black art many of the camps seemed to perfect, the greatest 'challenge' remained body disposal. Cremation was always the preferred method, either via crematoria or, more crudely, in huge open pits. Auschwitz-Birkenau, when it reached the point of maximum efficiency in 1942 and 1943, could gas and cremate up to 20,000 people a day. Those who had escaped gassing were in no sense reprieved – they were typically worked, starved or tortured to death.

Special duties

The process of killing was the paramount focus of the extermination camps, but as we have indicated in earlier chapters they were also the focus of huge volumes of economic activity for Himmler. The labour camps, and the labour sections of the extermination camps, provided endless slave labour for the SS. By the beginning of 1945, for example, the SS had 511,537 male prisoners and 202,674 female prisoners registered in the camps, all forced to work for the Reich.

For the inmates, the line between work and execution was a blurred one. A typical working day, such as in a quarry or factory, would last from around 5 a.m. or 6 a.m. (depending on the season) until around 8 p.m., at which point the ragged inmates would stand for hours in all weathers while they underwent roll call. The only food that they would receive in their working day was typically two or three bowls of thin gruel, occasionally augmented with some vegetables or a small piece of bread, cheese paste or gristly meat. All this combined with terrible hygiene and constant disease meant that conditions in the labour camps led to a minimum 10 per cent attrition amongst workers, rising much higher in the last years of war. More than 110,000 workers died between July 1942 and June 1943 alone.

For the SS, the relationship between prisoners and profit remained a healthy one. From March 1942, local factories run by the SS or private enterprises could order bulk volumes of prisoners for work duties, and the SS would charge the companies for each individual used. While many of the projects were soul-crushing manual labour, the SS also applied slave labour to production facilities for advanced armaments programmes, as Johannes Tuchel here illustrates:

In 1944 the network of concentration camps reached its zenith. Parts of the armament industry were moved below ground. Flossenbürg prisoners produced aircraft for Messerschmitt underground, and Neuengamme prisoners set up gigantic factory complexes in the caves of Porta Westfalica. In October 1944 the Dora-Mittelbau camp near Nordhausen in the Harz mountains, until then a satellite command of Buchenwald, was converted into an independent camp. Here,

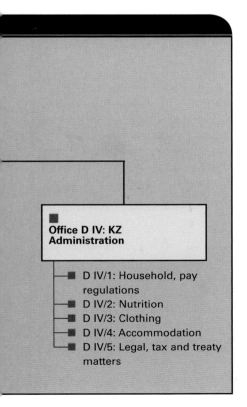

Office D IV: KZ Administration

- D IV/1: Household, pay regulations
- D IV/2: Nutrition
- D IV/3: Clothing
- D IV/4: Accommodation
- D IV/5: Legal, tax and treaty matters

components for the V-weapons were produced under unimaginable conditions.

(Dear, 1995)

The industrial outputs of Himmler's slave labour were based on mass turnover of personnel, not on individual productivity, so the SS guards had little concern with long-term decent treatment. Even those people sent to labour camps, rather than extermination centres, still suffered appallingly and lived short, brutal lives at the mercy of violent, dehumanized individuals.

Death toll

What is truly horrifying about the Final Solution is the scale of its twisted achievements. The estimated six million Jews who were murdered included three million Poles, 1.1 million Soviets, 596,000 Hungarians and 287,000 Romanians. Other

LIST OF NAZI CONCENTRATION CAMPS

Camp Name	Country (today)	Camp Type	Years
Amersfoort	Netherlands	Prison and transit camp	1941–45
Arbeitsdorf	Germany	Labour camp	1942
Auschwitz-Birkenau	Poland	Extermination and labour camp	1940–45
Banjica	Serbia	Concentration camp	1941–44
Bardufoss	Norway	Concentration camp	1944 – ?
Belzec	Poland	Extermination camp	1942–43
Bergen-Belsen	Germany	Collection point	1943–45
Berlin-Marzahn	Germany	Early a 'rest place' then labour camp	1936– ?
Bolzano	Italy	Transit camp	1944–45
Bredtvet	Norway	Concentration camp	1941–45
Breendonk	Belgium	Prison and labour camp	1940–44
Breitenau	Germany	'Early wild camp', then labour camp	1933–34, 1940–45
Buchenwald	Germany	Labour camp	1937–45
Chelmno (Kulmhof)	Poland	Extermination camp	1941–43, 1944–45
Crveni krst	Serbia	Concentration camp	1941–45
Dachau	Germany	Labour camp	1933–45
Falstad	Norway	Prison camp	1941–45
Flossenbürg	Germany	Labour camp	1938–45
Grini	Norway	Prison camp	1941–45
Gross-Rosen	Poland	Labour camp; Nacht und Nebel camp	1940–45
KZ Herzogen-busch (Vught)	Netherlands	Prison and transit camp	1943–44
Hinzert	Germany	Collection point and sub-camp	1940–45
Janowska (Lvóv)	Ukraine	Ghetto; transit, labour, and extermination camp	1941–43
Jasenovac	Croatia	Extermination camp	1941–45
Kaiserwald (Mezaparks)	Latvia	Labour camp	1942–44
Kaufering /Landsberg	Germany	Labour camp	1943–45
Kauen (Kaunas)	Lithuania	Ghetto and internment camp	?

Camp Name	Country (today)	Camp Type	Years
Klooga	Estonia	Labour camp	1943–44
Lager Sylt (Alderney)	Channel Islands	Labour camp	1943–44
Langenstein-Zwieberge	Germany	Buchenwald sub-camp	1944–45
Le Vernet	France	Internment camp	1939–44
Majdanek (KZ Lublin)	Poland	Extermination camp	1941–44
Malchow	Germany	Labour and transit camp	1943–45
Maly Trostenets	Belorussia	Extermination camp	1941–44
Mauthausen-Gusen	Austria	Labour camp	1938–45
Mittelbau-Dora	Germany	Labour camp	1943–45
Natzweiler-Struthof	France	Labour camp; Nacht und Nebel camp	1941–44
Neuengamme	Germany	Labour camp	1938–45
Niederhagen	Germany	Prison and labour camp	1941–43
Oranienburg	Germany	Collection point	1933–34
Osthofen	Germany	Collection point	1933–34
Plaszów	Poland	Labour camp	1942–45
Ravensbrück	Germany	Labour camp for women	1939–45
Risiera di San Sabba (Trieste)	Italy	Police detainment camp	1943–45
Sachsenhausen	Germany	Labour camp	1936–45
Sajmiste	Serbia	Extermination camp	1941–44
Salaspils	Latvia	Labour camp	1941–44
Sobibór	Poland	Extermination camp	1942–43
Soldau	Poland	Labour; transit camp	1939–45
Stutthof	Poland	Labour camp and extermination camp	1939–45
Theresienstadt (Terezín)	Czech Republic	Transit camp and ghetto	1941–45
Treblinka	Poland	Extermination camp	1942–43
Vaivara	Estonia	Concentration and transit camp	1943–44
Warsaw	Poland	Labour and extermination camp	1942–44
Westerbork	Netherlands	Collection point	1940–45

LOCATIONS OF MAJOR CONCENTRATION AND EXTERMINATION CAMPS, 1939–45*

KEY
- ■ Extermination camps
- ■ Concentration camps

Klooga
Vaivara
ESTONIA
LATVIA
Kaiserwald
LITHUANIA
Kaunas
Vilnius
Stutthof
Maly Trostenets
Neuengamme
Ravensbrück
Papenburg
Sachsenhausen
Plaszów
Treblinka
POLAND
Belsen
BERLIN
WARSAW
AMSTERDAM
Chelmno
Arbeitsdorf
Lvov
Sobibór
Dora-Mittelbau
Schileben
Majdanek
Belzec
Breendonk
Buchenwald
Auschwitz-Birkenau
Lvov
BRUSSELS
Ohrdruf
PRAGUE
Drancy
Lety
Hodonin
PARIS
GERMANY
Flossenbürg
Novaky
Natzweiler
VIENNA
Sered
Dachau
Mauthausen
Kistarcsa
Landsberg
Nartheim
BUDAPEST
HUNGARY
ROMANIA
Bolzano
FRANCE
Jasenovac
Sajmiste
Asti
Schabatz
Nisch
ITALY
Banjica
Le Vernet

* Shows 1939 borders

countries' Jewish populations suffered much fewer deaths, but as a percentage of the total national Jewish population the death toll of the Holocaust reveals the 'success' of the Nazi plan. Greece, for example, was stripped of 87 per cent of its Jewish population, the Netherlands of 71 per cent, Slovakia of 80 per cent and Germany itself of 36 per cent.

Poland, with its total Jewish population of 3.3 million, suffered a unique level of horror – 91 per cent of its Jews were murdered. Hitler nearly triumphed in eradicating Jews as a presence in Europe. In addition, 224,000 Sinti and Roma had also been murdered by 1945.

The peak of extermination camp activity was in 1942/43. After that,

▲ **CONCENTRATION AND EXTERMINATION CAMPS**
Poland was the principal location for the extermination camps. Partly this is because of the desire to eradicate Poland's Jews in their entirety, and partly because its location was a conveniently centralized destination for the deportation of Jews from other parts of Eastern Europe.

the changing fortunes of war disrupted the efficient transit of Jews to the gas chambers, and by late 1944 there was also increasing panic amongst the SS that their crimes were about to be discovered. Such fears did not stop the murders – if anything there seemed to be a desparate desire to eradicate the surviving Jews as potential witnesses. When the Soviets approached Poland in 1944, and then Germany in 1945, the concentration camp guards sometimes simply torched entire housing blocks with the prisoners inside, or forced the inmates on torturous marches deeper into Germany, executing all who fell by the wayside. During January 1945, for example, around 15,000 camp inmates died or were killed when some 60,000 prisoners were forced to make one such march. In total, it is estimated that some 100,000 people were killed during the evacuations of major Polish camps during the winter of 1945, and those that made it to Germany were often worked to death constructing the last-ditch defences of the Third Reich.

Liberation

The liberation of the extermination camps in 1945 brought salvation for many, but for thousands of others even liberation came too late – 13,000 people in Bergen-Belsen died of

DEPARTMENTS OF *AMTSGRUPPE* W, WVHA, WITH RESPONSIBILITIES

Division	Responsibility	Notes
Amt I	**Excavations and Quarries**	
Amt I(i)	Brickworks	Brickworks at Buchenwald, Neuengamme, Sachsenhausen and Stutthof labour camps
Amt I(ii)	Quarries	Granite mined at Gross-Rosen, Mauthausen and Natzweiler camps; stone quarried at Rotau and Linz
Amt I(iii)	Porcelain and Pottery	Allach factory main producer; other factories in Bohemia-Moravia
Amt II	**Building Materials**	
Amt II(i)	Building materials	Posen, Bielitz and Zichenau
Amt II(ii)	Cement	Auschwitz provided labour for Golleschau factory
Amt II(iii)	Eastern businesses	Controlled businesses captured from the Soviets
Amt III	**Food Industry**	
Amt III(i)	Mineral waters	SS controlled several mineral water companies, including Sudentenquell, Mattoni and Apollinaris, plus Rheinglassfabrik bottling plant
Amt III(ii)	Meat	Meat processing operations at Auschwitz, Dachau and Sachsenhausen
Amt III(iii)	Bread	Major bakeries at Auschwitz, Dachau, Herzogenbosch, Lublin, Plasnow and Sachsenhausen
Amt IV	**German Equipment**	
Amt IV(i)	Military equipment	Camps such as Auschwitz, Neuengamme, Dachau and Sachsenhausen involved in weapons/equipment manufacture and repair; camps provided contract labour for major aircraft companies
Amt IV(ii)	Carpentry	Both military and civilian furniture produced
Amt IV(iii)	Clothing	Produced uniforms and webbing for *Wehrmacht* and the SS
Amt V	**Land, Forestry and Fisheries**	
Amt V(i)	Food and nutrition	Investigations into animal breeding programmes, diet and alternative medicine
Amt V(ii)	Forestry	Controlled SS-owned forests and land
Amt V(iii)	Fisheries	Fish-processing operations
Amt VI	**Textiles and Leatherwork**	Repairs and reworkings of uniforms and leather items of kit, carried out at Dachau and Ravensbrück
Amt VII	**Books and Publishing**	
Amt VII(i)	Publishing	Ran Germanic-culture publishing house, Nordland-Verlag
Amt VII(ii)	Art restoration	Ran art restoration company Bauer und Cie; acquired artworks for Himmler
Amt VIII	**Cultural Buildings**	
Amt VIII(i)	Historic buildings and monuments	Conducted renovation and maintenance of important buildings
Amt VIII(ii)	King Heinrich Memorial Trust	Ran special historical trust established by Himmler

disease and the effects of their ill-treatment after the Allies took over the camps. By this time, many SS guards had simply vanished back into wider society, there to don civilian clothes and live regular lives. Those caught in the camps could be treated to summary justice – after Dachau was liberated in April 1945, horrified US soldiers summarily shot some 122 SS guards in a spontaneous act of vengeance. Camp commandants often attempted to evade justice. *SS-Obersturmbannführer* Rudolf Franz Ferdinand Höß, the commander of Auschwitz, eluded his pursuers for the best part of a year, disguising

himself as a farmer. Only when betrayed by his wife and captured did he give up his real identity, going on

to stand trial and face the hangman. For Höß and others, retribution had come home.

EXPERIMENTS CONDUCTED AT SELECTED CONCENTRATION CAMPS	
Experiment	*Known centre of experimentation*
Immersion hypothermia	Dachau and Auschwitz
Malaria infection	Dachau
Mustard gas exposure	Sachsenhausen, Natzweiler
Sulfonamide experiments	Ravensbrück
Sea water ingestion	Dachau
Sterilization experiments	Dachua, Auschwitz, Ravensbrück
Poisoning	Buchenwald
Phosphorus burns	Buchenwald
Altitude effects	Dachau
Genetic experiment on twins	Auschwitz

War Crimes Trials

With the end of the war and the revelation of the Holocaust came the Allied desire for retribution. Dozens of SS camp guards and commanders were apprehended, tried and executed, but hundreds more remained free.

The post-war trials of German war criminals are famously known as the Nuremberg trials, although not all of the court proceedings were conducted at Nuremberg. There were essentially two waves of trials. The first ran from November 1945 to October 1946, and were targeted at the big names of the Nazi leadership. Some 22 key figures were put on trial, including Göring, Hess, Ribbentrop, Kaltenbrunner, Rosenberg, Frank and Neurath. This prolonged trial went to the heart of ultimate responsibility for the Holocaust, and resulted in most of the defendants being either executed or imprisoned. The second wave of trials ran from November 1946 to April

1949, during which US Military Tribunals brought a further 185 people to court. Arranged according to 12 different categories of trial, this second wave was much more concerned with the people who delivered the Holocaust in the field, and was fundamentally targeted at SS personnel. The 12 categories of cases, and their foci, were as follows:

1) Medical Trial – Nazi medical experiments
2) Milch Trial – forced labour and medical experiments at Dachau
3) Justice Trial – Nazi legal abuses
4) Pohl Trial – SS officers involved in running concentration camps

5) Flick Trial – industrial use of forced labour
6) I.G. Farben Trial – offences by members of the industrial chemicals company
7) Hostages Trial – abuses of civilians in southeastern Europe
8) RuSHA Trial – crimes by officials of the RuSHA
9) *Einsatzgruppen* Trial – crimes committed by *Einsatzgruppen*.
10) Krupp Trial – use of slave labour by Krupp
11) Ministries Trial – officials responsible for facilitating war crimes
12) High Command Trial – high-ranking officers responsible for

EINSATZGRUPPEN TRIAL', DEFENDANTS

Name	Rank/Function	Sentence	1951 Amnesty
Adolf Ott	SS-Obersturmbannführer, member of the SD; commander of *Sonderkommando* 7b of *Einsatzgruppe* B	Death by hanging	Commuted to lifetime imprisonment; released 9 May 1958
Eduard Strauch	SS-Obersturmbannführer, member of the SD; commander of *Einsatzkommando* 2 of *Einsatzgruppe* A	Death by hanging	handed over to Belgian authorities; died in hospital 11 September 1955
Erich Naumann	SS-Brigadeführer, member of the SD; commander of *Einsatzgruppe* B	Death by hanging	Executed 7 June 1951
Ernst Biberstein	SS-Obersturmbannführer, member of the SD; commander of *Einsatzkommando* 6 of *Einsatzgruppe* C	Death by hanging	Commuted to lifetime imprisonment; released 1958
Erwin Schulz	SS-Brigadeführer, member of the *Gestapo*; commander of *Einsatzkommando* 5 of *Einsatzgruppe* C	20 years	Commuted to 15 years; released 9 January 1954; died 1981
Eugen Steimle	SS-Standartenführer, member of the SD; commander of *Sonderkommando* 7a of *Einsatzgruppe* B and of *Sonderkommando* 4a of *Einsatzgruppe* C	Death by hanging	Commuted to 20 years; released June 1954; died 1987
Franz Six	SS-Brigadeführer, member of the SD; commander of *Vorkommando Moscow* of *Einsatzgruppe* B	20 years	Commuted to 15 years; released 30 September 1952
Gustav Nosske	SS-Obersturmbannführer, member of the *Gestapo*; commander of *Einsatzkommando* 12 of *Einsatzgruppe* D	Lifetime imprisonment	Commuted to 10 years; died 1990
Heinz Jost	SS-Brigadeführer, member of the SD; commander of *Einsatzgruppe* A	Lifetime imprisonment	Commuted to 10 years; died 1964
Martin Sandberger	SS-Standartenführer, member of the SD; commander of *Sonderkommando* 1a of *Einsatzgruppe* A	Death by hanging	Commuted to lifetime imprisonment; released 1958
Otto Ohlendorf	SS-Gruppenführer, member of the SD; commander of *Einsatzgruppe* D	Death by hanging	Executed 7 June 1951
Otto Rasch	SS-Brigadeführer, member of the SD and the *Gestapo*; commander of *Einsatzgruppe* C	Removed from the trial on 5 February 1948 due to medical reasons	

offences against POWs and civilians

The *Einsatzgruppen* Trial in particular brought to light documents and witnesses that stunned the listening world with their revelations and testimony. Of the 24 *Einsatzgruppen* personnel charged, 13 were sentenced to death by hanging.

In addition to the Nuremberg trials, numerous other trials were conducted by local military tribunals throughout the occupied zones. Such trials brought to light many concentration camp guards and commanders, including the female guards who were brutally responsible for all-female sections of

extermination and concentration camps. At the Belsen Trial held by the British in Lüneburg from 17 September 1945, 45 former SS men, women and *kapos* (prisoner functionaries) from the Bergen-Belsen and Auschwitz camps were brought to face charges of crimes against humanity. All except one (who had to be removed from the trial owing to illness) were either executed or imprisoned.

Rudolf Höß, following his capture and his appearances as a witness at the Nuremberg trials, was handed over to the Supreme National Tribunal in Poland, found guilty of his crimes, and hanged. His appearances at Nuremberg, however, illustrated

the depths to which the SS mentality could degenerate. Here is an excerpt from his testimony concerning 'improvements' made in gassing operations at Auschwitz:

Another improvement we made over Treblinka was that we built our gas chambers to accommodate 2,000 people at one time, whereas at Treblinka their 10 gas chambers only accommodated 200 people each. The way we selected our victims was as follows: we had two SS doctors on duty at Auschwitz to examine the incoming transports of prisoners. The prisoners would be marched by one of the doctors who would make spot decisions as they

Name	Rank/Function	Sentence	1951 Amnesty
Paul Blobel	*SS-Standartenführer*; member of the SD; commander of *Sonderkommando* 4a of *Einsatzgruppe* C	Death by hanging	Executed 7 June 1951
Walter Blume	*SS-Standartenführer*; member of the SD and the *Gestapo*; commander of *Sonderkommando* 7a of *Einsatzgruppe* B	Death by hanging	Commuted to 25 years; released 1955
Walter Hänsch	*SS-Obersturmbannführer*; member of the SD; commander of *Sonderkommando* 4b of *Einsatzgruppe* C	Death by hanging	Commuted to 15 years
Werner Braune	*SS-Obersturmbannführer*; member of the SD and the *Gestapo*; commander of *Sonderkommando* 11b of *Einsatzgruppe* D	Death by hanging	Executed 7 June 1951
Willy Seibert	*SS-Standartenführer*; member of the SD; deputy chief of *Einsatzgruppe* D	Death by hanging	Commuted to 15 years
Emil Haussmann	*SS-Sturmbannführer*; member of the SD; officer of *Einsatzkommando* 12 of *Einsatzgruppe* D	Committed suicide before the arraignment on 31 July 1947	
Waldemar Klingelhöfer	*SS-Sturmbannführer*; member of the SD; officer of *Sonderkommando* 7b of *Einsatzgruppe* B	Death by hanging	Commuted to lifetime imprisonment; released 1956
Lothar Fendler	*SS-Sturmbannführer*; member of the SD; deputy chief of *Sonderkommando* 4b of *Einsatzgruppe* C	10 years	Commuted to 8 years
Waldemar von Radetzky	*SS-Sturmbannführer*; member of the SD; deputy chief of *Sonderkommando* 4a of *Einsatzgruppe* C	20 years	Released
Felix Rühl	*SS-Hauptsturmführer*; member of the *Gestapo*; officer of *Sonderkommando* 10b of *Einsatzgruppe* D	10 years	Released
Heinz Schubert	*SS-Obersturmführer*; member of the SD; officer in *Einsatzgruppe* D	Death by hanging	Commuted to 10 years
Mathias Graf	*SS-Untersturmführer*; member of the SD; officer in *Einsatzkommando* 6 of *Einsatzgruppe* D	Time already served	

walked by. Those who were fit for work were sent into the Camp. Others were sent immediately to the extermination plants. Children of tender years were invariably exterminated, since by reason of their youth they were unable to work. Still another improvement we made over Treblinka was that at Treblinka the victims almost always knew that they were to be exterminated and at Auschwitz we endeavored to fool the victims into thinking that they were to go through a delousing process. Of course, frequently they realized our true intentions and we sometimes had riots and difficulties due to that fact. Very frequently women would hide their children under the clothes but of course when we found them we would send the children in to be exterminated. We were required to carry out these exterminations in secrecy but of course the foul and nauseating stench from the continuous burning of bodies permeated the entire area and all of the people living in the surrounding communities knew that exterminations were going on...

Such testimony revealed the full extent of the horror, but many of its perpetrators would remain at liberty. Some, such as Eichmann, were later tried and executed, but others remained at large, free to live out their lives in anonymity. With the liberation of the camps, the wider world was stunned by what had occurred. As well as the obvious culpability of the Nazi leadership and the SS, the question remained as to the level of complicity amongst the general European population. The fact remains that the sheer logistics of deportation were only achieved through the assistance of civilian authorities and accomplices. Sometimes this assistance was forced, but sometimes it came willingly – Germany was not the only nation with anti-Semitic tendencies. Holocaust guilt, it is sad to say, does not lie purely on the shoulders of the Germans.

CHAPTER 6

Police and Intelligence

The Nazi system of policing the Third Reich was labyrinthine in the extreme. There were multiple security and police organizations, some of them legacies from the Weimar Republic and older police institutions, while others were new creations established after Hitler's taking of power in 1933.

What came to unite all the police and security services of the Third Reich was the SS. When the Nazis took control in 1933, the police forces of Germany were arranged on an individual state basis. This arrangement was not suited to a centralized dictatorship, so Hitler, Göring and Himmler began to shift existing Landespolizei (State Police) under SS control, while also establishing new security services such as the Sicherheitspolizei (Security Police; Sipo) and Sicherheitsdienst (Security Service; SD).

The German police and security services would become both instruments of terror and order, integral to the ideological and daily life of the Third Reich.

■ The Gestapo often used dogs for lightning swoops on homes and snatches of suspects. Here, dogs are being trained at the Gestapo School of Canine Intelligence at Rotengal.

Structuring a Police State

Himmler's goal from 1933 was to transfer all the primary law enforcement instruments in Nazi Germany to his control. He largely achieved this in 1934, when he became head of Germany's police and security services.

The first major change to the German police system under the Nazis came from Göring in 1933. Göring was the newly appointed head of the Prussian Police, Germany's most powerful police unit, with national jurisdiction. In a restructuring of major future significance, he reordered the force's *Amt* III into the *Geheime Staatspolizei* (Secret State Police; *Gestapo*), an organization that would become a much feared tool of political policing in the Third Reich.

But it was Himmler, rather than Göring, who would become the

ORGANIZATION OF THE *SICHERHEITSHAUPTAMT* (SECURITY MAIN OFFICE), 1935

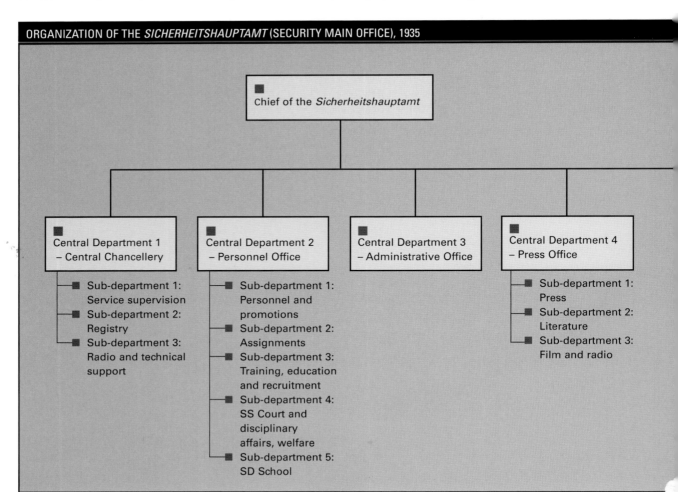

Chief of the *Sicherheitshauptamt*

Central Department 1 – Central Chancellery
- Sub-department 1: Service supervision
- Sub-department 2: Registry
- Sub-department 3: Radio and technical support

Central Department 2 – Personnel Office
- Sub-department 1: Personnel and promotions
- Sub-department 2: Assignments
- Sub-department 3: Training, education and recruitment
- Sub-department 4: SS Court and disciplinary affairs, welfare
- Sub-department 5: SD School

Central Department 3 – Administrative Office

Central Department 4 – Press Office
- Sub-department 1: Press
- Sub-department 2: Literature
- Sub-department 3: Film and radio

supreme police authority in the new Germany. Himmler relentlessly accrued power. Once established as RFSS, he began developing a comprehensive unified police and intelligence system, including the civilian security services known as the *Sicherheitspolizei* (*Sipo*) and *Sicherheitsdienst* (SD). (See the next section for a more detailed discussion of the SS-controlled security and intelligence services.) He became the police chief in Munich in 1933, and acting chief of the *Gestapo* a year later, effectively making him the overlord of political policing in Nazi Germany. Yet the regular police forces still remained outside his control.

Extended reach

In April 1934, Himmler's reach over local, regional and state police forces, including the uniformed and criminal branches (see table below), was completed. He took a new position – *Chef der Deutschen Polizei* (Chief of German Police) – an encompassing office that put him at the head of all uniformed and detective branches of the German state, as well as the security services already under his jurisdiction. His final extension of power would come much later, in August 1943, when he was promoted to Minister of the Interior – a position that enabled him to interfere more directly in the judicial processes.

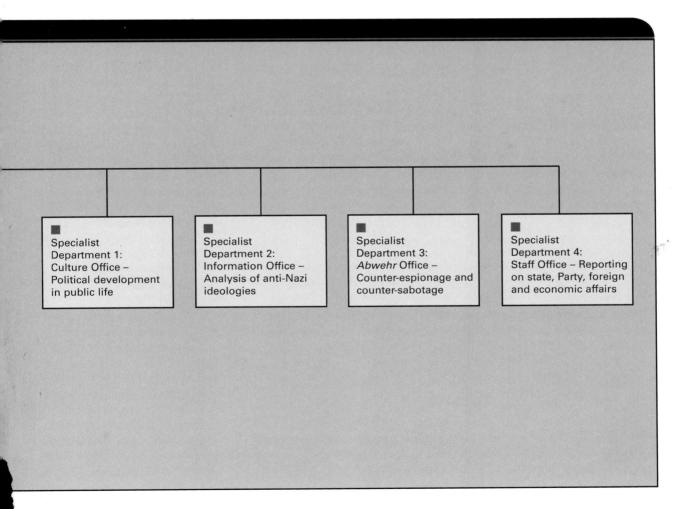

Specialist Department 1:
Culture Office – Political development in public life

Specialist Department 2:
Information Office – Analysis of anti-Nazi ideologies

Specialist Department 3:
Abwehr Office – Counter-espionage and counter-sabotage

Specialist Department 4:
Staff Office – Reporting on state, Party, foreign and economic affairs

---

UNITS WITHIN THE *ORDNUNGSPOLIZEI* (ORDER POLICE; *ORPO*)

Baupolizei (Buildings Police)
Feuerschutzpolizei (Fire Protection Police)
Feuerwehren (Fire Brigades)[1]
Luftschutzpolizei (Air Raid Police)
Technische Nothilfe, TeNo (Technical Emergency Service)
Feldjägerkrops, FJK (Auxiliary Police)
Verwaltungspolizei (Administrative Police)
Gesundheitspolizei (Health Police)
Gewerbepolizei (Factory & Shops Police)
Hochgebirgs Gendarmerie (Mountain Gendarmerie)
Kasernierte Polizei (Barrack Police)
Schutzpolizei der Gemeinden (Municipal Police)
Landespolizei (Barracked Territorial Police)[2]
Landwacht (Rural Guards)[3]
Stadtwacht (City Guards)[4]

Motorisierte Gendarmerie (Motorized Traffic Gendarmerie)
Polizei Fliegerstaffeln (Police Flying Units)
Polizei Nachrichtenstaffeln (Police Signal Units)
Gendarmerie (Rural Police)
Polizei Reiterstaffeln (Mounted Police Units)
Schutzpolizei des Reichs (Reich Protection Police)[5]
Schutzpolizei, Schupo (Protection Police)
Verkehrsbereitschaften (Traffic Police)
Verkehrskompanien (mot) zbV (Motorized Special Duty Traffic Police)
Wasserschutzpolizei (Waterways Protection Police)

1. Served as an auxiliary force to the *Feuerschutzpolizei*
2. Under *Wehrmacht* authority from 1935
3. Assisted the *Gendarmerie*
4. Assisted the *Schutzpolizei*
5. Responsible for cities and large towns

In a sense, the regular street-level policing continued much as it had always done, but there were distinct signals that it was now the SS that was in ultimate control, as Gordon Williamson here points out:

> Himmler would ensure that the majority of senior and middle-level Police posts were filled by men who were also members of the SS and thus owed obedience to him... Senior ranks who remained in the Police and who were not already members of the SS were pressured into joining; membership became a prerequisite for a successful Police career.
>
> (Williamson, 2006)

Williamson also goes on to note that from 1942 all police were issued with a pay book 'bearing the SS runes rather than the Police eagle on the cover'. There was no doubt as to who was in charge.

Another major organizational change in policing during the 1930s came with the formation of the *Reichssicherheitshauptamt* (Reich Main Security Office; RSHA), which was established in September 1939 as the supreme security office in the Third Reich. (The previous security office had been known as the *Sicherheitshauptamt*.) Headed by Reinhard Heydrich until his assassination in 1942, the RSHA became the umbrella organization for suppressing 'enemies of the state'.

Structured law enforcement

The RSHA was divided into seven major departments, including two SD departments (*Amt* III and *Amt* VI) responsible for domestic and foreign intelligence respectively, and *Amt* IV – the *Gestapo*. It also included the *Kriminalpolizei* in *Amt* V (see below).

In terms of their regional and local arrangements, the police forces within Germany were split into the following administrative divisions. At the regional level was the *Landespolizeibehörde* (Regional Police Authority), controlled by the *Länder* authorities or, in the case of Prussia and Bavaria, by the *Regierungspräsident* (Government President). The next level of command came with the *Kreispolizeibehörde* (City/County Police Authority), headed by various civic officials depending on the nature of the territory, and finally the *Ortspolizeibehörde* (Local Police Authority), controlled typically by a local mayor. While the security services were the most feared elements of policing, the main interface of law and order – and therefore the most pervasive tool of the domestic SS – was the regular police forces.

Ordnungspolizei

The two major regular police forces in the Third Reich were the

▼ *KRIPO* OFFICES

The *Kripo* maintained offices in most of the major towns and cities across the *Reich*. The offices at a sub-regional level would report back to the relevant regional office headquarters. In turn, the reports from regional offices were then passed on to the central office in Berlin, part of the RSHA.

Kriminalpolizei – the Criminal Police, better known as the *Kripo* – and the *Ordnungspolizei* (Order Police; *Orpo*). The *Orpo* was commanded from 1936 to 1945 by *SS-Oberstgruppenführer* Kurt Daluege, an unpleasant and brutish man who was generally unpopular with the civilian career policemen who made up the service's ranks. Daluege purged *Orpo* officials

who were not oriented towards the Nazi Party, in the process depriving the force of thousands of excellent officers and consequently reducing its efficiency.

He also encouraged members of the *Allgemeine-SS* to join the police ranks, breeding tensions and suspicions amongst the older officers and the new intake.

LOCATION OF *KRIPO* REGIONAL OFFICES

GERMAN POLICE RANKS

Ranks of the Polizei

- Generaloberst
- General
- Generalleutnant
- Generalmajor
- Oberst
- Oberstleutnant
- Major
- Hauptmann
- Oberleutnant
- Leutnant
- Meister
- Hauptwachtmeister
- Zugwachtmeister
- Oberwachtmeister
- Wachtmeister
- Rottwachtmeister
- Unterwachtmeister
- Anwärter

The command structure of the *Orpo*, below the regional SS levels, was centred on the *Hauptamt Ordungspolizei* (Order Police Headquarters), which was the official command HQ in Berlin and included various inspectorates and training schools. Below this office were the *Befehlshaber der Ordnungspolizei* (Chiefs of the Order Police), which

were district command positions. The more local sub-divisions were the responsibility of the *Kommandeure der Orpo* (Commanders of the Order Police). The police officers themselves were broadly split into two categories: the *Polizeivollzugsbeamten* (Uniformed Police) and the non-uniformed *Polizeiverwaltungsbeamten* (Administrative Police).

The *Orpo's* duties were those of any regular police force, from policing towns, cities and rural areas to managing traffic and monitoring waterways. The *Schutzpolizei* (Protection Police), for example, functioned as the standard municipal police force.

The numbers of *Schutzpolizei* officers were established according to the size of the local population, typically one officer for every 1000–2000 head of population. The *Schutzpolizei* was divided into *Reviere Polizei* (Precinct Police) – units of about 20–40 officers that patrolled a designated locality; five or more of these would form a *Polizei Abschnitt* (Police Sector). In turn, large and heavily populated cities or districts might then arrange several police sectors into a *Polizei Gruppe* (Police Group).

Yet there were also several specialist sections. The *Kasernierte*

Polizei (Barrack Police), for example, was a trained civil emergency unit, heavily armed with automatic weapons and armoured cars to handle riots and similar breakdowns in social order. The *Technische Nothilfe* (Technical Emergency Service) was a further emergency response unit, but it was dedicated to restoring public services should they be disrupted through social disorder.

Kriminalpolizei

Falling under *Sipo* authority, the *Kripo* was essentially the plain-clothes detective force of the regular German police. As such, the *Kripo* was mainly concerned with high-end non-political crimes – murders, rapes, fraud etc. It was also heavily engaged in tackling Germany's thriving black market economy.

Because the *Kripo* had also come under SS jurisdiction during the 1930s, and combined with the expanding emergencies of the war years, there is a sense in which every police unit had political policing implications. There was a regular flow of personnel from the *Kripo* to the *Gestapo*, the civilian detectives having applicable investigative skills and local intelligence of great use to the security agency.

Indeed, many *Kripo* members held a rank in the *Allgemeine-SS* that was equivalent to their *Kripo* rank, and some *Kripo* members even joined the ghastly *Einsatzgruppen* forces in their murder campaigns in the occupied territories. (The commander of *Einsatzgruppe* B, attached to Army Group Centre during *Barbarossa*, was Artur Nebe, a former head of the *Kripo*.) In the wider police force, from

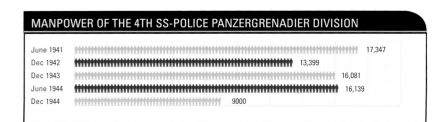

MANPOWER OF THE 4TH SS-POLICE PANZERGRENADIER DIVISION

June 1941	17,347
Dec 1942	13,399
Dec 1943	16,081
June 1944	16,139
Dec 1944	9000

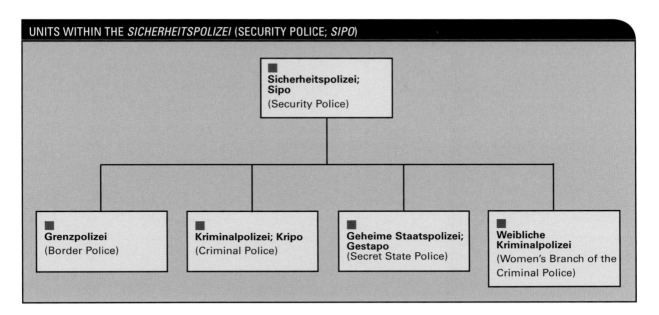

UNITS WITHIN THE *SICHERHEITSPOLIZEI* (SECURITY POLICE; *SIPO*)

- Sicherheitspolizei; Sipo (Security Police)
  - Grenzpolizei (Border Police)
  - Kriminalpolizei; Kripo (Criminal Police)
  - Geheime Staatspolizei; Gestapo (Secret State Police)
  - Weibliche Kriminalpolizei (Women's Branch of the Criminal Police)

1942 police generals were also given an equivalent SS rank, and wore SS insignia in police colours.

Special and military police

There were numerous other forms of specialist policing in the Third Reich, too many to explore in depth here. The *Sonderpolizei* (Special Police), for example, incorporated a range of units dedicated to distinct policing scenarios, often run by government offices rather than coming under the general police command structure. These units included the *Eisenbahnpolizei* (Railway Police), under the jurisdiction of the Ministry of Transport, the *Bergpolizei* (Mines Police – Ministry of Economic Affairs), *Jagdpolizei* (Game Conservation Police – Forestry Office) and the *Hafenpolizei* (Harbour Police – Ministry of Transport).

Another interesting police unit was the *Luftschutzpolizei* (Air Raid Police).

The duties of this police force – responding to the crises of air raids on urban areas – were similar to those of the British Air Raid Precaution (ARP) wardens, and were originally performed by a mix of *Luftwaffe* and Civil Defence organizations. Even this seemingly most politically irrelevant force was brought under Himmler's direct control as Allied air raids began to take a heavier toll on Germany's people and on its infrastructure.

Out in rural communities, policing was conducted by the *Gendarmerie*. Away from the fearful power of city police, the *Gendarmerie* had something approaching a parochial charm – a typical *Gendarmerie* officer would serve a small community on his own, working from his own home. There were larger strutural divisions of the *Gendarmerie*, however, and overall authority for all *Gendarmerie* rested

with the *Generalinspekteur der Gendarmerie*, which was in turn part of the *Hauptamt Orpo*.

The SS police presence extended into every community, regardless of size, although we should not regard every uniformed officer as having a *Gestapo*-like eye for political crimes. It should also be noted that the SS was not exclusive in running its own police and intelligence services. German Army military police duties were performed by the *Feldgendarmerie* (Field Police). Both the Army and later the *Luftwaffe* also formed their own *Geheime Feldpolizei* (Secret Field Police; GFP).

In essence, these bodies were internal military equivalents of the *Gestapo*, investigating crimes such as sabotage, treason, spying and black marketeering. Many of the GFP members were from the *Kripo*, and they often worked together with *Sicherheitsdienst* operatives.

Security Services

Himmler's SS security services were a typically complex arrangement consisting of numerous branches. Nevertheless, they managed to create a genuine mechanism of control throughout Germany and the occupied territories.

Unpacking the SS intelligence apparatus of the Third Reich is a complicated exercise. To give full explanation of all the departments within this apparatus would and does take up whole separate volumes. The easiest way to map the security services under Himmler's command is to look at them in their post-1939 hierarchy, by which time they had been assembled under the auspices of the RSHA, mentioned above.

The RSHA

The RHSA was the overarching body for the whole of the SS security services, and was formed in September 1939 under the command of Reinhard Heydrich, then, after his assassination, *SS-Obergruppenführer* Ernst Kaltenbrunner. It was organized into seven main departments:

Amt I – responsible for issues relating to personnel, training and organization.

Amt II – responsible for budgets, administration, legal issues and finance.

Amt III – the *Inland-SD*; dealt with civilian security issues within Germany.

Amt IV – the *Gestapo*; the main Nazi political police, dealing with any issues relating to 'enemies of the state', and therefore involved in many aspects of implementing the Holocaust.

Amt V – the *Kripo*; dealt with non-political serious crimes.

Amt VI – the *Ausland-SD*; responsible for foreign intelligence.

Amt VII – 'Written Records'; ideological research and producing propaganda literature.

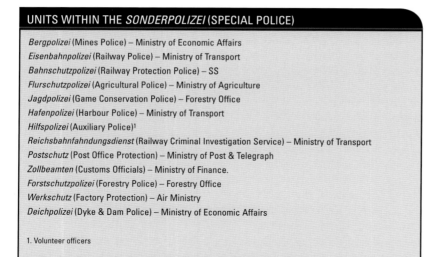

UNITS WITHIN THE *SONDERPOLIZEI* (SPECIAL POLICE)

Bergpolizei (Mines Police) – Ministry of Economic Affairs
Eisenbahnpolizei (Railway Police) – Ministry of Transport
Bahnschutzpolizei (Railway Protection Police) – SS
Flurschutzpolizei (Agricultural Police) – Ministry of Agriculture
Jagdpolizei (Game Conservation Police) – Forestry Office
Hafenpolizei (Harbour Police) – Ministry of Transport
Hilfspolizei (Auxiliary Police)[1]
Reichsbahnfahndungsdienst (Railway Criminal Investigation Service) – Ministry of Transport
Postschutz (Post Office Protection) – Ministry of Post & Telegraph
Zollbeamten (Customs Officials) – Ministry of Finance.
Forstschutzpolizei (Forestry Police) – Forestry Office
Werkschutz (Factory Protection) – Air Ministry
Deichpolizei (Dyke & Dam Police) – Ministry of Economic Affairs

1. Volunteer officers

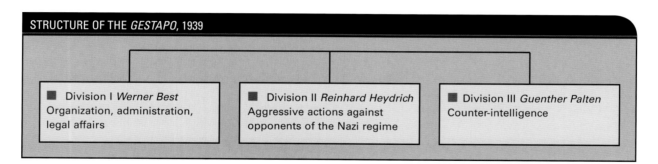

STRUCTURE OF THE *GESTAPO*, 1939

■ Division I *Werner Best*
Organization, administration, legal affairs

■ Division II *Reinhard Heydrich*
Aggressive actions against opponents of the Nazi regime

■ Division III *Guenther Palten*
Counter-intelligence

Amt III and *Amt* VI together constituted the SD organization, while *Amt* IV and *Amt* V came under the umbrella of the *Sipo*. The structure encompassed every major facet of security work, but there were, as we shall see, some significant tensions between the branches, especially between the SD and *Gestapo*.

Before looking at the individual organizations, however, it is worth a brief diversion to explore the man who bound it all together, Reinhard Heydrich.

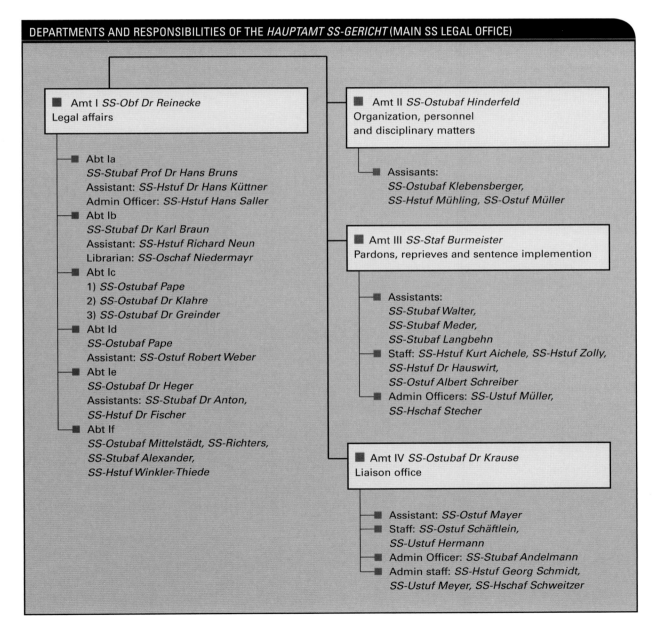

DEPARTMENTS AND RESPONSIBILITIES OF THE *HAUPTAMT SS-GERICHT* (MAIN SS LEGAL OFFICE)

Amt I *SS-Obf Dr Reinecke*
Legal affairs

- Abt Ia
  SS-Stubaf Prof Dr Hans Bruns
  Assistant: *SS-Hstuf Dr Hans Küttner*
  Admin Officer: *SS-Hstuf Hans Saller*
- Abt Ib
  SS-Stubaf Dr Karl Braun
  Assistant: *SS-Hstuf Richard Neun*
  Librarian: *SS-Oschaf Niedermayr*
- Abt Ic
  1) *SS-Ostubaf Pape*
  2) *SS-Ostubaf Dr Klahre*
  3) *SS-Ostubaf Dr Greinder*
- Abt Id
  SS-Ostubaf Pape
  Assistant: *SS-Ostuf Robert Weber*
- Abt Ie
  SS-Ostubaf Dr Heger
  Assistants: *SS-Stubaf Dr Anton,*
  SS-Hstuf Dr Fischer
- Abt If
  SS-Ostubaf Mittelstädt, SS-Richters,
  SS-Stubaf Alexander,
  SS-Hstuf Winkler-Thiede

Amt II *SS-Ostubaf Hinderfeld*
Organization, personnel
and disciplinary matters

- Assisants:
  SS-Ostubaf Klebensberger,
  SS-Hstuf Mühling, SS-Ostuf Müller

Amt III *SS-Staf Burmeister*
Pardons, reprieves and sentence implemention

- Assistants:
  SS-Stubaf Walter,
  SS-Stubaf Meder,
  SS-Stubaf Langbehn
- Staff: *SS-Hstuf Kurt Aichele, SS-Hstuf Zolly,*
  SS-Hstuf Dr Hauswirt,
  SS-Ostuf Albert Schreiber
- Admin Officers: *SS-Ustuf Müller,*
  SS-Hschaf Stecher

Amt IV *SS-Ostubaf Dr Krause*
Liaison office

- Assistant: *SS-Ostuf Mayer*
- Staff: *SS-Ostuf Schäftlein,*
  SS-Ustuf Hermann
- Admin Officer: *SS-Stubaf Andelmann*
- Admin staff: *SS-Hstuf Georg Schmidt,*
  SS-Ustuf Meyer, SS-Hschaf Schweitzer

Heydrich's fiefdom

Reinhard Tristran Eugen Heydrich was born in 1904. Ironically given his future career, there were persistent rumours of Jewish ancestry on his father's side, rumours that he attempted to quash with a violent form of denial. Heydrich grew to be a handsome, charismatic and musically talented young man, who joined the German Navy, from which he was dismissed in 1931 after an affair with a young girl turned into a scandal. Heydrich joined the SS in 1932, and he largely bluffed his way into impressing Himmler with a knowledge of intelligence operations. Playing a leading role in the Blood Purge of the SA in 1934 secured his favour with the Nazi hierarchy, and in June 1936 he was appointed the head of the *Sipo* and of the SD, a curious split positioning that goes some way to explaining the structural tensions described below. When the RSHA was formed in 1939, he took overall control of all

LOCATIONS OF *GESTAPO* PRISONS*

EAST PRUSSIA

■ Farge

■ Fehrbellin

■ Hohensalza

■ BERLIN

■ Posen-Lenzingen

POLAND

GERMANY

■ Hunswinkel

■ Plan/Leinsitz

■ Rattwitz

■ Theresienstadt

Witkowitz ■

■ PRAGUE

■ Hradischko

■ Gross-Kunzendorf

■ Hinzert

■ Blechhammer

CZECHOSLOVAKIA

■ Rudersberg

■ Oberndorf-Aistaig

VIENNA ■

■ Ankenstein Schloss

AUSTRIA

■ Innsbruck-Reichenau

■ Vigaun

* Shows 1939 borders

the Reich's security sevices, while being directly subordinate to Himmler. Other high positions he achieved included the Deputy Reich Protector for Bohemia and Moravia, to which he was appointed in September 1941.

As we have seen, it was Heydrich who was chosen to implement the 'Final Solution of the Jewish Question', and he ran his personal Czechoslovakian responsibility with characteristic brutality. Then on 29 May 1942, three Czech resistance fighters threw a bomb under Heydrich's car on the outskirts of Prague. Heydrich died of his wounds several days later, and in vengeful response the SS destroyed the Czech village of Lidice.

Heydrich's legacy was an effective security service that brought fear and death to thousands of people within Germany and abroad. It is partly due to the efficiency of the RSHA organizations, plus Goebbels' propaganda ministry, that the German people remained politically

compliant until the very end of the war.

The SD and *Gestapo*

The original SS security agency was the *Sicherheitsdienst* (SD), formed in 1931 by Himmler as a security offshoot of his burgeoning SS organization. In terms of its role, Himmler himself described its activities primarily in terms of investigating crimes against Nazi ideology: 'The SD will discover the enemies of the National Socialist concept and it will initiate countermeasures through the official police authorities.' In short, it was to spy on the people, watching out for any individuals or activities considered subversive to the Nazi regime. To this end, it built up a major network of agents and informants throughout Germany and later into the occupied territories, filling out

thousands of confidential reports that were filtered through to the central office of the SD, headed by Heydrich.

The SD definition of a subversive individual became forbiddingly broad, especially once the full spectrum of Nazi racial policy came into play. Historian Louis L. Snyder here reflects on the varied hues of those targeted by the Reich security services:

Few could escape this monolithic organ of the Hitler terror. Its victims included Jews, Communists, pacifists, Seventh day Adventists, political criminals, professional criminals, beggars, antisocials, 'the work shy,' homosexuals, prostitutes, drunkards, swindlers and psychopaths. SD men were called on for such major tasks as arresting 67,000 'enemies of the state' in Vienna during the occupation of Austria in 1938.

◀ **GESTAPO PRISONS**

The *Gestapo* prison network was not only a system for the handling and processing of prisoners. It was also a means of social control, the prisons acting as physical warnings for local populations against political transgressions. Being taken into a *Gestapo* prison often meant not coming out alive, or deportation to a concentration camp. Furthermore, the *Gestapo* could enact the full range of legal processes – from arrest to sentencing – all within its own prison system.

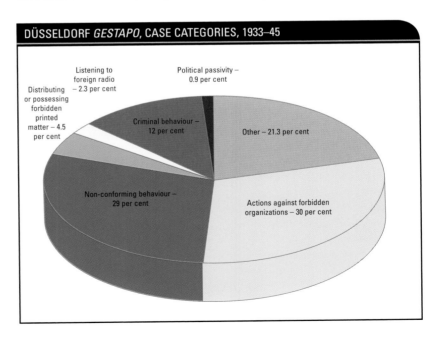

DÜSSELDORF *GESTAPO*, CASE CATEGORIES, 1933–45

Political passivity – 0.9 per cent
Listening to foreign radio – 2.3 per cent
Distributing or possessing forbidden printed matter – 4.5 per cent
Criminal behaviour – 12 per cent
Other – 21.3 per cent
Non-conforming behaviour – 29 per cent
Actions against forbidden organizations – 30 per cent

DEPARTMENTS OF THE *GESTAPO*, 1943

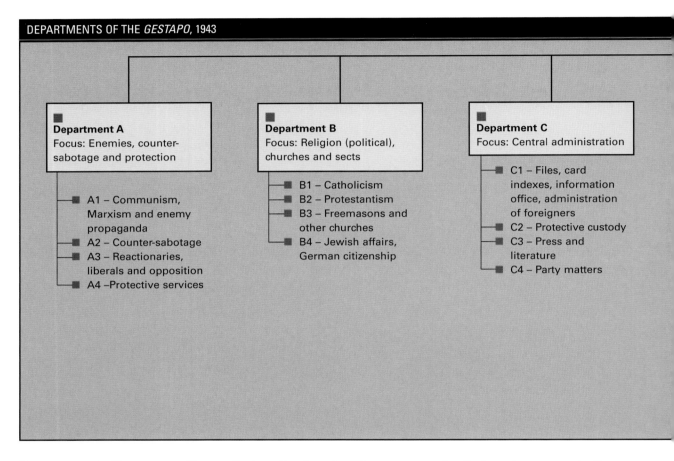

Department A
Focus: Enemies, counter-sabotage and protection

- A1 – Communism, Marxism and enemy propaganda
- A2 – Counter-sabotage
- A3 – Reactionaries, liberals and opposition
- A4 –Protective services

Department B
Focus: Religion (political), churches and sects

- B1 – Catholicism
- B2 – Protestantism
- B3 – Freemasons and other churches
- B4 – Jewish affairs, German citizenship

Department C
Focus: Central administration

- C1 – Files, card indexes, information office, administration of foreigners
- C2 – Protective custody
- C3 – Press and literature
- C4 – Party matters

Once a person had been arrested by the SD, a fast-track judicial system could process the prisoner and, with little respect for any human rights, have him or her tortured, imprisoned or executed.

SS Terror

Outside of Germany, in the occupied territories, the SD was able to implement more terror-based policies. It actively engaged in anti-Partisan actions, counter-espionage and the deportation of Jews to the ghettos, concentration camps and extermination camps. Alongside the *Gestapo*, therefore, the SD was a critical instrument in the SS crimes against humanity.

The *Gestapo* had different origins from the SD. Its precedent was the Prussian political police of the Weimar Republic, a part of the Prussian Interior Ministry although with Germany-wide authority. By 1933 the Prussian Interior Minister was none other than Göring, and in April he established the *Gestapo* as a state security force which, like the SD, was dedicated to protecting National Socialism against a variety of real and imaginary enemies. During 1934, the *Gestapo* also came under the spreading control of the SS.

The *Gestapo* was truly a law unto itself, and from its formation until the end of the war it terrorized the German people and the citizens of occupied lands. There was a definite overlap in SD and *Gestapo* responsibilities that was never entirely resolved. Relations between the two organizations could be frosty and competitive, especially in the field of foreign intelligence. The situation was complicated by the fact that, as we have seen, from June 1936 Heydrich was chief of both the

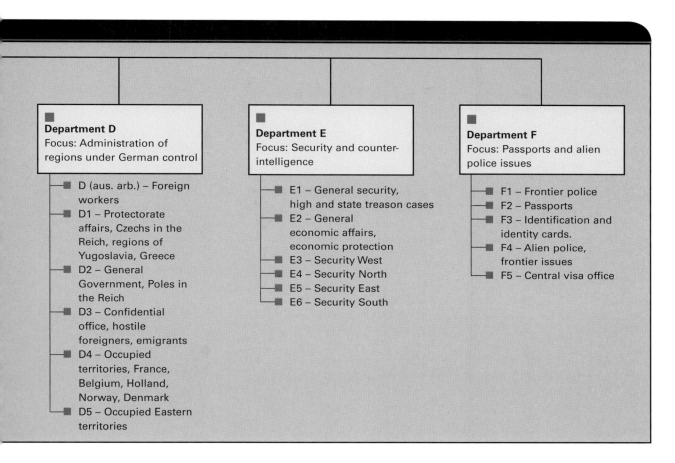

Department D
Focus: Administration of regions under German control

- D (aus. arb.) – Foreign workers
- D1 – Protectorate affairs, Czechs in the Reich, regions of Yugoslavia, Greece
- D2 – General Government, Poles in the Reich
- D3 – Confidential office, hostile foreigners, emigrants
- D4 – Occupied territories, France, Belgium, Holland, Norway, Denmark
- D5 – Occupied Eastern territories

Department E
Focus: Security and counter-intelligence

- E1 – General security, high and state treason cases
- E2 – General economic affairs, economic protection
- E3 – Security West
- E4 – Security North
- E5 – Security East
- E6 – Security South

Department F
Focus: Passports and alien police issues

- F1 – Frontier police
- F2 – Passports
- F3 – Identification and identity cards.
- F4 – Alien police, frontier issues
- F5 – Central visa office

SD and *Sipo*. A further complication was that another foreign intelligence organization existed, the *Abwehr* of Admiral Wilhelm Canaris, under the authority of the *Oberkommando der Wehrmacht* (OKW). Canaris was fired in early 1944, and his replacement was Major-General of Police (*SS-Brigadeführer*) Walter Schellenberg, an appointment that stripped the *Abwehr* of its OKW authority and brought all intelligence activities under Himmler's control.

Out of the competition between the *Gestapo* and the SD, the *Gestapo* undoubtedly emerged as the more powerful of the two agencies. For example, by 1939 the SD had 3000 operatives and 50,000 informers. The *Gestapo*, by contrast, had 20,000 members and 100,000 informers. The *Gestapo* also seemed to take the ear of the authorities more readily.

In terms of its structure, the *Gestapo* was split into six main departments by 1943, each with jurisdiction over a certain aspect of the security process, or with defined territorial responsibilities. As the diagram above shows, the *Gestapo* was an international organization, establishing offices in most major cities throughout the occupied territories. In doing so it established an independent legal system governed by its own rules, ensuring that any individual arrested by the *Gestapo* had no higher appeal authority. Yet although the *Gestapo* was certainly an influential organization, it was still spread thinly once the Third Reich expanded through war. In fact, recent research has indicated that many German cities were monitored by only a few dozen *Gestapo* agents, meaning that its reach was not universal, unlike the fear it instilled in Europe's peoples.

Operations and Powers

The police and security forces of the SS were instruments of terror as much as they were forces of order. Their operations ranged from the identification and arrest of political enemies, through to major anti-Partisan actions on the Eastern Front.

In the prosecution documents prepared for the Nuremberg trials, there was no doubt as to what the purpose of the SS security services was, and the magnitude of their crimes. The following is a significant excerpt from the 'Nazi Aggression & Criminality' documents prepared by the Office of United States Chief of Counsel For Prosecution of Axis Criminality:

> *The evidence shows that the GESTAPO was created by Goering in*

Prussia in April 1933 for the specific purpose of serving as a police agency to strike down the actual and ideological enemies of the Nazi regime, and that henceforward the GESTAPO in Prussia and in the other States of the Reich carried out a program of terror against all who were thought to be dangerous to the domination of the conspirators over the people of Germany. Its methods were utterly ruthless. It operated outside the law and sent its victims to the concentration camps.

Here the prosecution looks specifically at the *Gestapo*, and captures the essence of that organization's role as the thought police of the Nazi state. The document goes on to state that the *Gestapo* and SD were at the heart of both Hitler's ideological oppression and the crimes against humanity that defined the Nazi era:

> *The term "GESTAPO" became the symbol of the Nazi regime of force and terror. Behind the scenes, operating secretly, the SD, through its vast network of informants, spied upon the German people in their daily lives, on the streets, in the shops, and even within the sanctity of the churches.*
> *The most casual remark of a German citizen might bring him before the GESTAPO, where his fate and freedom were decided without recourse to law. In this government, in which the rule of law was replaced by a tyrannical rule of men, the GESTAPO was the primary instrumentality of oppression.*
> *The GESTAPO and the SD played an important part in almost every criminal act of the conspiracy. The categories of these crimes, apart from the thousands of specific instances of torture and cruelty in policing*

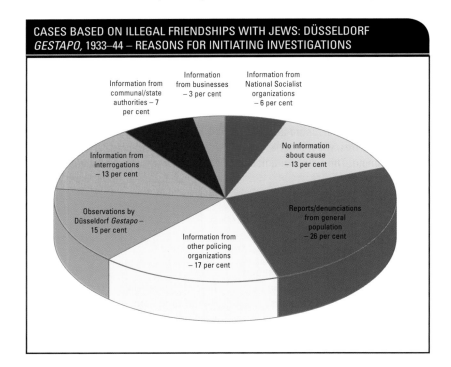

CASES BASED ON ILLEGAL FRIENDSHIPS WITH JEWS: DÜSSELDORF *GESTAPO*, 1933–44 – REASONS FOR INITIATING INVESTIGATIONS

- Information from communal/state authorities – 7 per cent
- Information from businesses – 3 per cent
- Information from National Socialist organizations – 6 per cent
- Information from interrogations – 13 per cent
- No information about cause – 13 per cent
- Observations by Düsseldorf *Gestapo* – 15 per cent
- Reports/denunciations from general population – 26 per cent
- Information from other policing organizations – 17 per cent

Germany for the benefit of the conspirators, indicate the extent of GESTAPO and SD complicity.

The security services under SS authority were certainly at the centre of the Nazi persecution of both Germans and the people of occupied countries. Their integral relationship to the *Einsatzgruppen* and the concentration/extermination camps, either as active participants or in directing operations, makes them directly culpable for the deaths of millions. So what was the extent to which the security services controlled society during the years of the Third Reich?

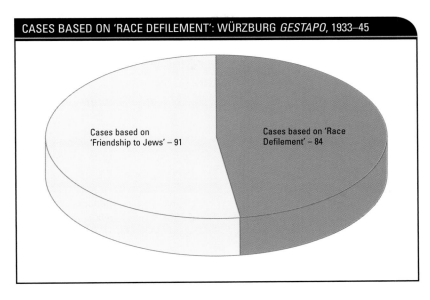

CASES BASED ON 'RACE DEFILEMENT': WÜRZBURG *GESTAPO*, 1933–45

Cases based on 'Friendship to Jews' – 91

Cases based on 'Race Defilement' – 84

Tools of coercion

In the Eastern territories, the *Sipo* and SD could give free reign to the imperatives of mass murder, aiding in the identification of Jews, Communists and other state enemies, and working with other bodies in the implementation of ghetto confinement and deportation to the death and labour camps. By looking at the *Gestapo*'s role in the West, however, we perhaps gain a more subtle sense of how they operated, and their level of influence.

One important point, already briefly acknowledged, was that the *Gestapo* operatives were far from all-pervasive. In Germany proper, most major towns and cities had fewer than 50 official *Gestapo* personnel in operation – just before the war, for example, Stettin and Frankfurt am Main had a total *Gestapo* of 41 combined. The simple maths of this situation was that the *Gestapo* could not do its job alone, and instead had

to rely upon officials in other agencies and, of course, its network of informants. Indeed, it is estimated that around 80 per cent of all *Gestapo* investigations originated in denunciations and betrayals. It was this phenomenon, rather than the *Gestapo* agents themselves, that gave the security services their seeming ubiquity. The greatest fear of many civilians under the *Gestapo*'s shadow was to be arrested and taken into the local *Gestapo* headquarters for questioning. The authorized use of torture, plus the very fact that in SS eyes arrest was largely the pre-acknowledgement of guilt, meant that people taken into a *Gestapo* prison would often simply disappear from society. The French philosopher Jean-Paul Sartre wrote of the sudden disappearance of citizens in his essay 'Paris Under Occupation':

One day you might phone a friend and the phone would ring for a long

time in an empty flat. You would go round and ring the doorbell, but no-one would answer it... If the wife or mother of the man who had vanished had been present at his arrest, she would tell you that he had been taken away by very polite Germans, like those who asked the way on the street. And when she went to ask what had happened to them at the offices in the Avenue Foch or the Rue des Saussaies [a Parisian Gestapo office and headquarters respectively] she would be politely received and sent away with comforting words.
(Quoted in Ousby, 1997)

In many cases, individuals were either interrogated to death within the *Gestapo* prison or office, or following interrogation they were deported to a concentration camp from which they were unlikely to emerge. Nuremberg trials testimony brought to light what happened to

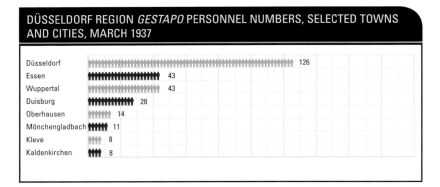

DÜSSELDORF REGION *GESTAPO* PERSONNEL NUMBERS, SELECTED TOWNS AND CITIES, MARCH 1937

Düsseldorf	126
Essen	43
Wuppertal	43
Duisburg	28
Oberhausen	14
Mönchengladbach	11
Kleve	8
Kaldenkirchen	8

those who went behind the *Gestapo* doors and were fortunate enough to survive. Here Hans Cappelen, a Norwegian citizen, recounts his terrifying interrogation by numerous *Gestapo* agents in the agency's Oslo headquarters. Bear in mind that Cappelen had already endured weeks of beatings:

> Then they placed a sort of home-made – it looked to me like a sort of home-made-wooden thing – with a screw arrangement, on my left leg; and they started to screw so that all the flesh loosened from the bones. I felt an awful pain and fainted away again. But I came back to consciousness again; and I have still big marks here on my leg from the screw arrangement, now, four years afterwards. So that led to nothing and then they placed something on my neck – I still have marks here [indicating] – and loosened the flesh here, but then I had a collapse and all of a sudden I felt that I was sort of paralyzed in the right side. It has otherwise been proved that I had a cerebral hemorrhage.

This ghastly account perfectly evokes why the *Gestapo* was so feared, and doubtless the rumours of what went on in the *Gestapo* prisons were powerful tools of political control in their own right.

Judicial process
In the case of an investigation actually warranting criminal trial, the individual might go before a local SS court or, if they had some stature, before the *Volksgerichtshof* (People's Court). A year after Hitler became Chancellor, he sought to establish a specialized high court that would deal exclusively with those charged with high treason or classified as traitors to the state. The *Volksgerichtshof* was the result, at first presided over by Fritz Rehn (July–September 1934), then by Otto Thierack (1934–42), Roland Freisler (1942–February 1945) and Harry Haffner (March–April 1945).

In its appearance alone the *Volksgerichtshof* stated its credentials, heavily adorned with swastikas and images of Hitler. Most of the court officials, including the panel of judges, were Party members or SS men. The trials conducted

therein worked largely on the basis of foregone conclusions – to appear before the court almost guaranteed a long prison sentence or death. Furthermore, the judges worked outside of independent scrutiny, and once the verdict was delivered, there was no further avenue of appeal. Many cases, however, were recorded for posterity on film, the films being a record for Hitler and his officials or for selective use in newsreels. The evidential process in the trials was highly skewed, and the proceedings placed a high emphasis on humiliation and verbal abuse, particularly under the rule of Freisler. The court's most famous case came with the trials of those implicated in the July 1944 bomb plot against Hitler, most of those accused destined for hideous executions, filmed for Hitler's pleasure.

Higher authorities – HSSPF
To give context to the operational structure of the SS and its police work, we need to explore in more depth the major regional command authority, the *Höherer SS- und Polizeiführer* (Higher SS and Police Leader; HSSPF). The HSSPF posts had been created in 1937 as an evolutionary development of the *SS-Oberabschnitt Führer* (SS Leaders of the Main Districts), and an HSSPF typically held both positions.

HSSPFs became, in the words of Mark Yerger, 'the most powerful (and feared) SS posts created by Himmler' (Yerger, 1997). These positions were not only related to the occupied territories – German HSSPFs were in control of *Oberabschnitt* districts within Germany, and as such governed all the related *Allgemeine-SS* units. In the right (that is, emergency) circumstances, the HSSPFs also had additional degrees of authority over local *Waffen-SS* and even Army formations, such as ad hoc battle groups. In terms of the various elements of the police and security services, the HSSPFs' overarching powers depended partly upon the challenges they faced and partly on the cooperation of various agencies:

Though the SD, Ordnungspolizei, Totenkopfverbände, and Sipo received orders from the respective main offices of which these groups were components of administrative direction, the HSSPF could bypass those command channels under the guise of an emergency situation and operationally control them directly or through administrative directives... Generally the Ordnungspolizei was more cooperative than the Sipo and SD or the RSHA and its precursor command offices, though this resistance eased following the death of Reinhard Heydrich in 1942.
(Yerger, 1997)

What constituted an 'emergency situation' could vary considerably, but such situations naturally became more common during the later years of the war, when desperation set into the German defence. A US Army

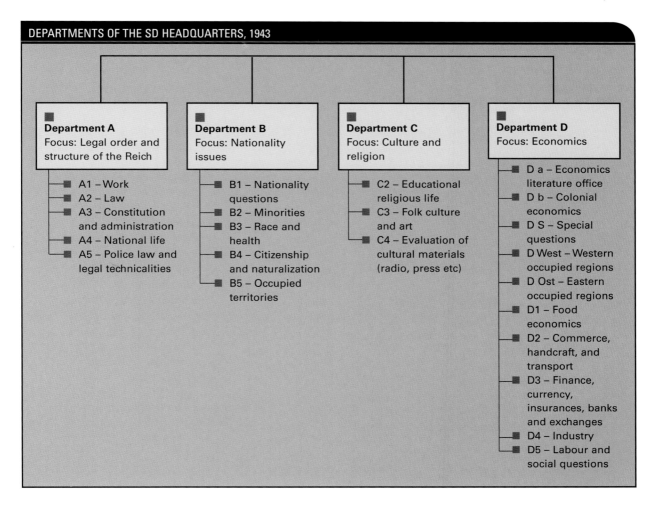

DEPARTMENTS OF THE SD HEADQUARTERS, 1943

Department A
Focus: Legal order and structure of the Reich

- A1 – Work
- A2 – Law
- A3 – Constitution and administration
- A4 – National life
- A5 – Police law and legal technicalities

Department B
Focus: Nationality issues

- B1 – Nationality questions
- B2 – Minorities
- B3 – Race and health
- B4 – Citizenship and naturalization
- B5 – Occupied territories

Department C
Focus: Culture and religion

- C2 – Educational religious life
- C3 – Folk culture and art
- C4 – Evaluation of cultural materials (radio, press etc)

Department D
Focus: Economics

- D a – Economics literature office
- D b – Colonial economics
- D S – Special questions
- D West – Western occupied regions
- D Ost – Eastern occupied regions
- D1 – Food economics
- D2 – Commerce, handcraft, and transport
- D3 – Finance, currency, insurances, banks and exchanges
- D4 – Industry
- D5 – Labour and social questions

intelligence document published in March 1945 noted how HSSPF roles had expanded as defeat closed around the Reich:

With the increasing danger to Germany proper, new responsibilities have been thrust upon the HSSPF, especially in the border areas. In some cases he has assumed active command of all units of the auxiliary organizations of the Reich and of the Party, except those of the Todt Organization (OT), so far as they have been organized for defensive combat tasks. In case of an invasion of his area he has been ordered to attach himself and all the units under him, including those of the SS and police, to the commander of the Wehrkreis and to act as his deputy for the latter if necessary.

(TM-E 30-451, March 1945)

HSSPF authorities were often central figures behind some of the major war crimes of the SS, at least in giving overall direction to the field units, either police or *Waffen-SS*. The HSSPF would, for example, launch anti-Partisan operations in given areas or would direct police units to acquire forced labour for given projects. Sometimes these operations would be conducted independently of the RFSS, but often Himmler himself would provide the directives, such as occurred with the liquidation of the Warsaw ghetto.

SSPF

The next level of subordinate command below the HSSPF was the *SS- und Polizeiführer* (SSPF). (Often commanders would serve as SSPFs before promotion took them up to HSSPF). SSPFs were powerful leaders in themselves, with immediate control over a substantial locality; indeed the reason behind the creation of these posts was to take away some of the excessive responsibilities placed upon the HSSPFs in Poland and the Soviet Union (SSPFs were only found in the occupied territories). Within their given areas, and like the HSSPFs, the SSPFs controlled multiple SS-directed agencies, including the *Orpo*, *Gestapo*, SD, *Kripo* and *Totenkopfverbände*.

The SS police commanders had a variable relationship with the local Party authorities, typically either a *Gauleiter* in Germany proper or a *Reichskommissar* in the occupied territories. (Poland was an exception, controlled by a govenor, Hans Frank.) On occasions, the relationship could degenerate into a non-cooperative squabble over personnel and policing

HÖHERE SS- UND POLIZEIFÜHRER (HSSPF) – REGIONAL COMMANDS

Höhere SS- und Polizeiführer Adriatisches Küstenland – HQ: Triest
Höhere SS- und Polizeiführer Albanien – HQ: Tirana
Höhere SS- und Polizeiführer Alpenland – HQ: Salzburg
Höhere SS- und Polizeiführer Belgien-Nordfrankreich – HQ: Brussels
Höhere SS- und Polizeiführer Böhmen und Mähren – HQ: Prague
Höhere SS- und Polizeiführer Danmark – HQ: Copenhagen
Höhere SS- und Polizeiführer Donau – HQ: Vienna
Höhere SS- und Polizeiführer Elbe – HQ: Dresden
Höhere SS- und Polizeiführer Frankreich – HQ: Paris
Höhere SS- und Polizeiführer Fulda-Werra – HQ: Arolsen
Höhere SS- und Polizeiführer Griechenland – HQ: Athens
Höhere SS- und Polizeiführer Kroatien – HQ: Zagreb
Höhere SS- und Polizeiführer Main – HQ: Nuremberg
Höhere SS- und Polizeiführer Mitte – HQ: Braunschweig
Höhere SS- und Polizeiführer Nord – HQ: Oslo
Höhere SS- und Polizeiführer Nordost – HQ: Königsberg
Höhere SS- und Polizeiführer Nordsee – HQ: Hamburg
Höhere SS- und Polizeiführer Nordwest – HQ: Den Haag
Höhere SS- und Polizeiführer Ost – HQ: Krakow
Höhere SS- und Polizeiführer Ostland und Rußland-Nord – HQ: Riga
Höhere SS- und Polizeiführer Ostsee – HQ: Stettin
Höhere SS- und Polizeiführer Rhein-Westmark – HQ: Wiesbaden
Höhere SS- und Polizeiführer Rußland-Mitte – HQ: Mogilev, then Minsk
Höhere SS- und Polizeiführer Rußland-Süd – HQ: Kiev
Höhere SS- und Polizeiführer Schwarzes-Meer – HQ: Nikolajew
Höhere SS- und Polizeiführer Serbien, Sandschack und Montenegro – HQ: Belgrade
Höhere SS- und Polizeiführer Slowakien – HQ: Pressburg
Höhere SS- und Polizeiführer Spree – HQ: Berlin
Höhere SS- und Polizeiführer Süd – HQ: Munich
Höhere SS- und Polizeiführer Südost – HQ: Breslau
Höhere SS- und Polizeiführer Südwest – HQ: Stuttgart
Höhere SS- und Polizeiführer Ungarn – HQ: Budapest
Höhere SS- und Polizeiführer Warthe – HQ: Posen
Höhere SS- und Polizeiführer Weichsel – HQ: Danzig
Höhere SS- und Polizeiführer West – HQ: Düsseldorf

– as was the case in the higher echelons of the Third Reich leadership, authority was often combative rather than cooperative.

Note, too, that there was an appointment that was superior to the SSPFs and HSSPFs. This was the post of *Höchste SS- und Polizeiführer* (Supreme SS and Police Leader; HöSSPF), which combined multiple HSSPF and other command regions into a single major command. There were two HöSSPF posts created during the war: HöSSPF 'Italien', essentially responsible for Italy, and HöSSPF 'Ukraine', which made up one of the largest SS territorial commands in the occupied Soviet territories.

Criminal minds

The people who occupied the police leader positions during the war included some of the architects, at least at a regional level, of the Holocaust and of various other forms of state-sponsored terror. For example, from November 1939 to August 1943, the SSPF 'Lublin', whose district fell within the General Government of Poland, was *SS-Gruppenführer und Generalleutnant der Polizei* Odilio Globocnik. Austrian-born Globocnik became a member of the SS in 1933, and then proceeded to embark on a twisted and corrupt political career, which saw him sacked as *Gauleiter* of Vienna in 1939. Globocnik then redeemed himself through service in the *Waffen-SS* in Poland and he was promoted to his SSPF position on November the same year.

Globocnik's behaviour in Poland was nothing short of terrifying for the

HÖCHSTE SS- UND POLIZEIFÜHRER (HöSSPF)

Höchste SS- und Polizeiführer 'Italien' – HQ: Rome, Verona and Bozen

Commander: *SS-Obergruppenführer* Karl Wolff (23 Sep 1943–8 May 1945)

District leaders:
- SSPF Bozen
- SSPF Mitteitalien-Verona
- SSPF Oberitalien-Mitte
- SSPF Oberitalien-West

Höchste SS- und Polizeiführer 'Ukraine' – HQ: Kiev

Commander: *SS-Obergruppenführer* Hans-Adolf Prützmann (29 Oct 1943–Sep 1944)

District leaders:
- SSPF Aserbeidschan
- SSPF Awdejewka
- SSPF Bergvolker-Ordshonikidse
- SSPF Charkow
- SSPF Dnjepropetrowsk-Krivoi-Rog
- SSPF Kaukasien-Kuban
- SSPF Kertsch-Tamanhalbinsel
- SSPF Kiew
- SSPF Nikolajew
- SSPF Nord-Kaukasien
- SSPF Rowno
- SSPF Shitomir
- SSPF Stalino-Donezgebiet
- SSPF Stanislav-Rostow
- SSPF Taurien-Krim-Simferopol
- SSPF Tschernigow
- SSPF Wolhynien-Brest-Litowsk

populations who fell foul of his command. He was responsible for the violent liquidation of the Warsaw ghetto in April and May 1943, during which more than 50,000 people were either killed in the ghetto or deported to the death camps for execution. Incidentally, the field commander for this operation was *Brigadeführer* Jurgen Stroop, an equally prejudiced man who would himself go on to become the SSPF for Warsaw from April to September 1943, then HSSPF *Griechenland* (Greece) during September and October 1943.

Other career high points, but moral low points, in Globocnik's service included the destruction of the Bialystok ghetto in August 1943 (an action that condemned another 60,000 Jews to certain death) and numerous general resettlement actions against the Polish civilian population, all conducted with a violent sense of purpose.

These actions were just part of Globocnik's integration into the Holocaust, and were indeed the smaller part. On 13 October 1941, Globocnik was given the order to begin construction of Belzec extermination camp in southeastern Poland. Globocnik duly set the wheels in motion, and oversaw the creation of a camp that would kill more than 400,000 Jews from the Lublin and Galicia districts before the war's end.

Nor was Belzec the end of his creations. Globocnik went on to oversee the creation of Majdanek, Sobibór and Treblinka. All told it is estimated that the camps and programmes he implemented were responsible for the deaths of some 1.5 million people. Following his lethal service to Poland, Globocnik was promoted to HSSPF *Adriatisches-Küstenland* (Adriatic Coastland), a position that he occupied from September 1943 to May 1945.

When the end came for Globocnik, he managed to cheat justice.

Although caught and arrested by British troops and secret service agents, he killed himself via a cyanide capsule. This atrocious man was buried in an unmarked and forgotten grave.

Military-style police units

One notable aspect of the *Orpo*'s wartime existence was that it provided the manpower to form around 80 military-style police units, organized as battalions and equipped with light infantry weapons rather than standard police-issue firearms. Indeed, police personnel were even channelled into forming a fully established *Waffen-SS* combat division, the *4.SS-Polizei-*

Panzergrenadier-Division. This formation saw front-line combat deployment, but many of the smaller units were used principally in anti-Partisan roles, fighting bitter battles behind the front lines.

These units were increasingly open to sympathetic volunteers from the occupied territories. The creation of German-controlled foreign police stemmed from the fact that any local police forces in an occupied country automatically came under the control of the relevant SS formations.

Himmler realized that the extent of the occupation zones meant that policing could not be provided purely by German units, despite the fact that Hitler had shown a gut opposition to

SS- UND POLIZEIFÜHRER (SSPF) – REGIONAL COMMANDS

Polizeigebietsführer Agram	SS- und Polizeiführer Mitteitalien-Verona
Polizeigebietsführer Banja-Luca	SS- und Polizeiführer Mitte-Norwegen
Polizeigebietsführer Copenhagen	SS- und Polizeiführer Mogilew
Polizeigebietsführer Essegg	SS- und Polizeiführer Montenegro
Polizeigebietsführer Knin	SS- und Polizeiführer Nikolajew
Polizeigebietsführer Sarajewo	SS- und Polizeiführer Nord-Kaukasien
SS- und Polizeiführer Aserbeidschan	SS- und Polizeiführer Nord-Norwegen
SS- und Polizeiführer Awdejewka	SS- und Polizeiführer Ober-Elsaß
SS- und Polizeiführer Bergvolker-Ordshonikidse	SS- und Polizeiführer Oberitalien-Mitte
SS- und Polizeiführer Bialystok	SS- und Polizeiführer Oberitalien-West
SS- und Polizeiführer Bozen	SS- und Polizeiführer Pripet
SS- und Polizeiführer Charkow	SS- und Polizeiführer Quarnero
SS- und Polizeiführer Dnjepropetrowsk-Krivoi-Rog	SS- und Polizeiführer Radom
SS- und Polizeiführer Estland	SS- und Polizeiführer Rowno
SS- und Polizeiführer Friaul	SS- und Polizeiführer Rostow-Awdejewka – See Stanislav-Rostow
SS- und Polizeiführer Görz	SS- und Polizeiführer Salzburg
SS- und Polizeiführer Istrien	SS- und Polizeiführer Sandschak
SS- und Polizeiführer Kattowitz	SS- und Polizeiführer Saratow
SS- und Polizeiführer Kaukasien-Kuban	SS- und Polizeiführer Shitomir
SS- und Polizeiführer Kertsch-Tamanhalbinsel	SS- und Polizeiführer Stalino-Donezgebiet
SS- und Polizeiführer Kiew	SS- und Polizeiführer Stanislav-Rostow
SS- und Polizeiführer Krakau	SS- und Polizeiführer Süd-Norwegen
SS- und Polizeiführer Lemberg	SS- und Polizeiführer Taurien-Krim-Simferopol
SS- und Polizeiführer Lettland	SS- und Polizeiführer Triest
SS- und Polizeiführer Litauen	SS- und Polizeiführer Tschernigow
SS- und Polizeiführer Lublin	SS- und Polizeiführer Warsaw
SS- und Polizeiführer Metz	SS- und Polizeiführer Weißruthenien
SS- und Polizeiführer Minsk – See Weißruthenian	SS- und Polizeiführer Wolhynien-Brest-Litowsk

allowing foreigners to bear arms and police the Reich. Yet Himmler got his way, and on 25 July 1941 ordered that SS occupation forces organize 'additional protective units from the ethnic groups suitable to us in the conquered area as soon as possible'. In November of that year, Himmler ordered that these auxiliary police be formed into units called the *Schutzmannschaften der Ordnungspolizei* (Detachments of Order Police). They were also known as *Hilfspolizei* (Auxiliary Police; *Hipo*) or, in the occupied Soviet territories, as *Hilfswillige* (Voluntary Assistants; 'Hiwis'). The enthusiasm for joining the police military units was impressive, as Gordon Williamson describes:

> From among the *Volksdeutsche* elements in Poland, some 12 polizei regiments were formed; in Estonia 26 regiments. Latvia and Lithuania between them raised 64 battalions totalling around 28,000 men, and in the Ukraine an astonishing 70,000 volunteers came forward, sufficient to form 71 battalions. In the Balkans the Croats produced some 15,000 volunteers, the Serbs some 10,000, and even Albania was able to produce sufficient volunteers to form two police battalions.
>
> (Williamson, 1994)

The *SS-Polizei-Regimenter* (SS Police Regiments), as they became known from 1943, and the various foreign auxiliary police units, were generally used in anti-Partisan, ghetto policing, Jewish deportation and general order

roles in the Eastern theatres. The battalions were typically about 500 men strong, divided into one command and four regular companies, each with its own machine-gun support group.

Some of the foreign auxiliary police units, as we have seen, were also deployed in assisting the *Einsatzgruppen* (Task Forces) during extermination and deportation operations.

In fact, their behaviour in support of *Wehrmacht* and SS units could shock even racially hardened German sensibilities. In Poland in 1939, for example, *Volksdeutsche* (Ethnic Germans) serving with the *Orpo* behaved with such violent prejudice against Jews and other elements of the Polish community that the local *Gauleiter* recommended they be immediately disbanded.

COMMAND STRUCTURE OF THE HAUPTAMT ORPO WITH RESPONSIBILITIES

Haupamt Orpo

Amt I: *Kommandoamt* (Command Department)
Amtsgruppe I: Organization
Amtsgruppe II: Personnel
Amtsgruppe III: Medical

Amt II: *Verwaltung und Recht* (Adminstration and Rights)
Amtsgruppe I: Pay, allowances, finance, legal
Amtsgruppe II: Civilian registration, entertainment, trades and handicrafts, traffic control
Amtsgruppe III: Police billetting and accommodation

Amt III: *Wirtschaftverwaltungsamt* (Economics Department)
Amtsgruppe I: Clothing and rations
Amtsgruppe II: Finance, wages
Amtsgruppe III: Quartering
Amtsgruppe IV: Pensions and allowances
Amtsgruppe V: Personnel financial issues

Amt IV: *Technische Nothilfe* (Technical Emergency Service)

Amt V: *Feuerwehren* (Fire Brigades)

Amt VI: *Kolonialpolizei* (Colonial Police)

Amt VII: *Technisches SS under Polizeiakademie* (SS and Police Technical Training Academy)

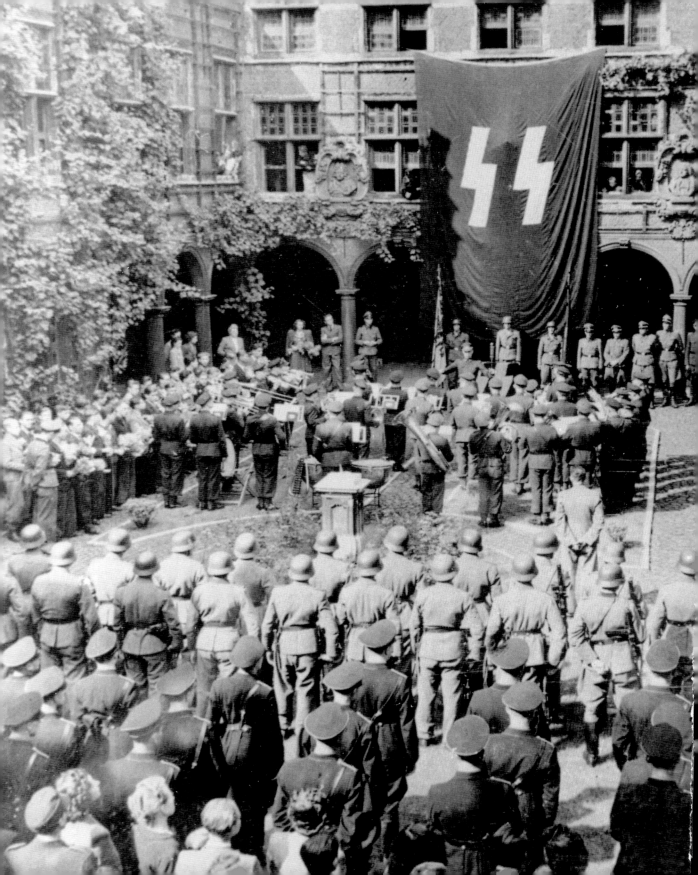

CHAPTER 7

SS Culture & Ideology

To be a member of the SS was to join a unique brotherhood, complete with its own systems of identity, symbolism and ideology. Indeed, it is one of the central ironies of the SS that an organization capable of such major atrocities, and which disdained orthodox faith, should actually be ingrained with the language and rituals of religion.

Himmler himself, notwithstanding his ordered and pedantic mind, had an almost mystical perception of his SS and of the racial project upon which the Nazis were embarked. Concepts such as 'Blood and Soil' were mixed in Himmler's mind with a desire for some ill-defined form of Nordic deism, a faith of strength and racial power but without the moral obligations of most other religions.

Although this philosophy did not percolate down to every SS man, the clothes he wore and oaths he made all emphasized almost spiritual bonds with his comrades.

■ **New SS volunteers take part in a parade in Brussels in July 1944. Even at this late stage in the war, Himmler was seeking new recruits for his**

Mythology and Identity

The Nazi state was generally hostile towards any sort of organized faith, although it tolerated the practices of Germany's large Christian population. Yet Himmler, a lapsed Catholic, seems almost to have attempted to develop a new brand of SS faith.

Q: Why do we believe in Germany and the *Führer*?

A: Because we believe in God, we believe in Germany which He created in His world and in the *Führer* Adolf Hitler, whom he has sent us.

Q: Whom must we primarily serve?

A: Our people and our *Führer* Adolf Hitler.

Q: Why do you obey?

A: From inner conviction, from belief in Germany, in the *Führer*, in the Movement, and in the SS, and from loyalty.

These words, a translation of the catechism recounted by new recruits to the *Allgemeine-SS*, are difficult to tie down in terms of a core philosophy. On the one hand, they clearly state a belief in God, and that God created Germany. Yet unlike the catechisms of regular religions, this passage veers away from placing loyalty to God above everything, and instead locates Adolf Hitler at the centre of the recruit's universe.

Here we see the balancing act of what we might call an SS spiritualism. On the one hand, Himmler clearly felt that the ritualistic and unifying themes of religion were beneficial to his organization. On the other hand, he pulls back from making the divine the primary source of authority for the SS soldier – such

would clearly be unacceptable in a nation where Hitler himself was practically ascribed divine status.

Nazi theology

To make sense of SS 'spirituality' (if it is appropriate to call it that), it is useful to set it in the context of the religious life of the Nazi Party. There is no doubt that Hitler was essentially opposed to the practice of Christianity. Yet Germany's long history of Catholicism, and its legacy as the birthplace of the Protestant Reformation, meant that it was a presence he could not openly attack (that attention was the preserve of the Jewish faith, of course). His chosen course, therefore, was de facto persecution and begrudging tolerance.

It is easy to see why Hitler was antagonistic towards Christianity. Here was a faith that not only had Jewish roots and scriptures (the Old Testament), but also promoted ideas of conciliation, love of enemies, kindness, mercy and forgiveness – all of which notions were anathema to Nazi ideologies of war, violence, hard hearts and racial enmity.

At first, however, the Nazis seemed to buy into a much modified version of Christianity, emphasizing racial and heroic notes at the expense of its gentler doctrines, aided by support from many of the churches, who

believed Hitler had rescued German faith from the clamp of Bolshevism. The Nazi Party Programme even expressed support for the practice of 'positive Christianity'.

Later, however, Nazi theologians attempted to reshape core Christian theology to match their own world view. Professor Ernst Bergmann, for example, wrote several books on the topic, several of which ended up on the Catholic list of banned titles. Bergmann published *Die 25 Thesen der Deutschreligion* ('The Twenty-five Points of the German Religion'), a work of breathtakingly outlandish theology that amongst its premises claimed that Christ was not Jewish but Nordic, Adolf Hitler was the new messiah and the Old Testament was no longer considered part of scripture. Bergmann also argued that 'Either we have a German God or none at all.' The construction of a new German neo-pagan religion based on Nordic deities rather than the Christian God, termed the *Deutsche Glaubensbewegung* (German Faith Movement) and headed by 'Reich Bishop' Ludwig Müller, rankled with Germany's regular Christians, who saw the Nazi religious charade for what it was.

The new Nazi religiosity never achieved anything like official status, as Hitler was generally atheistic in outlook, although with an almost

NAZI SYMBOLISM

Symbol		Origins	Nazi Meaning and SS Applications
	Hakenkreuz (Swastika)	Uncertain – prevalent across Indo-European cultures from the Bronze Age	National flags and offical emblem of NSDAP
	Sonnenrad ('Sunwheel' Swastika)	Old Norse symbol for the sun	Divisional sign for Waffen-SS divisions Wiking and Nordland
	Eagle	Roman Empire	Represented Nazi Party (when looking to right) and Nazi Germany (when looking to left)
	Totenkopf (Death's Head)	Ancient; eighteenth-century European military symbol	Used by SS as official badge
	Sig rune	Ancient/medieval Germanic alphabets	Symbolized victory. Two side by side became the official emblem of the SS
	Opfer rune	Ancient/medieval Germanic alphabets	Symbolized self-sacrifice. Used in SA Sports Badge for War Wounded
	Odal rune	Ancient/medieval Germanic alphabets	Symbolized family and racial cohesion. Used by the SS Race and Settlement Department
	Ger rune	Ancient/medieval Germanic alphabets	Symbolized faith. Alternative divisional sign for Waffen-SS Division Nordland
	Heilszeichen	Ancient/medieval Germanic alphabets	Symbolized success. Used on SS Death's Head ring
	Wolfsangle (Wolf's Hook)	Medieval German	Symbolized liberty. Early motif of NSDAP and used by Waffen-SS Division Das Reich
	Toten rune	Ancient/medieval Germanic alphabets	Symbolized death, hence used on official SS documents alongside date of death
	Tyr rune	Ancient/medieval Germanic alphabets	Symbolized leadership in battle. Used on SS grave markers
	Eif rune	Ancient/medieval pagan Germanic alphabets	Symbolized enthusiasm, passion. Worn by SS adjutants in the 1930s
	Hagall rune	Ancient/medieval Germanic alphabets	Symbolized fidelity (to Nazi cause). Featured on SS Death's Head ring
	Leben rune	Ancient/medieval Germanic alphabets	Symbolized life. Used by SS Lebensborn Society

LEBENSBORN FACILITIES OR FIELD OFFICES

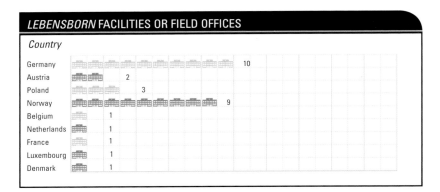

Country		
Germany		10
Austria		2
Poland		3
Norway		9
Belgium		1
Netherlands		1
France		1
Luxembourg		1
Denmark		1

divine sense of destiny. Himmler, meanwhile, was forming his own sense of reality.

Pseudo-religion

Himmler, a lapsed Catholic, had three major influences in his spiritual life. First, he was deeply wedded to the worlds of Nordic identity and mythology, seeing in Nordic paganism the violent and heroic models for his SS. Second, Himmler was fascinated by the Jesuit Order, particularly in terms of their devotion to serving the Pope with total loyalty. Third, he was utterly convinced of Nazi racial theory, seeing the need to produce a pure Aryan race, and to extirpate 'contaminating' races, as a profound destiny.

The three elements of paganism, Catholic ritualism and racism were all present in the daily lives and identities of the SS. First, consider the SS insignia. As the table on the previous page displays, the SS was deeply indebted to pagan symbolism, applying age-old runic symbols to denote division, regiment or branch of service, or as parts of badges and awards. The SS awarded deserving officers silver rings decorated with

the Death's Head, the double lightning-flash runes and an asterisk rune that signified the word *Heil*. (The inside of the ring featured Himmler's signature.) Indeed, inanimate objects took on a life of their own in the SS. Standards were 'consecrated', *Allgemeine-SS* recruits laying their hands on such artefacts as they were sworn into the service.

Many SS rituals were religious in both their symbolism and their language. For example, new recruits to the *Waffen-SS* would be sworn in at 10 p.m. on 9 November each year, the anniversary of the Munich Putsch taking on the status of a religious festival. The occasion was given gravitas and emotion through torchlight illumination and the sombre incantations of the SS pledge, which included the promise of 'obedience unto death'.

One interesting aspect of SS culture was Himmler's attempt to replace Christian festivities with pagan holidays. The winter and summer solstices therefore became focal points in the SS calendar, as well as the Munich Putsch date noted above and Hitler's birthday on 20 April. Himmler even tried to create

an SS alternative to Christmas, the Festival of Midsummer, celebrated through the exchange of decorative plates and candlesticks. It never caught on, as the tradition of Christmas was too powerful for even Himmler to quash.

Himmler could, however, have a more direct influence over the classic rite of marriage. In a truly bizarre system, Himmler created a paganistic Order of Germanic Clans. SS men intending to marry had to fill out an RSHA questionnaire proving the Aryan ancestry of both bride and groom, and including photographs of the happy couple looking suitably Aryan. If the application was approved, the couple could be entered into the Order of Germanic Clans, and they would be wed through both a standard civil ceremony and an additional ceremony conducted by the local SS commander. SS officers also presided over the SS version of christenings, laying hands on the child as it was officially given its name. At the other end of life, funerals for SS personnel might include candlelit vigils around the open coffin.

The grandeur of Himmler's spiritual visions for the SS was most garishly represented by Wewelsburg Castle in Westphalia, which essentially became the high temple of the SS. An enthusiast for the legend of King Arthur and his Knights of the Round Table, Himmler replicated the 12-seat table in an imposing dining hall, each seat for one of his own 'knights'. Graber explains that beneath the dining room was a crypt that contained 12 stone pedestals:

If an Obergruppenführer were to die, an urn containing his ashes was placed on the appropriate pedestal. The smoke was directed upward into the vents in the ceiling so that those assembled could watch the spirit ascend into a type of Valhalla.

(Graber, 1978)

It is obvious that Himmler saw his SS as more than just a military organization. The value of such spirituality is ambiguous, but regardless of the rites and services that Himmler established, it does seem to be the case that SS personnel had an acute sense of belonging.

Breeding the warrior

The racial element of Himmler's belief system had, as we have seen, many disturbing qualities. An unsettling expression of this element was the *Lebensborn* ('Fount of Life') programme, which was founded in December 1935. Crudely put, *Lebensborn* was essentially a breeding project, a facility for getting the best of SS manhood to breed with true Aryan women. The purposes of *Lebensborn* were spelt out by Himmler in a directive of 13 September 1936:

(1) aid for racially and biologically-hereditarily valuable families.
(2) the accommodation of racially and biologically-hereditarily valuable mothers in appropriate homes, etc.
(3) care of the children of such families.
(4) care of the mothers.

It is the honourable duty of all leaders of the central bureau to become members of the organization 'Lebensborn e. V.'.

The women selected for the programme were not necessarily married – perpetuation not propriety was the goal of the programme – and in 1940 some 70 per cent of the mothers were unmarried. The pregnant women were cared for by the SS for the duration of their pregnancy. Once the children were born, they were taken into special SS nurseries, where they would be brought up as good specimens of physically and racially pure German nationhood.

As the programme developed, these nurseries actually became meeting places for eligible SS men and eager German women. Furthermore, the *Lebensborn* programme spread out from the confines of Germany and into the occupied countries of Western Europe. Outside of the 10 *Lebensborn* homes established in Germany, there were also nine in Norway, two in Austria, and one each in Belgium, the Netherlands, France, Luxembourg and Denmark.

The *Lebensborn* programme was neither effective nor, in the end, popular. Himmler's encouragement for young women to have children out of wedlock smacked of male fantasies, and the widespread incorporation of foreigners into the *Waffen-SS* gave the lie to Himmler's idea that the SS embodied racial purity.

KNOWN LOCATIONS OF LEBENSBORN FACILITIES (1944)

Country	Town	Country	Town
Germany/Austria	Bad Polzin	Netherlands	Nijmegen (planned)
	Bofferding bei Luxemburg*		
	Gmunden/Traunsee*	Norway	Bergen
	Hohenhorst		Geilo
	Klosterheide		Godthaab*
	Nordrach		Hurdalsverk
	Pernitz/Muggendorf		Klekken
	Schalkhausen/Krs. Ansbach*		Os*
	Steinhöring		Oslo
	Wernigerode/Harz		Stalheim*
	Wiesbaden		Trondheim
Belgium	Wegimont bei Lüttich	* The places marked with an asterisk indicate	
		orphanages or children's homes, while the	
Denmark	Kopenhagen	remained indicate maternity homes.	
France	Lamorlaye bei Chantilly		
General Government	Cracow		
	Otwock		
	Warsaw		

SS Racial Culture

The SS was, as we have seen repeatedly, an organization with tortured racial logic. Himmler, in his desire to define the racial purity of true Germans, involved his SS in curious and often horrible experiments in massaging history and in racial engineering.

An SS pocket diary and information book entitled *Der Soldatenfreund* ('The Soldier's Friend'), published in 1943, gave the following explanation of the *SS-Hauptamt*, emphasizing its role in preserving SS racial quality:

It is the task of the SS Main Office to create a strictly organized elite order. Therefore it is charged with the selection of suitable men for the SS and with the recording of the SS members and their families, furthermore with the ideological and political guidance, schooling, and education of the entire SS and police as well as the care of the organizations committed within the frame of the SS and police. A further task is the physical education and the physical training of the SS before and after military duty. Of special importance is the selection, the establishment, and the leadership of the SS in the Germanic countries, and the prevailing of the Germanic idea in all spheres of life.

As this passage makes clear, in one way or another, physical 'quality' and racial health were at the core of SS culture and thinking. Although, as we have seen, clear racial purity was not borne out in practice, particularly within the *Waffen-SS*, there was a definite sense that the SS was on a racial mission. We have already seen several ways in which this was expressed, including the ultimate horror that was the Holocaust and more benign programmes such as *Lebensborn*. Yet the SS desire to create a pure Aryan society developed in other, often bizarre

---

RuSHA CASE – DEFENDANTS, 1947–48

Ulrich Greifelt – *SS-Obergruppenführer*; General of Police; Chief of the Staff Main Office (*Stabshauptamt*) of the *Reichskommissar für die Festigung des Deutschen Volkstums* (Reich Commissioner for the Strengthening of the German Nation; RKFDV); Chief of *Amtsgruppe* B of the Staff Main Office.

Rudolf Creutz – *SS-Oberführer*; Deputy to Greifelt; Chief of *Amtsgruppe* A of the Staff Main Office of the RKFDV.

Konrad Meyer-Hetling – *SS-Oberführer*; Chief of *Amtsgruppe* C of the Staff Main Office of the RKFDV.

Otto Schwarzenberger – *SS-Oberführer*; Chief of *Amt* V in *Amtsgruppe* B of the Staff Main Office of the RKFDV.

Herbert Hübner – *SS-Standartenführer*; Chief of Branch Office Poznan of the Staff Main Office of the RKFDV; representative of the *SS-Rasse- and Siedlungshauptamt* (SS Race and Settlement Main Office; RuSHA) for the Warthegau.

Werner Lorenz – *SS-Obergruppenführer*; General of the *Waffen-SS* and Police; Chief of the *Hauptamt Volksdeutsche Mittelstelle* (Ethnic German Main Assistance Office; VOMI) of the SS.

Heinz Brückner – *SS-Sturmbannführer*; Chief of *Amt* VI of VOMI.

Otto Hofmann – *SS-Obergruppenführer*; Chief of RuSHA, 9 July 1940–20 April 1943; Higher SS and Police Leader (HSSPF) for southwestern Germany.

Richard Hildebrandt – *SS-Obergruppenführer*; General of Police; Chief of RuSHA, 20 April 1943–May 1945.

Fritz Schwalm – *SS-Obersturmbannführer*; Chief of Staff of RuSHA and principal RuSHA representative at the *Einwandererzentrale* Lodz (Immigration Centre, Lodz; EWZ).

Max Sollmann – *SS-Standartenführer*; Chief of *Lebensborn*, e.V. ('Fount of Life' Society) of the SS; Chief of Main Department A of *Lebensborn*.

Gregor Ebner – *SS-Oberführer*; Chief of the Main Health Department of *Lebensborn*.

Günther Tesch – *SS-Sturmbannführer*; Chief of the Main Legal Department of *Lebensborn*.

Inge Viermetz – Deputy Chief of Main Department A of *Lebensborn*.

---

ways. Some were mere exercises in academic curiosity, while others were cruel attempts at genetic engineering.

Foreign strains

On 30 September 1947, the US Military Tribunal at Nuremberg sat to consider the 'RuSHA Case', the trial of 14 members of the *SS-Rasse- und Siedlungshauptamt* (SS Race and Settlement Main Office; RuSHA). The indictments contained a broad sweep of crimes against humanity in the occupied countries, and contained some chillingly unusual charges read out by the prosecution, including:

a. Kidnapping the children of foreign nationals in order to select for Germanization those who were considered of 'racial value';

b. Encouraging and compelling abortions on Eastern workers for the purposes of preserving their working capacity as slave labor and of weakening Eastern nations;

c. Taking away, for the purpose of extermination or Germanization, infants born to Eastern workers in Germany;

d. Executing, imprisoning in concentration camps, or Germanizing Eastern workers and prisoners of war who had had sexual intercourse with Germans, and imprisoning the Germans involved;

e. Preventing marriages and hampering reproduction of enemy nationals.

RuSHA CASE VERDICTS	
Name	*Sentence*
Ulrich Greifelt	Life Imprisonment
Rudolf Creutz	15 Years Imprisonment
Konrad Meyer-Hetling	Acquitted & Released
Otto Schwarzenberger	Acquitted & Released
Herbert Hübner	15 Years Imprisonment
Werner Lorenz	15 Years Imprisonment
Heinz Brückner	15 Years Imprisonment
Otto Hofmann	25 Years Imprisonment
Richard Hildebrandt	25 Years Imprisonment
Fritz Schwalm	10 Years Imprisonment
Max Sollmann	Acquitted & Released
Gregor Ebner	Acquitted on two charges, convicted on the third but released for time served
Günther Tesch	Acquitted & Released
Inge Viermetz	Acquitted & Released

As is evident from these charges, the RuSHA Case covered a lot of ground, too much to cover in detail here. Yet one aspect is particularly worthy of exploration – the kidnap of children as part of an extension of the *Lebensborn* programme.

In a speech at Bad Schachen in October 1943, Himmler acknowledged that the occupation had brought Germany into contact with a huge range of peoples and cultures, a fact that threw up some new possibilities for racial engineering:

Obviously in such a mixture of peoples there will always be some racially good types. Therefore I think that it is our duty to take their children with us, to remove them from their environment, if necessary by robbing or stealing them. Either we win over any good blood that we can use for ourselves and give it a place in our people or we destroy this blood.

In terms of the options that Himmler presents in the last sentence, he obviously invested heavily in the latter. Yet his attempt to find 'good blood that we can use for ourselves' had terrible repercussions for thousands of children and their families from the Eastern occupied territories.

Following the occupation of Poland, the Baltic states and the Soviet Union, Himmler's RuSHA agents spread out through the territories, on the lookout for children who physically matched the Aryan ideal – blonde hair, blue eyes, strong physique. In an attempt to 'Germanize' these young people, they were literally kidnapped from their parents (the parents were themselves often destined for concentration camps). Orphans – of which there were plenty owing to the massive death toll amongst Eastern European civilians – were another major source.

MAJOR EXPEDITIONS BY THE *AHNENERBE*, 1936–43

Destination	Date	Key Figures	Purpose
Italy	1937	Franz Altheim (archaeologist); Erika Trautmann (researcher)	Study prehistoric rock inscriptions
New Swabia (Antarctica)	December 1938– February 1939	Alfred Ritscher (leader)	Stake German claim over New Swabia, to secure whaling rights and activities
Bohuslän (Sweden)	August–November 1936	Wolfram Sievers (organizer)	Study prehistoric rock art
Eastern Europe, Balkans, Middle East	1938	Franz Altheim (archaeologist); Erika Trautmann (researcher)	Study supposed Nordic and Semitic conflicts within the Roman Empire
Karelia (Finland)	June 1936	Yrjö von Grönhagen (leader); Ola Forsell (illustrator); Fritz Bose (musicologist)	Investigate pagan sorcerers and witches
Murg Valley (Germany)	Various expeditions between 1936 and 1938	Wiligut and Gunther Kirchhoff; Gustav Riek (archaeologists)	Study ancient civilizations in the Black Forest
Mauern (Germany)	1936–37	R.R. Schmidt (archaeologist); Dr Assien Bohmers (archaeologist and expedition leader)	Study Cro-Magnon sites
France (various cave sites)	Late 1930s	Dr Assien Bohmers (archaeologist)	Investigate prehistoric cave art
Tibet	1939	Ernst Schäfer (leader); Karl Wienert (geologist); Ernst Krause (filmmaker; entomologist); Bruno Beger (anthropologist)	Explore Tibetan geology and culture; establish Aryan connections with Asia, including an attempt to prove the Aryan ancestry of Buddha
Crimea	July 1942	Dr Herbert Jankuhn; Karl Kersten; Baron Wolf von Seefeld (team members)	Search for Gothic artefacts
Ukraine	June 1943– February 1945	Heinz Brücher (botanist; leader)	Botanical studies

The numbers of children taken are hard to ascertain, as the records have either been destroyed, lost or not compiled in the first place. It is thought that up to 100,000 children from Poland alone were extracted, and tens of thousands from the Soviet territories. The total figure may be in the region of 250,000. Additional numbers were also taken from other parts of the occupied territories. Although the Germans utterly destroyed the village of Lidice in Czechoslovakia in 1942 (the reprisal action for the assassination of Reinhard Heydrich), for example, and killed most of its population, some 91 children were still selected for Germanization, and were sent back to infant camps in Germany.

Once in the hands of the Germans, the infants were to be raised in SS homes or nurseries under strict educational guidelines. (While the majority of children went en masse into special SS-run centres, decent numbers were adopted directly by SS families. Those raised from babies would never know their origins.) The word 'strict' was operative – in SS eyes the growing children had to have the contamination of their original parentage and upbringing worked out of them. Beatings were commonly administered to those children who, doubtless emotionally scarred by their fractured childhoods, displayed behavioural problems. In fact, an extremely high percentage of the children taken by the SS were ultimately sent on to extermination camps like so much troublesome garbage to be disposed of. At the end of the war, only 25,000 children were identified and sent back to their families. In a horrible twist to the strory, many of the children had indeed had their characters reshaped by their SS education, and no longer fitted back into the societies from which they came.

Exploring the world
Another side to SS culture was the work of the *Ahnenerbe* (Ancestral Heritage) organization. Its pompous full title was *Studiengesellschaft für Geistesurgeschichte Deutsches Ahnenerbe* (The Society for Research into the Spiritual Roots of Germany's Ancestral Heritage), and it was founded in July 1936 by Himmler, Nazi 'Blood and Soil' ideologist Walter Darré, and a German-Dutch lecturer, Herman Wirth, whose primary interests were ancient religions and their symbolic systems.

The general purpose of the *Ahnenerbe* was basically to provide scientific and historical proof for the Nazis' ideas of racial supremacy, mainly by searching for evidence of Germany's Aryan spiritual and cultural heritage. Numerous expeditions were commissioned (see table opposite), with purposes ranging from discovering ancient 'Nordic' burial sites through to analysing ancient cave art for evidence of ancestral links. Much of the history and cultural research the *Ahnenerbe* produced was laughably skewed by its Nazi agenda, and

generated little of consequence or worth. Of darker significance, however, were the scientific research elements of the organization. Most of the experimental work of this sector was aimed at proving the racial inferiority of Jews, Slavs etc, and to do so it

commissioned some of the most heinous medical experiments in the concentration camps. A phrenological study, for example, required the collection of 120 Jewish skulls. It seems there was little the SS did without involving death for someone.

SOCIAL SCIENCES RESEARCH INSTITUTES IN THE AHNENERBE

Institute	Translation
Alte Geschichte	Ancient History
Ausgrabungen	Excavation
Deutsche Volksforschung und Volkskunde	German Ethnic Research and Folklore
Germanisch-deutsch Volkskunde	Germanic-German Folklore
Germanische Kulturwissenschaft und Landschaftskunde	Germanic Cultural Studies and Landscape Science
Germanische Sprachwissenschaft und Landschaftskunde	Germanic Linguistics and Landscape Science
Germanisches Bauwesen	Germanic Architecture
Griechische Philologie	Greek Philology
Hausmarken und Sippenzeichen	House Brands and Family Marks
Indogermanisch-arische Sprach- und Kulturwissenschaft	Indogermanic-aryan Language and Cultural Studies
Indogermanisch-deutsche Musik	Indogermanic-German Music
Indogermanische Glaubengeshichte	Indogermanic Faith history
Indogermanische Rechtsgeschichte	Indogermanic Historical jurisprudence
Indogermanisch-finnische Kulturbeziehungen	Indogermanic-Finnish cultural relations
Indogermanisch-germanische Sprach- und Kullturwissenschaft	Indogermanic-Germanic Language and Cultural Studies
Innerasien und Expeditionen	Inner Asia and Expeditions
Keltische Volksforschung	Celtic ethnic research
Klassische Altertumswissenschaft	Classical Antiquity
Klassische Archäologie	Classic Archaeology
Lateinische Philologie	Latin Philology
Mittellatein	Medieval Latin
Mittlere und Neuere Geschichte	Middle and Modern History
Nordwestafrikanische Kulturwissenschaft	Northwest African Cultural Studies
Orientalistische Indologie	Oriental Indology
Ortung und Landschaftssinnbilder	Location and Landscape symbols
Ostasien-Institut	East Asian Institute
Philosophie	Philosophy
Runen, Schrift und Sinnbildkunde	Runes, Alphabets, and Symbols
Urgeschichte	Prehistory
Volkserzählung, Märchen und Sagenkunde	Folktales, Fairytales and Myths
Vorderer Orient	Near East
Wurtenforschung	Dwelling Mound Research

Conclusion

The SS was a complex organization at many levels – ideological, military, organizational and operational. Its place is history, however, is principally assured because of its crimes against humanity.

It is one of the great ironies of SS history that as the war closed in on the Reich in 1945, its leader, Heinrich Himmler, actually began to make peace overtures to the Allies. These were ineffectually done through Swedish channels, and they included a commitment to free Jews from the extermination camps. Hearing the news, Hitler stripped Himmler of his titles and ordered his arrest, an event prevented by Hitler's suicide the very next day.

Realizing that his unparalleled crimes against humanity were about to be revealed, Himmler went on the run, unintelligently impersonating a discharged *Gestapo* agent (he shaved off his moustache and wore an eye patch to complete his disguise). Nevertheless, he was apprehended near the Danish border at Bremervörde, and incarcerated. While in detention, he was recognized for who he was. Realizing that his destiny was now set in stone – the world's cinema audiences had already seen the truly horrific pictures from the concentration and extermination camps – Himmler played his ace card.

On 23 May, while under examination by a British doctor, he bit down on a cyanide capsule hidden in his mouth, and died on the spot. The greatest mass murderer in history would never face justice.

SS MARSCHIERT – MARCHING SONG LYRICS

German	English
SS marschiert in Feindesland	SS marches into the enemy country
Und singt ein Teufelslied	Singing a devilish song
Ein Schütze steht am Wolgastrand	A marksman stands at the Wolgastrand
Und leise summt er mit	And he is also humming quietly
Wir pfeifen auf Unten und Oben	We don't give a damn about up and down
Und uns kann die ganze Welt	And the whole world
Verfluchen oder auch loben,	can praise or curse us
Grad wie es jedem gefällt	how everybody likes to
[Refrain:]	[Refrain:]
Wo wir sind da geht's immer vorwärts	Where we are it's advancing
Und der Teufel, der lacht nur dazu	And the devil is laughing
Ha, ha, ha, ha, ha, ha.	Ha, ha, ha, ha, ha, ha.
Wir kämpfen für Deutschland	We fight for Germany
Wir kämpfen für Hitler	We fight for Hitler
Der Rote kommt niemals zur Ruh'	The Commie never comes to rest
Wir kämpften schon in mancher Schlacht	We fought already in some battles
In Nord, Süd, Ost und West	In North, South, East and West
Und stehen nun zum Kampf bereit	We're ready to fight
Gegen die rote Pest	Against the Bolshevik pest
SS wird nicht ruh'n wir vernichten	SS won't rest. We destroy
Bis niemand mehr stört Deutschlands Glück	Until nobody disturbs Germany's luck
Und wenn sich die Reihen auch lichten	And also when the rows thin out
Für uns gibt es nie ein zurück	There's never a turning back for us
[Refrain...]	[Refrain...]

Yet the scale of Himmler's crimes meant that any form of human justice would have been inadequate. Himmler had not just overseen the administration of the Holocaust, he had also created a military organization whose raison d'etre was essentially racial war.

Of course, the SS undoubtedly contained brave soldiers, in the form of the *Waffen-SS*. The reality of human nature does mean that good and evil can sit side by side. In the case of the SS, however, the latter side triumphed.

TEXT OF HIMMLER'S POZNAN SPEECH, 4 OCTOBER 1943

I also want to mention a very difficult subject before you here, completely openly. It should be discussed amongst us, and yet, nevertheless, we will never speak about it in public. Just as we did not hesitate on June 30 to carry out our duty, as ordered, and stand comrades who had failed against the wall and shoot them. About which we have never spoken, and never will speak. That was, thank God, a kind of tact natural to us, a foregone conclusion of that tact, that we have never conversed about it amongst ourselves, never spoken about it, everyone shuddered and everyone was clear that the next time, he would do the same thing again, if it were commanded and necessary.

I am talking about the 'Jewish evacuation': the extermination of the Jewish people. It is one of those things that is easily said. 'The Jewish people is being exterminated', every Party member will tell you, 'perfectly clear, it's part of our plans, we're eliminating the Jews, exterminating them, ha!, a small matter.' And then along they all come, all the 80 million upright Germans, and each one has his decent Jew. They say: all the others are swine, but here is a first-class Jew. And none of them has seen it, has endured it. Most of you will know what it means when 100 bodies lie together, when there are 500, or when there are 1000. And to have seen this through, and – with the exception of human weaknesses – to have remained decent, has made us hard and is a page of glory never mentioned and never to be mentioned.

Because we know how difficult things would be, if today in every city during the bomb attacks, the burdens of war and the privations, we still had Jews as secret saboteurs, agitators and instigators. We would probably be at the same stage as 1916–17, if the Jews still resided in the body of the German people. We have taken away the riches that they had, and I have given a strict order, which Obergruppenführer Pohl has carried out, and we have delivered these riches completely to the Reich, to the State. We have taken nothing from them for ourselves. A few, who have offended against this, will be [judged] in accordance with an order, that I gave at the beginning: He who takes even one Mark of this is a dead man.

A number of SS men have offended against this order. There are not very many, and they will be dead men – WITHOUT MERCY! We have the moral right, we have the duty to our people to do it, to kill this people who want to kill us. But we do not have the right to enrich ourselves with even one fur, with one Mark, with one cigarette, with one watch, with anything. That we do not have. Because at the end of this, we don't want, because we exterminated the bacillus, to become sick and die from the same bacillus. I will never see it happen, that even one bit of putrefaction comes in contact with us, or takes root in us. On the contrary, where it might try to take root, we will burn it out altogether. But altogether we can say: We have carried out this most difficult task for the love of our people. And we have taken on no defect within us, in our soul, or in our character.

THE FATE OF THE WAFFEN SS DIVISIONS, MAY 1945

DIVISION	STRENGTH (Jan 1945)	FATE
1st SS-Panzer Division *Leibstandarte SS Adolf Hitler*	22,000	As part of the Sixth SS Panzer Army the division fought at the siege of Budapest. The remnants retreated to Austria where they surrendered to U.S. forces near Steyr on 8 May 1945.
2nd SS-Panzer Division *Das Reich*	18,000	Involved in the failed attempt to break the siege of Budapest, the division fled to Vienna and westwards to surrender to American forces in Austria.
3rd SS-Panzer Division *Totenkopf*	15,400	After surrendering to U.S. forces at Linz, the remnants of the division were turned over to the Soviets.
4th SS-Panzergrenadier Division *Polizei*	9000	Surrendered to U.S. forces near Wittenberge-Lenzen, west of the Elbe River.
5th SS-Panzer Division *Wiking*	14,800	The division carried out a fighting withdrawal through Czechoslovakia, then surrendered to U.S. forces near Fürstenfeld, Austria on 9 May.
6th SS-Gebirgs Division *Nord*	15,000	In May 1945, the unit's survivors surrendered to American forces in Austria.
7th SS-Volunteer Mountain Division *Prinz Eugen*	20,000	The division retreated towards Celje in Slovenia where it surrendered on 11 May 1945 to Yugoslav forces.
8th SS-Cavalry Division *Florian Geyer*	13,000	The division was virtually destroyed in the fighting around Budapest in early 1945.
9th SS-Panzer Division *Hohenstaufen*	19,000	The division surrendered to U.S. forces in the Steyr-Amstetten area of Austria on 8 May 1945.
10th SS-Panzer Division *Frundsberg*	15,500	Fought the Red Army in Pomerania and later in Saxony, where the remnants surrendered in May 1945.
11th SS-Volunteer Panzergrenadier Division *Nordland*	9000	Most of the division died in the battle for Berlin, with a few survivors being taken into captivity by Soviet forces.
12th SS-Panzer Division *Hitlerjugend*	19,500	As part of the Sixth SS Panzer Army, 10,000 survivors surrendered to the Americans near Enns, Austria, on 8 May 1945.
13th Waffen Mountain Division of the SS *Handschar* (Croatian No 1)	12,700	After frontline action in Hungary, the remnants of the division surrendered to British forces in Austria. Many Muslim volunteers were handed over to Tito's partisans.
14th Waffen Grenadier Division of the SS *Galizien* (Ukrainian No 1)	22,000	Transferred to the newly-formed Ukrainian National Army in April 1945. Surrendered to U.S. forces near Klagenfurt, Austria, in May 1945.

DIVISION	STRENGTH (Jan 1945)	FATE
15th Waffen Grenadier Division of the SS (Latvian No 1)	16,800	Involved in the defence of Berlin, the division surrendered to U.S. forces on the Elbe River.
16th SS-Panzergrenadier Division *Reichsführer-SS*	14,000	The division surrendered to British forces near Klagenfurt, Austria.
17th SS-Panzergrenadier Division *Götz von Berlichingen*	3500	Most of the division were captured by U.S. forces after fighting around Moosburg, Germany, at the end of April 1945.
18th SS-Volunteer Panzergrenadier Division *Horst Wessel*	11,000	After fighting around Budapest, the division moved westward to surrender to U.S. forces.
19th Waffen Grenadier Division of the SS (Latvian No 2)	9000	The division was surrounded in the Courland Pocket until the end of the war when it surrendered to the Red Army.
20th Waffen Grenadier Division of the SS (Estonian No 1)	15,500	Fighting in Silesia and Czechoslovakia until the end of the war, the majority of the division surrender to Soviet forces north of Prague in May 1945.
21st Waffen Mountain Division of the SS *Skanderbeg* (Albanian No 1)	5000	Operational only from February 1944, most of the division's men deserted as the Soviet advance threatened their homeland, with the remnants making their way to Austria to surrender in May 1945.
22nd Waffen Mountain Division of the SS *Maria Theresia*	8000	Most of the division was destroyed in the siege of Budapest in early 1945.
23rd SS-Volunteer Panzergrenadier Division *Nederland* (Netherlands No 1)	6000	After fighting around Berlin, the remaining elements of the division were captured by U.S. forces.
24th Waffen Mountain Division of the SS *Karstjäger*	3000	The remains of the unit surrendered to British forces in northern Italy on 9 May 1945, one of the last German formations to lay down its arms.
25th Waffen Grenadier Division of the SS *Hunyadi* (Hungarian No 1)	15,000	Formed only in November 1944, the division surrendered to the US Third Army at Salzkammergut, Austria, on 5 May 1945.
26th Waffen Grenadier Division of the SS *Hungaria* (Hungarian No 2)	13,000	Surrendered to the Western Allies at Attersee, Austria, where many of the division's surviving troops were handed over to Soviet forces.
27th SS-Volunteer Grenadier Division *Langemarck* (Flemish No 1)	7000	Involved in heavy fighting around the Oder River, the remnants of the division surrendered to Soviet forces at Mecklenburg on 8 May 1945.
28th SS-Volunteer Grenadier Division *Wallonien* (Walloon No 1)	4000	After fighting around Berlin, remnants of the division surrendered to British forces near Lübeck in May 1945.
29th Waffen Grenadier Division of the SS (Italian No 1)	15,000	On 30 April 1945 the remnants of the division surrendered to U.S. troops in Gorgonzola, Lombardy.
30th Waffen Grenadier Division of the SS (Russian No 2)	4500	The unit was disbanded at the beginning of 1945, with officers being transferred to the Nibelungen Division.
31st Waffen Grenadier Division of the SS *Böhmen-Mähren*	11,000	Formed only in September 1944, the division fought in Hungary until February 1945, later surrendering to Soviet forces near Königgrätz, east of Prague.
32nd SS-Volunteer Grenadier Division *30. Januar*	2000	The division was mostly destroyed in the Battle of Berlin while some members surrendered to the Western allies.
33rd Waffen Grenadier Division of the SS *Charlemagne* (French No 1)	7000	The division was destroyed in the Battle of Berlin, with some members being the last defenders of Hitler's HQ, the *Führerbunker*.
34th SS-Volunteer Grenadier Division *Landstorm Nederland* (Netherlands No 2)	7000	The remnants of the division surrendered to British forces near Oosterbeek on 5 May 1945.
35th SS-Police Grenadier Division	5000	The division was badly mauled during the Battle of the Seelow Heights, and remnants surrendered to both U.S. and Soviet forces near the Elbe River.
36th Waffen Grenadier Division of the SS *Dirlewanger*	6000	Involved in fighting around the Oder River, most of the division deserted in the final months of the war or were captured by the Red Army.
37th SS-Volunteer Cavalry Division *Lützow*	1000	As part of the Sixth SS Panzer Army in Austria the division surrendered to U.S. forces in May 1945.
38th SS-Panzergrenadier Division *Nibelungen*	1000	Existing for just a few weeks, the division surrendered to U.S. forces near Oberwössen, southern Germany, on 8 May 1945.

Bibliography

Books

Christopher Ailsby. *Hell on the Eastern Front, the Waffen-SS War in Russia 1941–1945*. Staplehurst: Spellmount, 1998.

Bishop, Chris. *Hitler's Foreign Divisions – Foreign Volunteers in the Waffen-SS, 1940–1945*. London: Amber Books, 2005.

Bishop, Chris. *Essential ID Guide: Waffen-SS Divisions 1939–45*. Stroud: Spellmount, 2007.

Burleigh, Michael. *Germany Turns Eastward*. London: Pan Books, 2002.

Carruthers, Bob (ed.) *Servants of Evil*. London: André Deutsch, 2001.

Davis, Brian. *The German Home Front*. Oxford: Osprey, 2007.

Dearn, Alan. *The Hitler Youth 1933–45*. Oxford: Osprey Publishing, 2006.

Deighton, Len. *Blitzkrieg – From the Rise of Hitler to the Fall of Dunkirk*. Fakenham: Book Club Associates, 1979.

Estes, Kenneth. *A European Anabasis – Western European Volunteers in the German Army and SS, 1940–1945*. Columbia University Press e-book: http://www.gutenberg-e.org/esk01/index.html.

Evans, Richard J. *The Third Reich in Power 1933–1939 – How The Nazis Won Over The Hearts and Minds of a Nation*. London: Penguin Books, 2006.

Flaherty, Thomas (ed.) *The SS*. London: Time-Life, 2004.

Graber, G. S. *History of the SS*. London: Robert Hale, 1978.

Grunberger, Richard. *A Social History of the Third Reich*. London: Phoenix, 2005.

Kogon, Eugen, et al (eds.) *Nazi Mass Murder: A Documentary History of the Use of Poison Gas*. New Haven, CT: Yale University Press, 1993.

Layton, Geoff, *Germany: The Third Reich 1933–45*. London: Hodder & Stoughton, 2000.

Lucas, James. *Germany Army Handbook 1939–1945*. Stroud: Sutton Publishing, 1998.

Mayer, S. L. (ed.) *Signal – Hitler's Wartime Magazine*. London: Bison, 1976.

Ousby, Ian. *Occupation – The Ordeal of France, 1940–1944*. London: Pimlico, 1997.

Rees, Laurence. *The Nazis – A Warning From History*. London: BBC Worldwide, 2002.

Rikmenspoel, Marc. *Waffen-SS Encyclopedia*. Bedford, PA: Aberjona Press, 2004.

Snyder, Louis L. *Encyclopedia of the Third Reich*. Ware: Wordsworth Edition Limited, 1998.

Trevor-Roper, Hugh. *Hitler's Table Talk 1941–1944*. London: Phoenix Press, 2000.

Trigg, Jonathan. *Hitler's Jihadis – Muslim Volunteers of the Waffen-SS*. Stroud: The History Press, 2008.

Van Hoesel, A. F. G. *Die Jeugd die wij vreesden*. Utrecht: St Gregorinschuis, 1948.

Williamson, Gordon. *The SS: Hitler's Instrument of Terror*. London: Sidgwick & Jackson, 1994.

Williamson, Gordon. *Waffen-SS Handbook 1933–1945*. Stroud: Sutton, 2003.

Williamson, Gordon. *World War II German Police Units*. Oxford: Osprey 2006.

Yerger, Mark. *Allgemeine-SS – The Commands, Units and Leaders of the General SS*. Atglan, PA: Schiffer Publishing, 1997.

Useful web sites

Axis History Factbook – http://www.axishistory.com
Feldgrau.com – http://www.feldgrau.com
United States Holocaust Memorial Museum – http://www.ushmm.org
German Police in World War II – http://www.germanpolice.org
The Nizkor Project – http://www.nizkor.org

Glossary

Abteilung – Battalion/Detachment
Admiral (Adm) – Admiral
Ahnenerbe – Ancestral Heritage (see *Studiengesellschaft für Geistesurgeschichte Deutsches Ahnenerbe*)
Allgemeine-SS – General SS
Amtsgruppe – Group Office
Anschluss – Union with Austria, March 1938
Arbeitsgaue – Divisional Work Districts

Armee – Army
Armeegruppe – Army Group
Auftragstaktik – Mission-oriented Tactics
Ausbildung – Training
Autobahn – Motorway
Bataillon – Battalion
Befehlshaber der Ordnungspolizei (BDO) – Chief of the Order Police
Befehlshaber der Waffen-SS (BdWSS) – Chief of the Waffen-SS
Bekenntniskirche – Confessional Church

Bergpolizei – Mountain Police
Bewaffnete-SS – Armed SS
Blitzkrieg – Lightning War
Blockwart – Block Warden
Blut und Boden – 'Blood and Soil'
Bodenständige – Static
Brigadeführer – Brigade Leader (equivalent to an Army Major-General)
Bund Deutscher Mädel (BDM) – League of German Girls
Chef der Deutschen Polizei im

Reichsministerium des Innern – Chief of the German Police in the Reich Ministry of the Interior

Christliches Landvolk – Christian Agrarian Party

Deutsche Arbeiterpartei (DAP) – German Workers Party

Deutsche Arbeitsfront (DAF) – German Labour Front

Deutsche Glaubensbewegung – German Faith Movement

Deutsches Jungvolk – German Young People

Deutsches Nachrichtenburo (DNB) – German News Bureau

Deutschnationale Volkspartei (DNVP) – German National People's Party

Die Endlösung – 'The Final Solution'

Dienststelle Ribbentrop – Ribbentrop Bureau

Dienstverpflichtung – Compulsory service

Einsatzgruppen (der Sicherheitspolizei und des SD) – Task Forces

Einsatzkommando – Sub-unit of an *Einsatzgruppen*

Eisenbahnpolizei – Railway Police

Ersatz – Replacement

Ersatzheer – Replacement Army

Fallschirmjäger – Paratroops

Feld-Division (Luftwaffe) – Field Division (Luftwaffe) (from 1943)

Feldgendarmerie – Field Police

Feldgerichtsabteilung – Court-Martial Department

Feldheer – Field Army

Feldjäger – Sharpshooters

Feldkommandostelle RFSS – Field Command Staff RFSS

Flakkorps – Anti-Aircraft Corps

Fliegerdivision – Air Division

Flieger-HJ – Hitler Youth Paramilitary Aviation Enthusiasts

Fliegerkorps – Air Corps

Frankfurter Zeitung – 'Frankfurt Newspaper' (newspaper)

Fregattenkapitän (Fkpt) – Captain (junior)

Freikorps – Free Corps

Freiwillig – Volunteer/voluntary

Fremdarbeiter – Foreign Workers

Führer – Leader

Führerbunker – Hitler's bunker

Führerkanzlei – Führer Chancellery

Führerprinzip – Leadership Principle

Fuß-Standarte – (SS) Foot Regiment

Gastarbeitnehmer – Guest Workers

Gau – District

Gauinspektor – District Inspector

Gauleiter – District Leader

Gebiet der Kriegsverwaltung – Military Administrative Zone

Gebietskommissar – Area leader

Gebirgs – Mountain

Gebirgsjäger – Mountain Light Infantry

Gefechtsgebiet – Combat Zone

Geheime Feldpolizei (GFP) – Secret Field Police

Geheime Staatspolizei (Gestapo) – Secret State Police

Gendarmerie – Local/Rural Police

Generaladmiral (Gen-Adm) – General-Admiral (equivalent to an Army Colonel-General)

Generalbevollmächtigter für den Arbeitseinsatz – General Plenipotentiary for Labour Deployment

Generalbezirke – General Regions

Generalfeldmarschall – Field Marshal

Generalgouvernement – General Government (of Central Poland)

Generalinspekteur der Gendarmerie – Inspector of Police

Generalkommissar – Commissar general

Generalleutnant – Lieutenant-General

Generalmajor – Major-General

Generaloberst – Colonel-General

Germania – latin term for Germany. *Welthauptstadt* ('World Capital') *Germania* was the name Adolf Hitler gave to the projected renewal of the German capital Berlin, part of his vision for the future of Germany after the planned victory in World War II.

Gestapo Leiststellen – Gestapo Regional HQs

Gleichschaltung – Forcible Coordination

Großadmiral – Grand Admiral

Großdeutsches Reich – Greater Germany

Gruppenführer – Group Leader (equivalent to an Army Lieutenant-General)

Hafenpolizei – Harbour Police

Hakenkreuz – 'Hook Cross', Swastika

Hauptamt/Hauptämter – Main Office(s)/Headquarters

Hauptamt Ordnungspolizei – Order Police Headquarters

Hauptamt Persönlicher Stab Reichsführer-SS (Pers. Stab RFSS) – Headquarters Personal Staff RFSS

Hauptamt SS-Gericht – Main SS Legal Office

Hauptamt Volksdeutsche Mittelstelle (VOMI) – Ethnic German Main Assistance Office

Hauptgebiete – Main Districts

Hauptkommissar – Commissar captain

Hauptmann – Captain

Hauptsturmführer – Head Storm Leader (equivalent to an Army Captain)

Haus der deutschen Kunst – House of German Art (Munich)

Heeresgruppe – Army Group

Heimatsgebiet – Home Zone

Heiliges Römisches Reich deutscher Nation – Holy Roman Empire of the German Nation

Herrenvolk – Master Race

Hilfspolizei (Hipo) – Auxiliary Police

Hilfswillige ('Hiwis') – Voluntary Assistants

Hitlerjugend (HJ) – Hitler Youth

Hochseeflotte – High Seas Fleet

Höchste SS- und Polizeiführer (HöSSPF) – Supreme SS and Police Leader

Höherer SS- und Polizeiführer (HSSPF) – Higher SS and Police Leader

Inspekteur der Konzentrationslager und SS-Wachverbände – Inspector of Concentration Camps and SS Guard Formations

Inspektion der SS-VT – Inspectorate of SS-VT

Jagdpolizei – Game Conservation Police

Jäger – Chasseur, Light (of infantry)

Jungmädelbund – League of Young Girls

Junker – landowner; SS Officer Cadet

Kaiserlich – Imperial

Kaiserliche Marine – Imperial Navy

Kampfgruppe – Battle Group

Kapitän zur See (KptzS) – Captain of the Sea

Kapo – Prisoner functionary

Kasernierte Polizei – Barrack Police

Kavallerie – Cavalry

KdF-Wagen – 'KdF-Car' (later the Volkswagen)

Kommandeure der Orpo – Commanders of the Order Police

Kommandostab RFSS – Command HQ RFSS

Kommodore (Kom) – Commodore

Kompanie – Company

Konteradmiral (KAdm) – Rear-Admiral

Korps – Corps

Kraft durch Freude (KdF) – 'Strength through Joy'

Kreis – Local Council

Kreisgebiete – Area Districts

Kreisleiter – County Leader

Kreispolizeibehörde – City/County Police Authority

Kriminalpolizei (Kripo) – Criminal Police
Kristallnacht – 'Night of the Broken Glass'
Landdienst – Land Service
Länder – States, Provinces
Landesinspekteur – Regional Inspector
Landespolizei – State Police
Landespolizeibehörde – Regional Police Authority
Landsturm – Land Storm
Landtag – Provincial Parliament
Lebensborn – 'Fount of Life'
Lebensraum – 'Living Space'
Luftflotte – Air Fleet
Luftschutzpolizei – Air Raid Police
Luftwaffe – (German) Air Force
Luftwaffe-Feld Division – Luftwaffe Field Division (to 1943)
Militärinternierte – Military Internees, POWs
Militärverwaltung – Military Administration
Minister für Kirchenfragen – Minister for Church Affairs
Motorisierte Infanteriedivision – Motorized Infantry Division
Nationalpolitische Erziehungsanstalten (NAPOLA) – National Political Education Institutes
Nationalsozialistische Deutsche Arbeiterpartei (NSDAP) – National Socialist German Workers Party
Nationalsozialistischer Deutscher Dozentenbund (NSDDB) – National Socialist Germany University Lecturers League
Nationalsozialistischer Deutscher Studentenbund (NSDSB) – National Socialist German Students League
Nationalsozialistischer Lehrbund (NSLB) – National Socialist Teachers League
NS Rechtswahrerbund – Nazi Lawyers Association
Oberabschnitt – Main District
Oberbefehlshaber des Heeres – Commander-in-Chief of the Army
Oberführer – Senior Leader (similar in rank to a British Army Brigadier)
Obergruppenführer – Senior Group Leader (equivalent to an Army General)
Oberkommando der Luftwaffe (OKL) – Luftwaffe High Command
Oberkommando der Marine (OKM) – Naval High Command
Oberkommando der Wehrmacht (OKW) – Armed Forces High Command
Oberkommando des Heeres (OKH) – Army High Command

Oberst – Colonel
Oberster SA-Führer – Supreme SA Leader
Oberstgruppenführer – Supreme Group Leader (equivalent to an Army Colonel-General)
Obersturmbannführer – Senior Storm Unit Leader (equivalent to an Army Lieutenant-Colonel)
Obersturmführer – Senior Storm Leader (equivalent to an Army Senior Lieutenant – Oberleutnant)
Olympiastadion – Olympic Stadium, Berlin
Operationsgebiet – Operations Zone
Ordnertruppe – Monitor Troops
Ordnungspolizei (Orpo) – Order Police
Ortsgruppenleiter – Local Group Leader
Ortspolizeibehörde – Local Police Authority
Ostarbeiter – Eastern Workers
Osthilfe – 'Help for the East'
Osttruppen – East Troops
Panzergrenadier – Motorized infantry, armoured infantry
Panzerschiff – Armoured Ship, Pocket Battleship
Parteikanzlei – Party Chancellery
Parteitage – Party Days (Rallies)
Pflichtjahr – Duty Year (BDM)
Politische Bereitschaften – Political Readiness Detachments
Polizei Abschnitt – Police Sector
Polizei Gruppe – Police Group
Polizeiverwaltungsbeamten – Administrative Police
Polizeivollzugsbeamten – Uniformed Police
Raum – Space
Regierungspräsident – Government President
Regiment – Regiment
Reichsarbeitsdienst (RAD) – Reich Labour Service
Reichsbank – Reich Bank
Reichsbevollmächtiger – Reich Plenipotentiary
Reichsfilmkammer – Reich Chamber for Film
Reichsführer-SS (RFSS) – Reich Leader SS (equivalent to an Army Field Marshal)
Reichsgau – Administrative district created in areas annexed by Nazi Germany
Reichsheer – Reich Army
Reichsjugendführer – Reich Youth Leader
Reichskammer der bildenden Künste – Reich Chamber for Fine Arts

Reichskassenverwalter – Chief Financial Officer
Reichskommissar – Reich Commissioner
Reichskommissar für die Festigung des Deutschen Volkstums (RKFDV) – Reich Commissioner for the Strengthening of the German Nation
Reichskommissariat – Reich Commission
Reichskulturkammer – Reich Chamber of Culture
Reichsleiter – Reich Leader
Reichsleitung der NSDAP – Reich Leadership of the NSDAP
Reichsmarine – Reich Navy
Reichsministerium für die besetzen Ostgebiete – Reich Ministry for the Occupied Eastern Territories
Reichssicherheitshauptamt (RSHA) – Reich Main Security Office
Reichstag – German parliament in Berlin
Reichstatthalter – Reich Governors
Reichstheaterkammer – Reich Chamber for Theatre
Reichswehr – Reich Defence Forces
Reiterstandarte – (SS) Cavalry Regiment
Reviere Polizei – Precinct Police
Richter – Judge, advocate
Rotte – (SS) File
Rottenführer – Section Leader
Rückwärtiges Gebiet – Rear Area
Schar – (SS) Section
Schutzmannschaften der Ordnungspolizei – Detachments of Order Police
Schutzpolizei – Protection Police
Schutzstaffel (SS) – Security Squad/Protection Squadron
Schwarze Reichswehr – Black Reichswehr
Sicherheitsdienst (SD) – Security Service
Sicherheitshauptamt – Main Security Office
Sicherheitspolizei (Sipo) – Security Police
Sonderkommando – Special Unit
Sonderpolizei – Special Police
SS-Abschnitt – SS District
SS-Amt – SS Office
SS-Feldgendarmerie – SS Field Police
SS-Führungshauptamt (SS-FHA) – SS Main Operational Office
SS-Gauführer – District Head
SS-Hauptamt (SS-HA) – SS Main Office
SS-Helferinnen – SS Helpers (all-female admin unit)
SS-Junkerschulen – SS Officer Cadet Schools

Index